MRP II: Making It Happen

The Implementers' Guide to Success with Manufacturing Resource Planning

SECOND EDITION

Thomas F. Wallace

John Wiley & Sons, Inc.

New York · Chichester · Brisbane · Toronto · Singapore

This book is dedicated, with
deep gratitude and an enduring
sense of loss, to

Ollie Wight

who led the way.

Contents

Acknowledgments

I'm deeply grateful to a large number of people for their help in writing the second edition of this book. Each and every member of the Oliver Wight group, both professional and administrative, has provided significant help either directly and/or indirectly. I thank you all.

Special thanks go to my colleagues on the Oliver Wight Process Improvement Task Force: Roger Brooks, Andy Coldrick, Norris Edson, Bruce Harvey, Dick Ling, Andre Martin, John Proud, Bill Sandras, John Schorr, and Steve Souza. Rachel Snyder, from our office in Vermont, made life very easy from the production end.

The people cited above helped enormously. However, there are several whose advice, encouragement, and commitment of time were above and beyond. Walt Goddard not only wrote the foreword to this book, but also provided excellent input. Ollie Wight referred to Walter as his "severest and best critic." Once again, Ollie hit it right on the button. Further, Walt's superb leadership made it possible for the Process Improvement team to do what it had to do—on time.

Darryl Landvater is owed special thanks for both his excellent input and for developing the Detailed MRP II Implementation Plan. The first edition of this book, as well as this one, owe much to Darryl's earlier work, which served as a foundation.

Pete Skurla provided superb help in the reviewing process. Our frequent dialogues helped greatly with shaping much of the material on Quick-Slice MRP that appears in chapters 11 and 12.

Thanks to my editor and publisher, Dana Scannell, who never fails to amaze me with his insight, his patience, and, most of all, with the enormous amount of courage and toughness he possesses.

Next, I send a tip of the hat and a deeply grateful thank you to my wife, lover, best friend, and valued adviser, Evelyn, for her help on this and all of the other ventures that have come and will come down the pike. Thanks and God bless.

Last, I'd like to quote directly from the Acknowledgment I wrote for the first edition of this book:

Most of all, I'm deeply indebted to the users, the people in manufacturing companies who've made it work. The early implementers in particular displayed great vision and courage to persevere, to take two steps forward and then maybe one step back, to keep the faith and to make it happen. Thanks largely to them, a trial-and-error approach to implementing MRP II is no longer necessary.

Thomas F. Wallace
Cincinnati, Ohio
and
Bryson City, North Carolina

Foreword

Avoid being a pioneer! That's good advice for executives of manufacturing companies. Those who go first have the painful "arrows of surprises" sticking out. Undertaking a major change is a tough enough challenge without having to be the trailblazer. A trailblazer must find the path and chart the course. Those who follow will improve it and eventually make it a routine journey.

Competition guarantees that a manufacturing executive cannot avoid challenges. What he or she can often do, however, is avoid surprises. Surprises, even the good ones, mean that you have lost control. This book addresses these issues—it describes a controlled approach to helping your company become more competitive. Manufacturing Resource Planning, MRP II, has proven to be an effective management weapon. It has enabled a great many companies to manage their business more professionally. With the excellent planning and scheduling information it provides, the successful MRP II users have made dramatic increases in customer service, significant gains in productivity, much higher inventory turns, and large reductions in purchase costs.

The two key terms that occur throughout this book are Class A MRP II and the *Proven Path*. Class A MRP II represents the destination and the *Proven Path* describes how to get there. Although Class A is not the ultimate (those that reach it continue to improve), it is a tough, attainable, and high-payback target. Although the *Proven Path* may not be the only way to attain Class A, it is the most traveled one.

For you, this is a book of foresight. It lays out a direction, identifies activities, describes significant milestones, and leads you to a specific destination. By following the steps, you take advantage of the hundreds of companies that have preceded you. Thus, it is really a book of hindsight. It reflects what has been learned, both the prerequisites to be successful as well as the pitfalls to be avoided.

Looking backwards, four trailblazing events deserve special mention.

In 1976, Ollie Wight asked Darryl Landvater, President of Oliver Wight Video Productions, Inc., to analyze how certain companies implemented MRP II so successfully. From this review, Darryl identified the critical activities and the sequence in which they should occur. Our current *Proven Path* has evolved from Darryl's original time-phased chart.

The second event was the creation of the *ABCD Checklist* by Ollie Wight in 1977. Ollie wanted to inspire users to operate MRP II to its full potential by focusing more on the operating aspects rather than the computer and software aspects. Installing an MRP II system simply means having an opportunity to help your company—what counts is how well you are using it to manage your business. With the help of the checklist, you can not only evaluate how well you are using these management systems, you can also identify the areas requiring improvement.

In 1979, the Oliver Wight Education Associates was formed to offer a complete curriculum of classes. George Bevis and Tom Wallace teamed up to teach MRP II: Successful Implementation. Tom had consulted with a wide variety of companies that had implemented MRP II systems and George, as senior vice president of the Tennant Company, had installed and operated one of the very best MRP II systems in our country. They put together a formal project plan containing the detailed steps required for the project team and the steering team. This was the third important event.

Andy Coldrick contributed the fourth one. While director of materials at Englehard Company in England, he implemented MRP II in an unconventional manner. Rather than utilizing the traditional company-wide approach, he elected to tackle one slice of the business at a time. Andy's success caused a number of our other associates to do the same with their clients. Again, the results were extremely successful—by concentrating on a small area, MRP II can be installed quickly and generates paybacks while the next area is being worked on. This fast-track approach is an implementation breakthrough. *Quick-Slice*

MRP is the term we use and Tom describes it in detail in this book.

Tom continues our tradition of helping practitioners. He has identified what it takes to become a Class A MRP II user and explains it clearly with real-world examples. Resist the "not invented here, let's do it our way" group. Blundering into MRP II, as too many companies do, will likely make your company better. Following the *Proven Path*, however, can make your company enormously better. Tom's advice is sound. His words and your actions can produce outstanding results for your company.

We wish you a successful journey.

Walter E. Goddard
Sunapee, New Hampshire

How to Use This Book

A large portion of the audience for this book falls into two categories:

• People from companies implementing MRP II who need a working guidebook.

• People from companies considering MRP II who want to learn about what's involved in implementing it.

For people in companies implementing MRP II, the primary audiences are the executive steering committee and the MRP II project team. (Both of these groups are described in chapter 5.) Ideally, all of these people should read the entire book but that may not always be practical. Therefore, I recommend the following as a workable minimum:

• The *torchbearer* (the chairman of the executive steering committee, also described in chapter 5): Read all chapters.

• Other members of the executive steering committee: Read chapters 2,4,5, and 6 and the section of chapter 9 which deals with implementing sales & operations planning. Further, if implementation is being done on a Quick-Slice basis (defined in chapter 2), rather than company wide, they should read chapters 11 and 12.

• All full-time members of the MRP II project team: Read all chapters.

• Other members of the project team: Read chapters 2 through 6, and 8 through 10. Here, also, in a Quick-Slice implementation, read chapters 11 and 12.

• People in the second category, from companies considering MRP II but not yet implementing it, may want to read the entire book, and that's fine. However, if pressed for time, they should get most of what they need to know from chapters 1 through 6, 11, and 12. If a subsequent decision is made to implement MRP II, they can read the remaining chapters and perhaps revisit some of the material already read.

THE IMPLEMENTERS' CHECKLISTS

This book is intended to be a working handbook for people involved in MRP II implementation. As such, it contains a series of Implementers' Checklists to help guide the company down the implementation path. The first checklist appears at the end of chapter 4, and there is one at the end of most of the remaining chapters. By using these checklists faithfully, a company can *ensure* a successful implementation and the benefits that result from it.

PART I

Introduction

Chapter 1

Manufacturing Resource Planning (MRP II)

Manufacturing Resource Planning is helping to transform our industrial landscape. It's making possible profound improvements in the way manufacturing companies are managed throughout North America, Japan, Western Europe, and Latin America. A hundred years from now, when the definitive industrial history of the twentieth century is written, the evolution of MRP II will be viewed as a watershed event.

A detailed and precise definition of Manufacturing Resource Planning[1] is contained in the glossary. A less-precise but perhaps more user-friendly definition of MRP II is:

a company-wide management system based on network scheduling, which enables people to run their business with high levels of customer service and productivity and simultaneously lower costs and inventories.

Or another:

organized common sense.

---

[1] The first word in the title—manufacturing—is used in the broadest sense. It refers to a manufacturing company—an organization that's in the business of designing, producing, and selling products. It does not refer only to the production function within such an organization.

3

Here are some other descriptions, perhaps not definitions but certainly darn-good examples.

MRP II is a company increasing its sales by 20 percent in the face of an overall industry decline. Discussing how this happened, the vice president of sales explains:

> We're capturing lots of business from our competitors. We can out-deliver 'em. Thanks to MRP II, we can now ship quicker than our competition, and we ship on time.

MRP II is a company building an excellent Just-in-Time[2] process on top of its already superb MRP II system. The production and inventory control manager:

> We were doing Just-in-Time before we ever heard that term. We're now turning our inventory over 40 times per year; we're on our way to 50; and I'm confident that we'll hit 100 turns before long. There's just no way we could be getting these kinds of Just-in-Time results in this plant without MRP II.

MRP II is a plant reducing its workweek from one of heavy overtime down to a normal 40 hours and simultaneously increasing output. The second-shift general foreman:

> Our overtime reduction is due to the good schedules and future visibility that we get from MRP II. We're getting more throughput out of this plant in *five* days than we used to get in seven.

MRP II is a purchasing department reducing its cost of purchased materials by 5 percent, in the face of heavy inflation. The director of purchasing:

> Thanks to MRP II, we're able to give our suppliers consistently valid due dates—for the first time ever—and that makes it a lot easier for them to supply us. Further, our buyers are no longer in order-launch-and-expedite mode. They now have time to do the really important part of their job, which is to save money for the company.

That's MRP II. Here's how it came to be.

[2] See Appendix A for an explanation of Just-in-Time and its relationship with MRP II.

THE EVOLUTION OF MRP II

MRP II began life in the 1960s as material requirements planning (MRP). Its inventors were looking for a better method of ordering material and parts, and they found it in this technique. The logic of material requirements planning asks the following questions:

- What are we going to make?
- What does it take to make it?
- What do we have?
- What do we have to get?

Ollie Wight called this the universal manufacturing equation. He pointed out that its logic applies wherever things are being produced—whether they be jet aircraft, tin cans, machine tools, chemicals, cosmetics . . . or Thanksgiving dinner.

Material requirements planning simulates the universal manufacturing equation. It uses the master production schedule (What are we going to make?), the bill of material (What does it take to make it?), and inventory records (What do we have?) to determine future requirements (What do we have to get?).

It quickly evolved, however, into something more than merely an ordering tool. Early users soon found that material requirements planning contained capabilities far greater than merely giving better signals for reordering. They learned this technique could help to *keep* order due dates valid *after* the orders had been released to production or to suppliers. MRP could also detect when the *due date* of an order (when it's scheduled to arrive) was out of phase with its *need* date (when it's required).

This was a breakthrough. For the first time ever in manufacturing, there was a formal mechanism for keeping priorities valid in a changing manufacturing environment.

In manufacturing, conditions change constantly. Change is not simply a possibility or even a probability. It's a certainty, the only constant, the only sure thing. The function of keeping order due dates valid and synchronized with these changes is known as *priority planning, or scheduling*. Did this breakthrough solve all the problems? Was this all that was needed? Hardly. In manufacturing, the issue of priority is only half the battle. Another factor—capacity—represents an equally challenging problem. (See figure 1-1.)

Techniques for helping plan capacity requirements were tied in with material requirements planning. Further, tools were developed to support the planning of aggregate sales and production levels (sales & operations planning); the development of the specific build schedule (master production scheduling); forecasting, sales planning and customer-order promising (demand management); and high-level resource analysis (rough-cut capacity planning). Systems to aid in executing the plan were tied in: various plant scheduling techniques for the inside factory and supplier scheduling[3] for the outside factory—the suppliers. These developments resulted in the next step in this evolution: closed-loop MRP. (See figure 1-2.)

Closed-loop MRP has a number of important characteristics:

1. It's a series of functions, not merely material requirements planning.

2. It contains tools to address both priority and capacity, and to support both planning and execution.

3. It has provisions for feedback from the execution functions back to the planning functions. Plans can then be altered when necessary, thereby keeping priorities valid as conditions change.

The fourth and most recent step in the evolution of MRP is called

Figure 1-1

Priority	Capacity
Which ones?	Enough?
Sequence	Volume
Scheduling	Loading

---

[3] Formerly called vendor scheduling. Either term is valid, but many people feel that the word *supplier* carries with it a more positive connotation, more in keeping with the important concept of customer/supplier partnerships and co-destiny.

Figure 1-2
Manufacturing Resource Planning (MRP II)

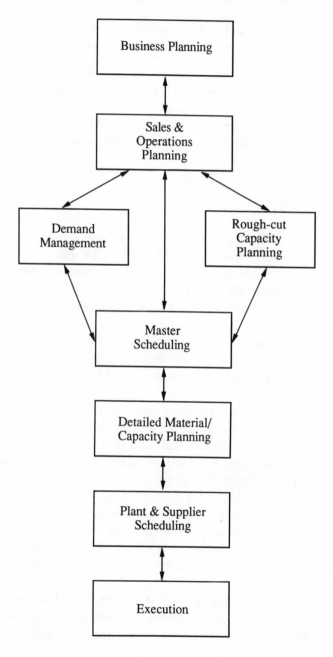

Manufacturing Resource Planning, or MRP II. A direct outgrowth and extension of closed-loop MRP, it involves two additional elements:

1. Finance—the ability to translate the operating plan (in pieces, pounds, gallons, or other units) into financial terms (dollars).

2. Simulation—the ability to ask what-if questions and to obtain comprehensive, detailed, actionable answers—in both units and dollars.

This book deals with how to implement Manufacturing Resource Planning—all the functions contained within closed-loop MRP, plus finance and simulation.

CLASS ABCD

By the mid-1970s the term MRP had become a buzzword. Almost everyone, it seemed, was "doing MRP." Many companies weren't happy with their results. On the other hand, some companies were achieving spectacular results. Companies' reactions to MRP ranged from: "It hasn't helped us at all" to "It's terrific; we couldn't run the business without it."

It became obvious that there were profound differences in how well companies were using this set of tools. To help focus on this issue, the Oliver Wight organization developed the ABCD classification. (See figure 1-3.)

Class D installations have often been viewed as "another computer failure." This strikes me as a bum rap for the computer, because the computer is the only element that's doing its job. Has the computer failed? No, it's working. Has MRP II failed? Not really; it hasn't had a chance. What has failed? The *people* in the company. They've failed to implement and operate this set of tools successfully.

Class C means a company has reduced its inventories, in some cases substantially, and probably is better able to manage engineering changes. The return on investment (ROI) for Class C MRP typically is very good. However, the company really hasn't changed the way it runs the business.

The company operating MRP II at a Class B level has dramatically improved its ability to deliver product on time to its customers, mini-mize shortages in the plant, avoid unplanned overtime, reduce the

Figure 1-3

Class A	Effectively used company-wide; generating significant improvements in customer service, productivity, inventory, and costs.
Class B	Supported by top management; used by middle management to achieve measurable company improvements.
Class C	Operated primarily as better methods for ordering materials; contributing to better inventory management.
Class D	Information inaccurate and poorly understood by users; providing little help in running the business.

inventories, and cope with the myriad of changes that typically confront a manufacturing organization.

Class A yields all of the Class B benefits and more. The business is managed with one consistent set of numbers, from top management's sales & operations plans down through the detailed schedules for the plant floor and the suppliers. Financial plans and reports are developed from the highly accurate operational numbers used to run the business on a day-to-day basis. Extensive use is made of simulation, performing what-if analyses using the MRP II data base, in both units and dollars.

This book deals with how to implement Manufacturing Resource Planning at a Class A level. Further, it applies to both first-time implementers and to *re-implementers,* companies whose first implementation resulted in Class C or D results and who now want to get the full bang for the buck. For those of you who'll be re-implementing, be of good cheer: many Class A and B companies got there via a re-implementation. The steps involved in a re-implementation are virtually identical to a first-time implementation; the main difference is that some of the necessary steps may have already been accomplished satisfactorily.

THE APPLICABILITY OF MRP II

Manufacturing Resource Planning has been successfully implemented in companies with the following characteristics:

- Conventional manufacturing (fabrication and assembly).
- Process manufacturing.
- Repetitive manufacturing.
- Job shop.
- Flow shop.
- Fabrication only (no assembly).
- Assembly only (no fabrication).
- High-speed manufacturing.
- Low-speed manufacturing.
- Make-to-stock.
- Make-to-order.
- Design-to-order.
- Complex product.
- Simple product.
- Multiple plants.
- Single plant.
- Manufacturers with distribution networks.
- Businesses heavily regulated by the government.

Manufacturing Resource Planning has virtually unlimited application potential.

This book deals with how to implement MRP II in any of the above environments.

MRP II AS A FOUNDATION

Today, there is a wide variety of tools and techniques that have been designed to help companies and their people produce their products better. These include Just-in-Time, Total Quality Control (JIT/TQC), Employee Involvement, CAD/CAM, Factory Automation, and more. These are excellent tools with enormous potential.

But . . . none of them will ever yield their full potential unless they're coupled with *an effective planning and scheduling system.* Here's why:

It's not good enough to be extremely efficient . . . if you're making the wrong items.

It's not good enough to make items at a very high level of quality . . . if they're not the ones needed.

It's not good enough to reduce setup times and cut lot sizes . . . if bad schedules prevent knowing what's really needed and when.

Manufacturing Resource Planning, when operating at a Class A or high Class B level, will do several things for a company. First, it will enable the company's people to generate enormous benefits. Many companies have experienced, as a direct result of MRP II, dramatic increases in on-time shipments and productivity, along with substantial decreases in lead times, purchase costs, quality problems, and inventories.

Further, MRP II can provide the foundation upon which additional productivity and quality enhancements can be built . . . an environment where these other tools and techniques can reach their full potential.

Scheduling—knowing routinely what is needed and when via the formal system—is fundamental to productivity. MRP II is the vehicle for getting valid plans and schedules, not only of materials and production. It also means valid schedules of shipments to customers, of manpower and machine requirements, of required engineering resources, of cash flow and profit. MRP/MRP II is the foundation, the bedrock, for true productivity.

Chapter 2

The Implementation Challenge

CATCH 22

There's an apparent catch 22 involved in implementing MRP II successfully. It goes like this:

It's a lot of work.

Implementing MRP II properly requires a great deal of time and effort on the part of many people throughout the company: Data must be made more accurate, people must be educated and trained, new software must be acquired and installed, new policies and procedures must be developed and made operational, and on and on.

It's a do-it-yourself project.

Successful implementations are done internally. In other words, virtually all of the work involved must be done by the company's own people. The responsibility can't be turned over to outsiders, such as consultants or software suppliers. That's been tried repeatedly, and hasn't worked well at all.

When implementation responsibility is decoupled from operational responsibility, who can be legitimately accountable for results? If results aren't forthcoming, the implementers can claim the users aren't operating it properly, while the users can say that it wasn't implemented correctly. Almost without exception, the companies who have become Class A or B are the ones where the users themselves implemented MRP II.

A key principle of implementation, therefore, is:

IMPLEMENTERS = USERS

The people who implement the various tools within Manufacturing Resource Planning need to be the same folks who will operate those tools after they're implemented.

The people who need to do it are already very busy, and MRP II is not their number one priority.

Their first priority is to make shipments, meet payroll, keep the equipment running . . . to run the business. All other activities must be subordinate. Implementing MRP II can't be priority number one, but it does need to be pegged as a high priority within the company, preferably the number two priority right below running the business.

This catch-22 is one of the reasons why many companies that implement MRP II never get beyond Class C. Other reasons include:

It's people-intensive.

MRP II is commonly misperceived as a computer system. Not so. It's a *people* system made possible by the computer.

Many early attempts at implementation focused on the computer and the software and neglected the people. Ollie Wight said it well: "If you consider MRP II as a computer system to order material, what you'll probably wind up with is . . . a computer system to order material. That means Class C. On the other hand, if you look upon MRP II as a set of tools with which to run the business far more effectively, and if you implement it correctly, that's exactly what you'll get."

Well, who runs the business? People do. People like foremen, production workers, engineers, marketers, buyers, planners—and their managers—and their managers' managers, up to and including the general manager.[1]

It requires top management leadership and participation.

If the goal is truly to run the business better, then the general manager and staff must be deeply involved because they and they alone have the real leverage over how the business is to be managed. Changes made at a lower level in the organization won't matter much if it's business as usual at the top.

It involves virtually every department within the company.

It's not enough for just Manufacturing or Materials or Distribution to be on board. Virtually all departments in the company must be deeply involved in implementing MRP II; those mentioned, plus marketing, engineering, quality, finance, personnel, etc.

It requires people to do their jobs differently.

Most companies implementing MRP II must undergo massive behavior change to be successful. MRP II requires a new set of values. Many things must be done differently, and this kind of transformation is never easy to achieve.

Experienced users say implementing MRP II is more difficult than building a new plant, introducing a new product, or entering a whole new market. Breaking through the catch-22, overcoming the people problems, making it happen—these are the challenges.

That's the bad news.

The good news is there's a way to meet these challenges. There's no mystery involved. Implementing MRP II successfully can be almost a sure thing—if it's done right. Yes, it is a lot of work. But it's virtually no risk—if you do it right. MRP II has never failed to work, not once,

---

[1] Throughout this book, I'll use the term general manager to refer to the senior executive in charge of the business unit (company, division, plant) implementing MRP II. In this context, general manager can be synonymous with president, chief executive officer, chief operating officer, managing director, division manager, and, in certain larger operations, plant manager.

when correctly implemented. It *will* work and users will realize enormous benefits.

Doing it right involves two major elements:

1. An aggressive implementation schedule, focused on achieving maximum benefits in minimum time.

2. The *Proven Path*. A set of steps that, if followed, will ensure a successful implementation.

AN AGGRESSIVE IMPLEMENTATION SCHEDULE

The question arises: "How long should it take to implement all of the functions of Manufacturing Resource Planning, throughout the entire company, from when we start until we're fully implemented?" First of all, it's difficult to implement all of MRP II, company wide, in less than a year. Some companies have achieved Class A status in less than 12 months, but not many. Why? Simply because so many things need to be done: massive education, data integrity, changing the way the business is run. And, all the while, it's not the number one priority.

On the other hand, for an average-sized or smaller-sized company (division, plant, unit), if it's taking longer than two years, it's probably not being done correctly. As a matter of fact, if a given business unit takes longer than two years to implement, the odds for achieving superior results decrease sharply. It becomes more and more difficult to maintain the intensity, the enthusiasm, the drive and dedication necessary, and thus harder to keep MRP II pegged as a very high priority.

Therefore, plan on a full implementation of Manufacturing Resource Planning taking longer than one year, but less than two. For purposes of simplicity and consistency, let's routinely refer to a 15-month implementation.

Some people feel a 15-month time frame is too aggressive—too ambitious. It's not. It's a very practical matter, and also necessary. Here's why:

Intensity and enthusiasm.

MRP II will be implemented by users, the people running the business. Their first priority *must* be running the business, a full-time job in itself. Now, their responsibilities for implementing MRP II will require more work and more hours . . . above and beyond running the business.

With a long, extended project, these people become discouraged. The payoff is too far in the future. There's no light at the end of the tunnel.

However, with an aggressive schedule, these people can see progress being made early on. They can expect that things will start to improve substantially within a relatively short time. In our experience, the operating people—sales and marketing people, foremen, buyers, engineers, planners, etc.—respond favorably to this environment.

Priority.

It's quite unlikely MRP II can hold the necessary high priority over three or four years. (Companies are like people; their attention spans are limited.) As the project's priority drops, so do the odds for success.

The best approach is to establish MRP II as a very high priority; implement it quickly and successfully. And then capitalize on it. Build on it. Use it to help run the business better and better.

Unplanned change.

Change of this type comes in two forms: changes in people and changes in operating environment. Each type represents a threat to the MRP II project.

Regarding people changes, take the case of a division whose general manager is MRP II-knowledgeable, enthusiastic, and leading the implementation effort. Suppose this person is suddenly promoted to the corporate office. The new general manager is an unknown quantity. That person's reaction to MRP II will have a major impact on the project's chances for success. He[2] may not be supportive of MRP II (usually because of a lack of understanding), and the entire implementation effort will be at risk.

Environmental change includes factors such as a sharp increase in

---

[2] The author believes that any job referenced in this book can be performed equally well by women or men. However, for purposes of simplicity and ease of reading, *he, him,* and *his* will be used throughout the book to refer to a person of either sex.

business ("We're too busy to work on MRP II"), a sharp decrease in business ("We can't afford MRP II"), competitive pressures, new governmental regulations, etc.

While such changes can certainly occur during a short project, they're much more likely to occur over a long, stretched-out time period.

Schedule slippage.

In a major project like implementing MRP II, it's easy for schedules to slip. Throughout this book, I'll discuss ways to minimize slippage. For now, let me just point out an interesting phenomenon: In many cases, tight aggressive schedules are actually *less* likely to slip than loose, casual, nonaggressive schedules.

Benefits.

Taking longer than necessary to implement defers getting the benefits. The lost-opportunity cost of only a one-month delay can, for many companies, exceed $100,000. A one-year delay could easily range into the millions. An aggressive implementation schedule, therefore, is very desirable. But . . . is it practical? Yes, almost always. To understand how, we need to understand the concept of the three knobs.

THE THREE KNOBS

In project management, there are three primary variables: the amount of *work* to be done; the amount of *time* available (calendar time, not man-years); and the amount of *resources* available to accomplish the work. Think of these as three knobs, which can be adjusted.

Figure 2-1

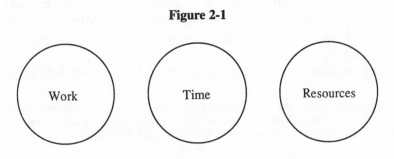

It's possible to hold any two of these knobs constant by varying the third. For example, let's assume the following set of conditions:

1. The work load is considered to be a constant, a given. There is a certain amount of work that simply has to be done to make this work.

2. The time can also be considered a constant, and, in this example, let's say it's fixed at about 18 months.

3. The variable then becomes the resource knob. By adjusting it, by providing resources at the necessary level, the company can accomplish the necessary amount of work in the defined time. (Developing a proper cost benefit analysis can put the resource issue into clearer focus, and I'll return to this issue in chapter 4.)

But . . . what if a company can't increase the resource knob. Sometimes, it's simply not possible. Maybe there's not enough money. Or the organization is stretched so thin already that consuming large blocks of many people's time on an implementation just isn't in the cards.

Well, there's good news. Within the Proven Path, there is provision for:

• *Company-wide* implementation: total company project; all MRP II functions implemented; time frame one to two years.

• *Quick-Slice MRP* implementation: confined to one or several pareto[3] high-impact product lines; most, but not all, MRP II functions implemented; time frame three to five months.

With Quick-Slice MRP, the resources are considered a constant, and they are limited. Further, the time is considered fixed and is a very short, aggressive period. The principle of urgency applies here also; since only a portion of the products/company will be cutting over to MRP II, it should be done quickly. This is because the company will need to move aggressively to the next step, which may be to do another Quick-Slice implementation on the next product family or perhaps to convert to a company-wide implementation.

---

[3] Pareto's law refers to the principle of the "vital few—trivial many." For example, in many companies 30 to 60 percent of their sales comes from 5 to 10 percent of their products. Pareto's law is also the basis for ABC inventory analysis, and is used extensively within Just-in-Time and Total Quality Control.

Resource constraints are only one reason why companies elect to begin implementation on a Quick-Slice basis. For other reasons, and for a detailed description of the Quick-Slice implementation process via the Proven Path, please see chapters 11 and 12. For now, let's examine the Proven Path methodology, realizing that it applies to either implementation approach.

THE PROVEN PATH

There's a tested, proven way to implement Manufacturing Resource Planning. Twenty or so years ago, no one could say that. Back then, people said:

It should work.

We really believe it'll work.

It stands a good chance of working.

It certainly ought to work.

No more. There's no longer any mystery about how to implement MRP II. There is a well-defined set of steps, which guarantees a highly successful implementation in a short time frame if followed faithfully and with dedication.[4] These steps are called the Proven Path.

If you do it right, it will work. Period. And you can take that to the bank.

How can we be so certain? How did this become such a sure thing? What happened along the way from then till now?

The main reason centers on some executives and managers in certain North American manufacturing companies. They had several things in common: a dissatisfaction with the status quo, a belief that better tools to manage their business could be developed, and an ample supply of courage. These early implementers led the way.

Naturally, they had some help. Consultants and educators—people like my colleagues and myself—assisted. Computer companies, most notably IBM in the early days, developed generalized software packages for material requirements planning, capacity requirements planning,

---

[4] *Faithfully* and *with dedication* are important words. They mean that this is not a pick-and-choose kind of process. They means skip no steps.

and shop floor control. But, fundamentally, the users did it themselves.

Over the past 25 years, thousands of companies have implemented MRP/MRP II. Many have implemented very successfully (Class A or B); even more companies less so (Class C or D). By observing a great variety of these implementation attempts and their results, it's become very clear what works and what doesn't. The methods that have proven unworkable have been discarded. The things that work have been refined, developed, and synthesized into what we call the Proven Path.

The Proven Path isn't theory; it's not blue sky or something dreamed up over a long weekend in Colorado Springs, where the air's really thin. Rather, it's a product of the school of hard knocks—built out of sweat, scar tissue, trial and error, learning, testing, refining.

Surprising? Not really. The Proven Path evolved the same way MRP II did—pragmatic, practical, straightforward. It wasn't created in an ivory tower or a laboratory, but on the floors of our factories, in our purchasing departments, in our sales and marketing departments, and on our shipping docks.

This evolution has continued, right into the 1990s, triggered by three factors:

1. New opportunities for improvement.

2. Common goals and processes.

3. Time pressures to make improvements quickly.

Keep in mind, when the original Proven Path was developed by Darryl Landvater in the mid-1970s, MRP II was close to being "the only game in town" for major improvements in manufacturing companies. Quality? That was viewed in the United States as the job of the quality control department, and people like W. Edwards Deming and others had to preach the gospel of Total Quality Control in other parts of the world. Just-in-Time? It hadn't yet hit the North American continent in any meaningful way. Other important tools like Design for Manufacturability, Activity-Based Costing, Gainsharing, and others hadn't been invented yet or existed in small and relatively unpublicized pockets of excellence.

Today, it's a very different world. No longer is it good enough to implement any one major initiative and then stop there. Tools like

Manufacturing Resource Planning, Just-in-Time, Total Quality Control, and others are all essential. Each one, by itself, is not sufficient. Companies must do them all, and do them very well, to be winners in the global marketplace of the 1990s. Winning companies will find themselves constantly in implementation mode, first one initiative, then another, then another. Change, improvement, implementation—these have become a way of life.

This was one trigger for a major evolutionary step in the Proven Path. A second has to do with the implementation process itself. There is far more similarity in implementing MRP II, JIT, TQC, DRP and others than there are differences. The implementation methodology is so similar because the processes and goals themselves are virtually the same: to enable people to change the way they do their jobs, so they can run the business better.

Third, as competitive pressures have increased so has the urgency to make rapid improvement. Time frames are being compressed, necessary not only for the introduction of new products but also for new *processes* to improve the way the business is run.

The current Proven Path, developed and refined during the mid- to late-1980s, reflects all three of the above factors. It is broader and more flexible. It applies to the implementation of Just-in-Time/Total Quality Control and Distribution Resource Planning, as well as MRP II.

Further, it offers an option on timing. The original Proven Path dealt with implementation on a company-wide basis: all products, all components, all departments, and all MRP II functions to be addressed in one major implementation project. However, the current Proven Path also includes the fast-track implementation route, which enables a company to make major improvements in a short time. We refer to these fast-track processes as Quick-Slice MRP, Breakthrough JIT/TQC, and Fail-Safe Mini-DRP.[5]

The Proven Path consists of 16 steps. We'll take a brief look at each of these steps now, and discuss them more thoroughly in subsequent chapters. (The fold-out chart in the back of the book is a graphic representation of the Proven Path. You may wish to refer to it as you read through this text.) The 16 steps are:

---

[5] Quick-Slice MRP will be covered in this book.

1. *Audit/Assessment I.*

An analysis of the company's current situation, problems, opportunities, strategies, etc. It addresses questions such as: Is Manufacturing Resource Planning the best step to take now to make us more competitive? If so, what is the best way to implement: company-wide or Quick-Slice? The analysis will serve as the basis for putting together a short-term action plan.

2. *First cut Education.*

A handful of executives and operating managers from within the company must learn how Manufacturing Resource Planning works; what it consists of; how it operates; and what is required to implement and use it properly. This is necessary to affirm the direction set by Audit/Assessment I and to effectively prepare the Vision Statement and Cost-Benefit Analysis.

3. *Vision Statement.*

A written document defining the desired operational environment to be achieved with the implementation of Manufacturing Resource Planning. It answers the question: What do we want this company to look like after the implementation?

4. *Cost/Benefit Analysis.*

A process to generate a written document that spells out the costs of implementation and the benefits of operating Manufacturing Resource Planning successfully, and results in a formal decision whether or not to proceed with MRP II.

5. *Project Organization.*

Creation of an Executive Steering Committee; an operational-level project team, consisting mainly of the managers of operating departments throughout the company; and the selection of the full-time project leader and other people who will work fulltime on the project.

6. *Performance Goals.*

Agreement as to which performance categories are expected to improve and what specific levels they are expected to reach.

7. *Initial Education.*

Ideally 100 percent, a minimum of 80 percent, of *all* of the people in the company need to receive some education on MRP II as part of the implementation process. For MRP II to succeed, many things will have to change, including the way that many people do their jobs. People need to know what, why, and how these changes will affect them. People need to see the reasons why they should do their jobs differently and the benefits that will result.

8. *Defining the Sales, Logistics, and Manufacturing Processes.*

A detailed statement of how the sales/marketing, logistics and manufacturing functions will operate following the implementation of MRP II, backed up by a detailed project plan necessary to achieve this.

9. *Planning and Control Processes.*

Development and implementation of policies and procedures necessary for effective planning and execution, from sales & operations planning down through the detailed schedules for the plants and suppliers.

10. *Data Management.*

Inventory records, bills of material, formulas, recipes, routings, and other data need to become accurate, complete, and properly structured.

11. *Process Improvement.*

Improvements in physical processes are the heart of a Just-in-Time implementation, and can play a significant role in Quick-Slice MRP. It's optional in an MRP II company-wide implementation, often not a major step. However, opportunities for improving physical processes should not be overlooked—before, during, and after—MRP II implementation.

12. *Software.*

Acquisition, installation, and maintenance of the necessary software to support all MRP II functions.

13. *Pilot and Cutover.*[6]

Beginning to operate the business with the new set of tools—on a very controlled and closely managed basis.

14. *Performance Measurements.*

Beginning to track actual results and compare them to the performance goals defined in step 6.

15. *Audit/Assessment II.*

A focused evaluation of the company's situation, problems, opportunities, and strategies following the implementation. It is the driver via which the company moves into its next improvement initiative (e.g., Just-in-Time, Total Quality Control, Distribution Resource Planning, or whatever).

16. *Ongoing Education.*

Initial education for new people coming into the company and refresher education for continuing employees. This is necessary so that MRP II can continue to be operated very well, and made even better as the company continuously improves further via Just-in-Time and Total Quality Control.

The Proven Path is a logical, straightforward implementation approach, based completely on demonstrated results. One more time: It is a lot of work but virtually no risk. If a company follows the Proven Path

---

[6] Cutover applies only to company-wide implementations. It entails adding the rest of the products/items onto the system following a successful operation of the pilot.

faithfully, sincerely, and vigorously, it *will* become Class A—and it won't take forever.

"Oh, really," you might be thinking, "how can you be so certain? What about all the 'MRP failures' I've heard about? You yourself said just a few pages ago there were more Class C and D users than Class A and B. That indicates that our odds for high success are less than 50 percent."

My response: It's up to you. If you want to have the odds for Class A or B less than 50 percent, you have that choice. On the other hand, if you want the odds for success to be near 100 percent, you can do so. Here's why.

The total population of Class C and D users includes *virtually zero* companies who followed the Proven Path closely and faithfully. Most of them are companies who felt that MRP was a computer deal to order parts, and that's what they wound up with. Others in this category tried to do it without educating their people and/or without getting their data accurate. Others got hung up on computer software. Or politics.

Here's the bottom line: Of the companies who've implemented via the Proven Path, who've sincerely and rigorously gone at it the right way, virtually all of them have achieved a Class A or high Class B level of success with MRP II. And they've realized enormous benefits as a result.

There are no sure things in life. Achieving superior results with MRP II, from following the Proven Path, is about as close as it gets.

PART II

Company-Wide Implementation

Chapter 3

Company-Wide Implementation— Overview

In chapter 2 we talked about the two different implementation approaches contained within the Proven Path methodology: Company Wide and Quick Slice. We'll get into the details of Quick Slice in chapters 11 and 12. For the next several chapters, let's look at how to implement MRP II on a company-wide basis for *all functions* of Manufacturing Resource Planning *throughout the company.*

To get started, let's consider the following:

It's possible to swallow an elephant . . . one chunk at a time.

Be aggressive. Make deliberate haste. Implement in 18 months or less.

Those two concepts may sound contradictory, but they're not. There's a way to "swallow the elephant one chunk at a time" and still get there in a reasonable time frame. Here's the strategy:

1. Divide the total MRP II implementation project into several major phases to be done *serially*—one after another.

2. Within each phase, accomplish a variety of individual tasks
simultaneously.

For most companies, implementing all of MRP II is simply too much
to handle at one time. The sum of the chunks is simply too much to
digest all at once. That's one reason for the multiphase approach. Further, in many cases, all of the activities in the subsequent phase are
dependent on the prior phase being completed. (There are some companies that can do it all in one phase, and we'll talk about them later in
this chapter.)

The use of simultaneous tasks within each phase is based on the need
for an aggressive implementation cycle of typically one year to 18
months. Doing each of the many tasks involved serially would simply
take too long.

For the time being, let's assume a three-phase project. Let's examine
what's to be done in each of the three phases:

Phase I - Basic MRP:

Sales & operations planning, demand management, rough-cut capacity planning, master production scheduling, material requirements planning and, in flow shops, plant scheduling.[1] Also included here are the
support functions of inventory accuracy, bill of material accuracy and
structure, plus anticipated delay reporting from the plant floor and
purchasing.

Basic MRP is not all of Manufacturing Resource Planning. Of and by
itself, it will produce substantial results; however, key elements such as
job-shop plant scheduling, supplier scheduling, complete financial integration, and perhaps others remain to be implemented.

This phase normally takes about ten months to complete.

---

[1] When we talk about plant schedules, it's necessary to recognize the differences in
manufacturing processes. Different processes often require different kinds of schedules.

Let's divide the universe of manufacturing processes into two broad categories: job
shop and flow shop. Job shops are often found in conventional fabrication and assembly
kinds of manufacturing. They tend to be more complex; they require the more complex
kinds of scheduling and control systems such as shop floor control, shop dispatching,
input-output control, and capacity requirements planning.

Flow shops, often referred to as process or repetitive kinds of manufacturing, tend to
be simpler, and thus the more complex tools usually aren't needed. Rough-cut capacity
planning, simple plant sequence lists, and output tracking often suffice.

Please see Appendix B for more information on the job-shop and flow-shop issue.

Phase II - Closing the Loop:

Supplier schedules for the outside factories (i.e., the suppliers and plant schedules for the job shops). This phase usually requires about three months.

Phase III - Finance and Simulation:

Completely integrating the financial systems into the MRP II operational data base, and activating the full what-if capability of MRP II. The elapsed time here is typically several months.

Other elements may also be included in Phase III that were identified earlier as very desirable but not absolutely necessary to achieve MRP II . . . automated-shop data collection, improved order-entry software, a supplier rating system, etc.

Let's consider elapsed time for a moment. From the above, we can see that basic MRP begins at time zero and continues through month 10, closed-loop MRP through month 13, and MRP II (financial planning and simulation) through about month 15.

Please be aware that these bar charts are generalized. They will not fit exactly into each and every company's situation. Examples:

• Some companies already have accurate and properly structured bills of material. They need to spend less time on this function than the chart indicates.

• Some companies don't have routings and standards. They have to start on them far earlier than what's shown, specifically back in phase I.

• Some companies already have shop floor control. This means that the loop can be closed in manufacturing simultaneously with basic MRP.

• Some companies don't need shop floor control, specifically flow shops. As we've just seen, plant schedules are much simpler, and can often be generated as a part of phase I.

On occasion, people question the location of time zero—the day the clock starts ticking. Should it follow the early and preliminary steps, as shown on the phase I bar chart? Or should it be at the very beginning of audit/assessment I?

I prefer it where it is, because that facilitates the consensus building, which is so important.

Some companies move through these early steps quickly, so for them the precise location of time zero is not terribly important. Other companies, however, find they need more time for these early activities than the several months implied by the chart. The principles to be considered are:

1. Take as much time as needed to learn about MRP II, and build a consensus among the management team. Set the vision statement and the performance goals. Do the cost/benefit analysis. Make sure this is the direction the company wants to go. Then commit to the project.

2. Once the decision is made to go for it, pursue it aggressively.

Occasionally, people have questions on the functional content of each of the three phases, such as: "Why isn't shop floor control in phase I? Can we move MRP to phase II and sales & operations planning to phase III?"

The timing of the implementation plan is structured to get the basic planning tools in place early. Companies (job shops, of course) that implement shop floor control first, before material requirements planning, may get better time and attendance data and a better handle on job location, but probably not much else. The biggest benefit from shop floor control comes from its ability to prioritize the jobs on the shop floor effectively. It simply can't do that without valid order due dates, which are done through material requirements planning.

Further, material requirements planning can't do its job without a valid master production schedule, which must be in balance with the sales & operations plan. That's why these functions are in phase I, and the execution functions (plus capacity requirements planning) are in phase II.

SCHEDULE BY FUNCTION, NOT SOFTWARE MODULES

Business functions and software modules are not the same. A business function is just that—something that needs to be done to run the business effectively. Examples include planning for future capacity needs; maintaining accurate inventory records, bills of material, and routings; customer order entry and delivery promising, and so on.

Software modules are pieces of computer software that support people in the effective execution of business functions.

Sometimes I see companies involved in an MRP II implementation effort scheduling their project around tasks like: "Implement the SOE (Sales Order Entry) module," "Implement the ITP (Inventory Transaction Processing) module," "Implement the PDC (Product Data Control) module," etc. This is a misguided approach for two reasons: sequence and message.

Companies that build their project plan around implementing software modules often do so based on their software vendor's recommendation. This sequence may or may not be the best one to follow. In some cases, it merely slows down the project, which is serious enough. In others, it can greatly reduce the odds for success.

One such plan recommended the company first install the material requirements planning module, then the shop floor control module, then the master production scheduling module. Well, that's backward. MRP can't work properly without the master schedule, and shop floor control can't work properly without MRP working properly. To follow such a plan would have not only slowed down the project but also would have substantially decreased the odds for success.

The second problem concerns the message that's sent out when the implementation effort is focused on software modules. Concentrating on implementing software modules sends exactly the wrong message to the people in the company. The primary emphasis is on the wrong thing— the computer. MRP II is *not* a computer system; it's a *people* system made possible by the computer. Implementing it is not a computer project or a systems project; it's a *management* project. The people in the company are changing the way they manage the business, so that they can manage it better than they ever could before.

THE ABCs OF IMPLEMENTATION

People talk about the ABCs of implementing Manufacturing Resource Planning. The concept is derived from the basic ABC approach to inventory control, in turn derived from Pareto's law. In that technique, the A items are considered very significant, costly, important, etc.

Hence, they deserve the most attention and the most careful planning and control. The B items are of less significance than the A items, and, hence, less time is devoted to each of them. The C items, while essential, are of least overall significance and are given proportionate attention.

This ABC approach, applied to implementation, identifies the C item as the computer, both the hardware and software.[2]

It's essential since MRP II can't be done manually, but it's of lesser significance overall than the other elements.

The B item is the data: the inventory records, the bills of material, the routings, etc. They are more significant and require more of the company's overall attention and managerial emphasis.

The A item is the people, the most important element in making it happen. If the people part of the implementation process is managed properly, the people will understand the objectives and how to get there. They'll take care of getting and keeping the data accurate. They won't allow the "computer tail" to wag the "company dog," as has been the case far too often. People are the key.

CUT THE CLOTH TO FIT THE PATTERN

Those of us within the Oliver Wight organization repeatedly point out MRP II is a generalized set of tools that applies to *any* manufacturing company.

We go to great lengths to help people break through the we're-unique[3] syndrome. When people recognize there is a well-defined, universally applicable body of knowledge in this field, they'll be able to use it to solve fundamental problems.

---

[2] This statement sometimes give systems people heartburn. Speaking as an ex-systems guy, I can understand that. But let me tell you—heartburn is better than scars. You systems people are critically important to the success of MRP II; the company can't get there without you because the computer is an essential element.

You are critically important, but you are not central. That's for the users. Systems people can keep it from working; only users can make it work. I still have scar tissue from failed attempts to implement systems from inside the MIS department. I batted for a much higher average when I was in an operating department.

A good way to define the role of the systems group in an MRP II implementation is: "Keep the C item the C item. Don't let it become the A item."

[3] The standard phrase is: "We're unique; we're different; it won't work for us." Believe it or not, I still hear that in the 1990s, from people who are talking about not only Manufacturing Resource Planning but also Just-in-Time, Total Quality Control, etc.

On the other hand, MRP II is a set of tools that must be tailored to fit individual companies. The implementation project must also reflect the individual company, its environment, its people, its processes, its history, etc. Here are some examples of special situations that can affect the specifics of implementation:

Flow shops.

Flow shops, as we've said earlier, are companies with manufacturing methods that can be described as purely process (chemicals, food, plastics, etc.) or as highly repetitive (tin cans, automobiles, razor blades, etc.).

The overall concept of MRP II definitely applies to these kinds of manufacturing environments. However, each and every function within MRP II may not be necessary. One good example is shop floor dispatching on an operation-by-operation basis, which is typically needed only where there is a functional job-shop form of organization. The technique known as detailed capacity requirements planning is another. In most flow shops, all of the necessary capacity planning can be done at the rough-cut level. Simple output tracking can be used instead of the more complex input-output control.

A company in this situation, not needing detailed shop dispatching and CRP, should exclude them from its implementation plan. Simple plant schedules (plant sequence lists, not shop dispatch lists) can usually be generated directly from the master schedule or material requirements planning as a part of phase I. Much of phase II can go away. And that's good news. It'll be easier to get to Class A—and quicker.

Financials already integrated.

Some companies, prior to implementing MRP II, already use operational data to drive much of their financial reporting. Numbers from the operating system are converted to dollars for certain financial planning and control purposes; product costing and inventory valuation are two functions often already integrated. At a minimum, of course, the current degree of financial integration must be implemented as part of phase I, not phase III.

Companies with high degrees of financial integration, prior to MRP II, are often seen in the process world (i.e., flow shops). For many of these companies, virtually all of their financial interface tasks for th _

MRP II project will occur in phase I. What happens then to phase III? Answer: It largely goes away. (Bringing up the simulation part of MRP II is important but not such a major task that it deserves its own phase.)

Now, hang on to that concept for a moment, and let's revisit what we just covered about flow shops not needing full-blown shop floor control, CRP, etc. We said that phase II, closing the loop, consisted mainly of supplier scheduling and even some of that could start in phase I. In other words, most of phase II goes away.

Here's a real opportunity for you flow shop folks with highly integrated financials. Your implementation of Manufacturing Resource Planning, Company Wide, might be done almost totally in *one* phase, not three. You may be able to *complete all, or virtually all,* of the implementation in *less than one year.* Audit/Assessment I can be helpful in getting a good focus on these kinds of possibilities.

Re-implementers.

Some companies have already attempted to implement MRP/MRP II, but it's not working properly. They have some or all of the technical pieces in place, yet they're not getting the results they should. Now they need to *re-implement,* but this time to do it right. Darryl Landvater said it well: "The jobs involved in *improving* an MRP II system are the same as those in implementing it correctly." As we said earlier, the difference is that, for re-implementers, some of the tasks may already be done.

For example, a re-implementer company may have acquired an adequate set of software for MRP II a few years before. Many of the software steps necessary for the first-time implementer wouldn't be required in this case.

That's perhaps the good news. However, in a re-implementation, there's one big issue that makes it tougher: how to convince all the people that it'll work the second time around[4] when it didn't work well after the first try. This will put more pressure on the education process, which we'll discuss later, and on top management's actions. Words alone won't do it. Their feet and their mouths must be moving in the same direction.

---

[4] Or third possibly? I've talked to people whose companies were in their third or fourth implementation. This gets really tough. The best number of times to implement MRP II is once. Do it right the first time.

Multiplant.

How about a company or division with more than one plant? How should it approach implementation?

Broadly, there are three choices: serial, simultaneous, or staggered.

Take the case of a company with four plants. Each plant employs hundreds of people, and has a reasonably complete support staff. The company wants to implement MRP II in all four plants.

The *serial* approach to implementation calls for implementing completely in a given plant, then starting in the second plant and implementing completely there, etc. The schedule would look like figure 3-1:

Figure 3-1

Plant 1	Plant 2	Plant 3	Plant 4

Month 0   15   30   45   60

This time span is not acceptable. Sixty months is five years, and that's simply too long.

The *simultaneous* approach is to do them all at the same time, as shown in figure 3-2.

Figure 3-2

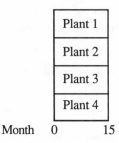

Plant 1
Plant 2
Plant 3
Plant 4

Month   0   15

This approach looks good because the entire project is finished in 15 months. However, there may be some problems. One would be availability of centralized resources, such as data processing, overall project management, etc. It may be impractical to support all four plants simultaneously.

Another potential problem gets back to the catch-22 of MRP II. Implementing MRP II is not the first priority. Some companies may wisely conclude that implementing simultaneously in all plants could be more than they want to bite off at one time. The effort and intensity required may be more than desired.

This leads most companies to choose the *staggered* method shown in figure 3-3.

This approach has several advantages:

1. MRP II gets implemented throughout the entire company fairly quickly (in this case, in slightly over two years for four plants).

2. The impact on centralized resources is lessened.

3. Only one plant is piloting and cutting over onto MPS/MRP at a time, so the overall level of effort and intensity is reduced.

4. Plant personnel can teach each other. For example, users from plant 2 may participate in the pilot and cutover at plant 1. In so doing, they can learn from the first plant's mistakes and avoid them. Plant 3 people can learn and help at plant 2, and so on.

One company we worked with brought all nine of its plants from time zero to Class A within three years. This was a very complex implementation, and the staggered method served them very well.

Distribution Resource Planning (DRP).

DRP is MRP II for a network of field warehouses. Companies that stock finished products, or perhaps spare parts, at a variety of remote

Figure 3-3

			15			
	Plant 1			18		
		Plant 2			21	
		Plant 3				24
		Plant 4				

Month 0   15   18   21   24 locations should seriously consider implementing DRP simultaneously with MRP II.[5] The functions involved are virtually identical: education, inventory accuracy, bill-of-material accuracy, item analysis, etc. However, different people are involved. For example, getting inventory accuracy at the branch warehouses should not affect the work load of the people getting inventory accuracy in the warehouses and stockrooms at the plant.

Further, in a company with a distribution network, master scheduling and material requirements planning will never work at full efficiency until DRP is operating. (Delaying DRP is analogous to implementing material requirements planning for some, but not all, levels in the bill of material.) Therefore, delaying DRP until the rest of MRP II is implemented means many months of less-than-complete benefits. Conversely, implementing DRP first, then MRP II, means some months of deferral of *all* of the benefits from MRP II.[6]

Necessary nonstandard functions.

Here, I'm referring to functions necessary to run the business, but which are peculiar to a given company or industry. Some examples are:

1. The pharmaceutical industry, among many others, requires lot traceability and lot number inventory control.

2. Firms supplying the U.S. Department of Defense must adhere to special contract accounting requirements.

3. Product shelf life is a major issue in many companies producing consumer package goods.

There are many other examples. The message here is obvious: Look very closely at the company, its industry and marketplace, its position within them, and its overall strategy. Don't make the serious error of assuming that if a given function isn't in the software package, it's not

---

[5] Here also audit/assessment I can be a big help.

[6] For additional details see Andre Martin, *DRP: Distribution Resource Planning— The Gateway to True Quick Response and Continuous Improvement*, 2nd ed. (Essex Junction, VT: Oliver Wight Publications, Inc. 1993).

needed for your company. The new software may need to be modified to support the function in question, ideally enabling it to be done even better. Perhaps the software will need modification merely to allow the function to be done as before. Or perhaps no software changes will be necessary for a given function.

It's important for companies to do their homework on such issues. They need to ask: "What special things are we doing today that we'll continue to do in the future after MRP II is on the air? Are they essential? If so, will they be handled within MRP II, or not? If not, how will we do them?"

Part of getting a better set of tools to run the business is to make certain that all of the necessary tools are in place.

TIME WASTERS

Nowhere on the Proven Path does one see things like:

- Document the current system in detail.

- Design the new system.

That's because these things are time wasters when done as separate activities.

Yes, it is necessary to identify those elements of today's operations that need to be blended into MRP II. What's *not* necessary is to spend time doing a detailed documentation of the current system, with piles of paper and flow charts covering many square feet of wall space. After all, the current system is going to be replaced.

And, yes, it's necessary to ensure that the details of how MRP II will be operated support the company's goals, operating environment and necessary functions. What's *not* necessary is to spend time re-inventing the wheel. The system is already designed; it's called MRP II. The issue is how, specifically and in detail, will the tools of MRP II be used to run the business.

The Proven Path approach makes provisions for these things to occur, not as separate steps but as part of an integrated, logical process of managing the implementation of MRP II. The details will come later, in chapters 5, 6, and 8.

In the following chapter, we'll closely examine the early steps on the Proven Path.

Chapter 4

Project Launch Part I

AUDIT/ASSESSMENT I

This step gets at questions like these:

We really want to improve our ability to manufacture; what should we do first?

We think we need MRP II, but we also feel we should get started on Just-in-Time. Can we do both at the same time?

We're a consumer package goods company, with a network of field warehouses. Do we need Distribution Resource Planning? If so, should we implement it before MRP II, after MRP II, or simultaneously?

We feel we're in big trouble. We can't ship on time, hardly ever. As a result, customers are unhappy and we're losing market share; we have major cash-flow problems; and morale throughout the company is really bad. What can we do to reduce the pain level, quickly?

We've just begun a major initiative with Total Quality Control. However, we're still in order-launch-and-expedite mode, with hot lists, red tags, and shortages like crazy. Some of us are convinced that we'll never get really good with quality until we learn how to plan and schedule well. But can we handle two major projects—TQC and MRP II—at the same time, and if so, how?

What to do, and how to get started? These are the kinds of issues addressed by audit/assessment I. Its purpose is to determine specifically which tools are needed (MRP II, JIT/TQC, or DRP), and in what manner they should be implemented (company wide or fast track). For example, a company may need Manufacturing Resource Planning badly. It may want to implement MRP II on a company-wide basis, mobilizing virtually all departments and people throughout the total organization. However, this may not be possible. Other time-consuming activities may already be underway, such as building a new plant, introducing a new product line, entering a new market, and/or absorbing an acquired company. Everything about MRP II may be perfect, except for the timing. Although the company may be willing to commit the necessary dollar resources to the project, the essential resource of people's time and attention simply might not be available. "Turning up the resource knob" is not an option.

In this case, the direction coming out of audit/assessment I might be to implement Quick-Slice MRP into one or several major product lines now. (A Quick-Slice MRP implementation involves far fewer people, and it's almost always possible to free up a handful of folks for a focused project like Quick Slice.) The early "slices," perhaps more than just one or two, would be followed by a Company-Wide implementation later, after completion of the other time-consuming high-priority project(s).

Audit/assessment I and its companion, audit/assessment II, are critically important to ensure that the improvement initiatives to be pursued by the company:

1. Match its true needs.

2. Generate competitive advantages in the short run.

3. Are consistent with the company's long-term strategy.

Participants in this step include the executives, a wide range of operating managers, and, in virtually all cases, outside consultants with Class A credentials in MRP II, JIT/TQC, and/or DRP. It's quite rare that a given business unit (company, group, division) possesses enough internal expertise and objectivity to put these important issues into focus.

The process is one of fact finding, identifying areas of consensus and disagreement, and matching the company's current status and strategies with the tools it has available for execution. The end result will be an action plan to move the company onto a path of continuous improvement. Typically, the recommended action plan is presented in a business meeting with the executives and managers who've been involved to date. The purpose for this session is to have the action plan explained, questioned, challenged, modified as required, and adopted.

Another very important activity should take place in this meeting, and I call it consciousness raising. The presentation must establish the connection between the company's goals and the set of tools called MRP II, and must outline how MRP II can assist the company in reaching those goals and objectives (increased sales, reduced costs, better product quality, improved quality of life, enhanced ability to cope with change, etc.). The general manager and other key people can then see the real need to learn about MRP II in order to make an informed decision about this potentially important issue. Learning about it is called first-cut education and we'll get into it in just a moment.

The time frame for audit/assessment I (elapsed time, not man-days) will range from several days to one month. Please note: This is not a prolonged, multimonth affair involving a detailed documentation of current systems. Rather, its focus and thrust is on what's *not* working well and what needs to be done now to become more competitive. (At this point, let's assume that the output from audit/assessment I has specified a company-wide implementation of MRP II.)

FIRST-CUT EDUCATION[1]

Key people need to learn about MRP II before they can do a proper job of creating the vision statement and estimating costs and benefits. They need to learn:

1. What is MRP II?

2. Is it for us? Does it make sense for our business?

3. What will it cost?

4. What will it save? What are the benefits we'll get if we do it the right way and get to Class A?

[1] Some individuals may go through first-cut education prior to audit/assessment I. Either they will not be aware of the value of the audit/assessment step or may want to become familiar with MRP II prior to audit/assessment. The sequence is not important; the critical issue is to make sure that both steps are done. A management team should make a decision to proceed with MRP II (or any other major initiative, for that matter) only after doing both audit/assessment I and first-cut education.

Figure 4-1
The Proven Path

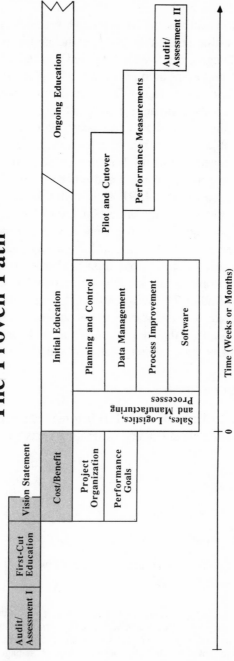

Time (Weeks or Months)

Some companies attempt to cost justify MRP II before they under-stand what it's all about. Almost invariably, they'll under-estimate the costs involved in implementation. They'll feel MRP is a computer system to order material. Therefore, most of the costs will be computer related. As a result, the project will not be properly funded.

Further, these companies almost always underestimate the benefits. They think MRP's a computer system to order material; therefore, most of the benefits will come from inventory reduction. It then becomes very difficult to peg the MRP II implementation as a high priority in the company.

The obvious moral of the story: First, learn about it; then, cost justify it.

Who needs first-cut education? For a typical company, these people would be:

1. *Top management.*

The general manager and the vice presidents of engineering, finance, manufacturing, and marketing/sales.

2. *Operating management.*

Sales (customer service) manager, production manager, systems man-ager, production control manager, purchasing manager, engineering manager, accounting manager.

Obviously, the composition of this group can vary greatly from company to company. In smaller companies, top management and oper-ating management are often one and the same. Larger companies may have senior vice presidents, directors, and others who would need early education on MRP II. The guidelines to follow are:

a. Don't send more people through first-cut education than neces-sary, since the final decision to implement hasn't yet been made.

b. On the other hand, be certain to include all key people who'll be held accountable for both costs and benefits. Their goal: To make an informed decision.

Sometimes companies have a difficult time convincing certain senior managers, possibly the general manager, to go through a first-cut education process. This can be a very serious problem, and chapter 6 will address it in detail.

VISION STATEMENT

In this step, the executives and operating managers who participated in first-cut education develop a written vision of the future. It describes what the company will look like and what new competitive capabilities will be in place following the implementation of Manufacturing Resource Planning. It does this in a way that can be measured easily, so it'll be obvious when you get there.

This step is easy to skip. It's easy to feel that it takes more time and effort than it's worth. Not true. The reverse is actually the case: It's not much work, and it's worth its weight in gold. It's an essential part of the process of laying the foundation for a successful project, along with the cost/benefit step.

The vision statement serves as a framework for consistent decision making over the life of the project, and can serve as a rallying point for the entire company.

More immediately, the vision statement will serve as direct input to downstream steps on the Proven Path: Cost/benefit analysis; establishment of performance goals; and definition of the sales, logistics, and manufacturing processes.

Input to the preparation of the vision statement includes:

1. The executives' and managers' knowledge of:

   - The company and its problems (where are we today?).

   - Its strategic direction (where are we going?).

   - Its operating environment (what does the marketplace require?).

   - Its competition (what level of performance would gain us a competitive advantage in that marketplace?).

2. The recommendations made in audit/assessment I.

3. What was learned in first-cut education.

Brevity is good; less is more. Ideally, the vision statement will consist of one or two pages. At most, there should be no more than one page for each major functional department—marketing, sales and distribution; manufacturing and materials, engineering/R & D; finance and accounting.

Since it's a relatively brief document, it shouldn't take a long time to prepare. One or several meetings should do the job, with heavy involvement by the general manager.

COST/BENEFIT ANALYSIS

Justifying the cost of an MRP II project is essential. Here are some reasons why:

1. *High priority.*

Job 1 is to run the business. Very close to that in importance should be implementing MRP II. It's very difficult to keep MRP II pegged as a very high priority if the relevant costs and benefits haven't been established and bought into. If MRP II doesn't carry this high priority, the chances for success decrease.

2. *A solid commitment.*

Implementing MRP II means changing the way the business is run. Consequently, top management and operating management must be committed to making it happen. Without a solid projection of costs and benefits, the necessary degree of dedication may not be attained, and the chances for success will decrease sharply.

3. *One allocation of funds.*

By identifying costs thoroughly and completely before implementation, the company has to process only one spending authorization. This avoids repeated "trips to the well" (the board of directors, the corporate office, the executive committee) and their attendant delays during the life of the project.

The people who attended first-cut education should now develop the cost justification. Their objective is to develop a set of numbers to use in deciding for or against MRP II. Do not, under any circumstances, allow yourselves to skip this step. Even though you may be convinced that you must do MRP II and its benefits will be enormous, it's essential that you go through this process, for the reasons mentioned above. To do otherwise is like attempting to build a house on a foundation of sand.

Let's first focus on the likely areas of costs and benefits. After that, we'll work through several sample cost justifications.

COSTS

A good way to group the costs is via our ABC categories: A = People, B = Data, C = Computer. Let's take them in reverse order.

C = Computer. Include in this category the following costs:

1. New computer hardware necessary for MRP II.

2. Purchased (or leased) software for MRP II.

3. Systems people and programmers to:

   • Write new software internally.

   • Install the purchased software on the computer, debug it, and make it work.

   • Enhance the purchased software to make it functionally complete.

   • Interface the purchased software with existing systems that will remain in place after MRP II is implemented.

   • Assist in user training.

   • Develop documentation.

   • Provide system maintenance.

These people may already be on staff, may have to be hired, and/or may be temporary contract personnel.

4. Forms, supplies, miscellaneous.

5. Software maintenance costs.

6. Other anticipated charges from the software supplier (plus perhaps some contingency money for unanticipated charges).

B = Data. Include here the costs involved to get and maintain:

1. Inventory record accuracy, which could involve:

   • New fences, gates, scales, shelves, bins, lift trucks, and other types of new equipment.

   • Costs associated with plant relayout, sometimes necessary to create and/or consolidate stockrooms.

   • Cycle counting costs.

   • Other increases in manpower necessary to achieve and maintain inventory accuracy.

2. Bill of material accuracy, structure and completeness.

3. Routing accuracy.

4. Other elements of data such as forecasts, customer orders, item data, work center data, etc.

A = People. Include here costs for:

1. The project team, typically full-time project leader and perhaps one or several assistants.

2. Education, including travel and lodging.

3. Professional guidance.

4. Increases in the indirect payroll, either temporary or ongoing, not reflected elsewhere. Examples include perhaps a new demand manager or master scheduler, additional material planning people, another dispatcher, etc. For most companies, this number is not large at all. For a few, usually those with no planning function prior to MRP II, it might be major.

These are the major categories of cost for MRP II. Which of them can be eliminated? None; they're all essential. Which one is most important? The A item, of course, because it involves the people. If, for whatever reason, it's absolutely necessary to shave some money out of the project budget, from where should it come? Certainly not the A item. How about cutting back on the C item, the computer? Well, if you absolutely have to cut somewhere, that's the best place to do it. Why? Because many companies have become very successful with MRP II with only very base, rudimentary, inexpensive sets of hardware and software. None to my knowledge has become highly successful without motivated, enthusiastic employees who received substantial amounts of education and training.

In general terms, for an average-sized business unit (about 500 to 1,000 people), it'll cost around $1 million. This number is not based on conjecture but rather on the direct experience of many companies.

A survey, taken during the latter half of 1988, captured results from more than 1200 companies who had implemented MRP/MRP II.[2] As a part of the survey, companies were asked to rate themselves as Class A, B, C, or D. Interestingly, the Class A companies reported implementation costs of $700,000 while the companies who identified themselves as Class D reported average costs of $800,000. Interesting, eh? Class D results cost even more than Class A![3].

BENEFITS

So much for the costs. Now let's look at the good news, the benefits.

1. *Increased sales,* as a direct result of improved customer service.[4] MRP II enables many companies to:

- Ship on time virtually all the time.

- Ship in less time than the competition.

- Have their salesmen spend their time selling, rather than expediting shipments and making excuses to customers over missed shipments.

---

[2] *Survey Results: MRP II/Just-in-Time* is available from Oliver Wight Publications.

[3] One major reason is that the Class D companies tend to overspend on the C item (the computer) and underspend on the A and B items (people and data).

[4] A variation on this theme: Some companies need to improve their customer service merely to hold onto the business they already have. This gets more and more important as one's competition gets tougher and tougher.

In short, MRP II can come to represent a significant competitive weapon. The user's survey cited above showed customer service gains of 15 percent for all respondents; 26 percent for the companies who identified themselves as Class A. For most companies, better customer service means more sales.[5]

2. *Increased direct labor productivity,* resulting from the valid, attainable schedules which MRP II can enable companies to have. Productivity is increased via:

• Providing matched sets of components to the assembly areas, thereby eliminating much of the inefficiency and idle time often present.

• Reducing sharply the amount of expediting, lot splitting, emergency changeovers, short runs, etc. in the fabrication areas.

• Requiring much less unplanned overtime, because the forward visibility provided by MRP II is so much better.

The survey results showed all respondents reporting an average productivity gain of 11 percent; the Class A users got 20 percent.

3. *Reduced purchase cost.* MRP II provides the tools to give suppliers valid schedules and better forward visibility. Once the customer company gets out of the order-launch-and-expedite mode, its suppliers can produce the customer's items more efficiently, at lower cost. A portion of these savings can be passed back to the buying company.

Further, valid schedules can free the buyers from a life of expediting and paper shuffling, so that they can do the important parts of their jobs—sourcing, negotiation, contracting, value analysis, cost reduction, etc.

Survey results: All companies reported an average purchase cost reduction of 7 percent; the Class A companies got 13 percent. In many companies, the single largest financial benefit from MRP II comes from purchase cost reduction.

---

[5] But not always. One exception would be a company already shipping at a high customer service level prior to MRP II. (There really are some like this but not many.) Another example: a defense contractor whose sales levels are determined primarily by what happens in Washington, DC, and not on its shipping dock.

4. *Reduced inventories.* Effective demand management and master scheduling result in valid schedules. Valid schedules mean matched sets of components, which means making the products on schedule and shipping them on time.

In the survey, all companies reported an average inventory drop of 16 percent, and Class A companies saw 30 percent.[6]

For most companies, the four benefit areas identified above are the big ones. However, there are other benefits from MRP II that are potentially very significant and should not be overlooked. They include:

5. *Reduced obsolescence,* from an enhanced ability to manage engineering changes, better forward visibility, and an overall smaller risk of obsolescence due to lower inventories in general.

6. *Reduced quality costs.* Valid schedules can result in a more stable environment, which can mean less scrap. Eliminating the end-of-the-month lump, where perhaps 75 percent of the shipments go out in the last 25 percent of the month, can mean reduced warranty costs.

7. *Reduced premium freight,* both inbound, by having a better handle on what's needed, and outbound, by being able to ship on time.

8. *Elimination of the annual physical inventory.* If the inventory numbers are accurate enough for MRP II, they'll be more than good enough for the balance sheet. Class A companies rarely take annual physical inventories. This can be a substantial savings in some companies. It can include not only the costs of taking the inventory itself but also the costs of disrupting production, since many companies can't produce while they count.

9. *Reduced floor space.* As raw material, work-in-process, and finished inventories drop sharply, space is freed up. As a result, you may not need to expand the plant or build the new warehouse or rent more

---

[6] These inventory numbers may strike some readers as too low. I agree. The survey measured absolute changes in inventory *levels;* as such it did not factor out price increases and increased volumes. My belief is that these inventory reduction numbers would be almost twice as large had the survey asked about inventory *turnover.* A 30 percent inventory reduction is not a Class A result; it is Class C. Typical inventory reductions in Class A situations range from 40 to 50 percent.

office space for some time to come. Do a mental connection between MRP II (and JIT, which you've either already started on or soon will) and your building plans. You may not need as much, or any, new brick and mortar once you get really good at manufacturing. Don't build a white elephant.

10. *Increased productivity of the indirect work force.* MRP II will help not only the direct labor people to be more productive but also the indirect folks. An obvious example is the large expediting group maintained by some companies. Under MRP II, this group should no longer be needed, and its members could be absorbed into other, more productive jobs.

Another aspect of this, more subtle and perhaps difficult to quantify, is the increased productivity of the supervisors and managers. That includes foremen, engineers, quality control people, production managers, vice presidents of marketing, and let's not forget about the guy in the corner office—the general manager. They should all be able to do their jobs better when the company is operating with a valid game plan and an effective set of tools to help them execute it.

They'll have more fun, also. More satisfaction from a job well done. More of a feeling of accomplishment. That's called quality of life. It's almost impossible to quantify that benefit, but it may be the most important one of all.

RESPONSIBILITY

A question often asked is: "Who should do the cost/benefit analysis? Who should put the numbers together?"

First of all, it shouldn't be a one-person process—it's much too important for that. Second, the process should not be confined to a single group. Let's look at several ways to do a cost/benefit analysis:

Method 1: Middle management sells up.

Operating managers put together the cost/benefit analysis and then attempt to sell the project to their bosses. If top management has been to first-cut education, there should be no need for them to be sold. Rather, they and their key managers should be evaluating specifically how MRP II will benefit their company and what it'll cost to get to Class A.

This method is not recommended.

Method 2: Top management decree.

The executive group does the cost justification and then decrees that the company will implement MRP II. This doesn't allow for building the kind of consensus and teamwork that's so important.

This method is not recommended.

Method 3: Joint venture.

This is the recommended approach. The cost justification should be done by those executives and managers who'll be held accountable for achieving the projected benefits within the framework of the identified costs. Here's how to do it:

1. A given department head, let's say the manager of sales administration and customer service, attends first-cut education.

2. The vice president of marketing attends first-cut education.

3. Upon returning to the company, both persons do some homework, focusing on what benefits the sales side of the business would get from a Class A MRP II system, plus what costs might be involved.

4. In one or several sessions, they develop their numbers. In this example, the most likely benefit would be increased sales resulting from improved customer service, and the biggest cost elements might be in education and training.

5. This process is done in the other key functional areas of the business. Then the numbers are consolidated into a single statement of costs and benefits in all of the key areas of the business.

Please note the participative nature of the joint venture approach. Since both top management and operating management are involved, it promotes consensus up and down the organization, as well as cross functionally. We've found it to be far better than the other approaches identified above.

A word of caution: Be fiscally conservative. When in doubt, estimate the costs to the high side and the benefits low. If you think some dollars may be required for a given item, but you're not certain, include them. Tag them as contingency if you like, but get 'em in there. There's little risk that this approach will make your cost/benefit numbers unattractive because MRP II is such a high payback project. Therefore, be conservative. Don't promise more than you can deliver.

JUSTIFICATION EXAMPLES

To illustrate the process, let's create a hypothetical company with the following characteristics:

Annual sales: $100 million
Employees: 700
Number of plants: 1
Manufacturing process: Fabrication and assembly
Product: A complex assembled make-to-order product, with many options (electronics, machinery, etc.)
Pretax net profit: 8 percent of sales
Annual direct labor cost: $10 million
Annual purchase volume (production materials): $30 million
Current inventories: $24 million

For convenience, we'll refer to this organization as Company T (for Typical). Let's take a look at its projected costs and benefits, but first, a warning:

Beware! The numbers that follow are not *your company's numbers. They are sample numbers only. Do not use them. They may be too high or too low for your specific situation. Using them could be hazardous to the health of your company and your career.*

With that caution, let's examine the numbers. Costs are divided into one-time (acquisition) costs and recurring (annual operating) costs . . . and are in our three categories: C = Computer, B = Data, A = People. (See figure 4-2.)

These numbers are interesting, for several reasons. First, they indicate the MRP II project will pay for itself in less than one year after full implementation, in fact, in just six and one-half months.

Figure 4-2
Company T Cost Justification

COSTS C-Computer	One Time	Recurring	Comments
Hardware	$60,000	$36,000	Company T will need to add some new hardware to its computers. Some of the new hardware will be purchased, and some leased.
Software	200,000	—	The most expensive software package being considered costs $200,000. They plan to maintain the software themselves.
Systems and programming	250,000	50,000	Data processing people costs to install, modify, interface, enhance, maintain, and document the software.

B-Data	One Time	Recurring	Comments
Inventory record accuracy	260,000	35,000	Includes new equipment and one full-time cycle counter.
Bill of material accuracy and structure	150,000	—	Bills will need to be restructured into the modular format. Experienced engineers will be required for this step.
Routing accuracy	35,000	—	Routings will need to be reviewed.

A-People	One Time	Recurring	Comments
Project team	$170,000	—	One full-time project leader and one assistant, for 18 months.
Outside education	700,000	12,000	Includes travel.
Inside education	80,000	30,000	Includes costs for video, overtime costs, plus vendor education.
Professional guidance	78,000	3,000	One-day visits, every four to eight weeks, by an experienced MRP II professional.
Total costs	$ 1,383,000	$166,000	

BENEFITS Function	Current	% Improvement	Annual Benefits	Comments
Sales	$100,000,000	5% at 8%	$ 400,000	Sales and marketing is projecting a 5% sales gain due to improved customer service. The company's net profit has been running at 8% of sales.
Direct labor productivity	10,000,000	5%	500,000	
Purchase cost reduction	30,000,000	3%	900,000	
Inventory reduction	24,000,000	20% at 15%	720,000	The inventory is projected to decrease by 20%. A carrying cost of 15% was used.
Obsolescence	300,000	20%	60,000	
Warranty cost reduction	500,000	25%	125,000	Quality currently suffers during the "end-of-month crunch," which will be eliminated.
Gross annual benefits			$2,705,000	
Subtracting: Recurring costs			−166,000	
Net annual benefits			$2,539,000	

	Divided by 12
Cost of a one-month delay	$211,583
Payback period (One-time costs/(net annual benefits/12))	6.5 Months, Following full implementation
Return on investment (Net annual benefits/one-time costs)	183%

Second, the lost opportunity cost of a one-month delay is $211,583. This very powerful number should be made highly visible during the entire project, for several reasons:

1. It imparts a sense of urgency. ("We really do need to get MRP II implemented as soon as we can.")

2. It helps to establish priorities. ("This project really is the number two priority in the company.")

3. It brings the resource allocation issue into clearer focus.

Regarding this last point, think back to the concept of the three knobs from chapter 2—*work* to be done, *time* available in which to do it, and *resources* which can be applied. Recall that any two of these elements can be held constant by varying the third.

Too often in the past, companies have assumed their only option is to increase the time. They assumed (often incorrectly) that both the work load and resources are fixed. The result of this assumption: A stretched-out implementation, with its attendant decrease in the odds for success.

Making everyone aware of the cost of a one-month delay can help companies avoid that trap. But the key people really must believe the numbers. For example, let's assume the company's in a bind on the MRP II project schedule. They're short of people in a key function. The choices are:

Figure 4-3
Company T Projected Cash Flow from MRP II

Year	Annual	Cumulative	
1	− $1,244,700	− $1,244,700	90% of one-time costs
2	− 138,300		Balance (10%) of one-time costs
	− 166,000		Annual recurring costs
	+ 1,352,500		50% of gross annual benefits
	+ 1,200,000		25% of inventory reduction
	+ $2,248,200	+ $1,003,500	
3	− 166,000		Annual recurring costs
	+ 2,705,000		Gross annual benefits
	+ 3,600,000		Balance (75%) of inventory reduction
	+ 5,848,200	+ 6,851,700	Total cash flow at end of year 3

1. Delay the implementation for three months. Cost: $633,000 ($211K x 3).

2. Stay on schedule by getting temporary help from outside the company (to free up the company's people to work on MRP II, not to work on MRP II themselves). Cost: $150,000.

No one will deny $150,000 is a lot of money. But, it's a whole lot less than $633,000.

So far in this example, I've been talking about costs (expenses) and benefits (income). Cash flow is another important financial consideration, and there's good news and bad news here.

First, the bad news.

A company must spend virtually all of the $1.4 million (one-time costs) before getting anything back.

The good news.

Enormous amounts of cash are freed up, largely as a result of the inventory decrease. The cost justification for Company T projects an inventory reduction of $4.8 million (20 percent of $24 million). This represents incoming cash flow. (See figure 4-3 for details.)

MRP II appears to be very attractive for Company T: An excellent return on investment (186 percent) and substantial amounts of cash being freed up.[7]

How might a different kind of company come out on cost justification? For example, one that's larger, with more locations, and in a different industry? Well, let's see.

Here's a profile on another manufacturer, this one called Company P & R (for Process and Repetitive):

Annual sales: $1 billion
Employees: 3,300
Plants: 3

---

[7] I haven't tried to quantify certain early benefits which often happen *during* an MRP II implementation. For example, sales & operations planning will frequently result in significant improvements to a company's operations even before any of the more detailed planning tools are in place. Another example: merely getting the inventory records and bills of material accurate has often resulted in substantial benefits early in the life of the project.

Distribution centers: 8
Manufacturing process: High-speed, high-volume flow processing
Product: Consumer package goods, make-to-stock
Pretax net profit: 12 percent
Annual direct labor cost: $24 million
Annual purchase volume (production materials): $200 million
Current inventories: Manufacturing (includes raw materials, WIP,
etc.): $33 Million; Distribution (finished goods): $65 million

Company P & R's cost justification is shown in figure 4-4. The
company is larger than Company T and more geographically dispersed.
Its products are simpler but made in much greater volume and much
faster. It has a network of eight distribution centers in place, and
Distribution Resource Planning (DRP) will be required.

Company P & R plans on implementing all of MRP II in all plants
within two years. DRP will be implemented simultaneously, as a part of
basic MRP.

Implementing MRP II/DRP in Company P & R will be more complex
and take longer than in a smaller one-location organization like Company T. The rewards are proportionately greater; typically the larger the
company, the more highly leveraged the benefits are from MRP II. This
can represent a very solid investment.

Company S (for Small) looks like this:

Annual sales: $10,000,000
Employees: 150
Plants: 1
Manufacturing process: Fabrication and assembly
Product: OEM components, make-to-order
Pretax net profit: 10 percent
Annual direct labor cost: $1,000,000
Annual purchase volume: $43,000,000
Current inventories: $2,000,000

See figure 4-5 for company S's cost justification. The bad news:
Benefits from MRP II are less highly leveraged in smaller companies.

The good news: Even in a small company, MRP II is a super investment.

Here are a few final thoughts on cost justification.

1. What I've been trying to illustrate here is primarily the *process* of cost justification, not how to format the numbers. Use whatever format the corporate office requires. For internal use within the business unit, however, keep it simple—two or three pages should do just fine. Many companies have used the format shown here and found it to be very helpful for operational and project management purposes.

2. I've dealt mostly with out-of-pocket costs. For example, the opportunity costs of the managers' time have not been applied to the project; these people are on the exempt payroll and have a job to do, regardless of how many hours will be involved. Some companies don't do it that way. They include the estimated costs of management's time in order to decide on the relative merits of competing projects. This is also a valid approach and can certainly be followed.

3. Get widespread participation in the cost-justification process. Have all of the key departments involved. Avoid the trap of cost justifying the entire project on the basis of inventory reduction alone. It's probably possible to do it that way and come up with the necessary payback and return on investment numbers. Unfortunately, it sends exactly the wrong message to the rest of the company. It says: "This is an inventory reduction project," and that's wrong. MRP II is a whole lot more than that.

4. To keep the examples as uncluttered as possible, I didn't add in any costs for contingency. Some companies prefer to include in the cost justification some dollars for unanticipated expenses. Their rationale is that if a surprise occurs, money is already in the budget to solve the problem. If there are no surprises, then, of course, the money isn't spent. I think that's a good idea. If your corporate culture allows, you may want to add in 5 percent or so for contingency.

5. A few companies, usually small and growing rapidly, have a difficult time cost justifying MRP II based on improvements to their *current* mode of operation. Because of their small size, the lack of effective formal systems isn't a major hindrance. However, they know that their rapid growth will soon get them to a size where the informal

Figure 4-4
Company P & R Cost Justification

COSTS C-Computer	One Time	Recurring	Comments
Hardware	$400,000	—	A hardware purchase, not lease.
Software	500,000	50,000	Includes purchase of DRP software. Software maintenance contract costs $35,000.
Systems and programming	650,000	60,000	Included here is the internal development of a new forecasting and order entry system.

B-Data	One Time	Recurring	Comments
Inventory records	900,000	100,000	This will be a major effort at the branch warehouses as well as the plants.
Bills of material	60,000	—	The bills are simple and fairly accurate.
Routings	—	—	The routings are simple, and currently very accurate.
Forecasting	100,000	70,000	Marketing will need to add a full-time person for sales forecasting. That person will come on board early.

A-People	One Time	Recurring	Comments
Project team	700,000	—	One full-time project leader at each plant, a corporate project leader, and an assistant—all for two years.
Outside education	300,000	30,000	
Inside education	290,000	90,000	
Professional guidance	150,000	3,000	
Total	$4,050,000	$403,000	

BENEFITS Function	Current	% Improvement	Annual Benefits	Comments
Sales	$1,000,000,000	0	—	The company's fill rate (% of orders shipped from stock) is already very high.
Direct labor productivity	24,000,000	7%	1,680,000	Mainly through reductions in idle time, overtime, layoff, and training. Costs caused by the lack of a good planning and scheduling system.
Purchase cost	200,000,000	2%	4,000,000	
Inventories Manufacturing	33,000,000	10% @ 15%	495,000	
Distribution	65,000,000	25 @ 15%	2,437,500	
Obsolescence	—	—	—	
Quality	—	—	—	
Premium freight	400,000	50%	200,000	Primarily outbound: from the plants to the branch warehouses and from the branches to the customers.

Other (Elimination of annual physical inventory)	50,000
Gross annual benefits	$8,862,500
Subtracting: recurring cost	− 403,000
Net annual benefits	$8,459,500
	divided by 12
Cost of a one-month delay	$704,950
Payback period	5.7 months
Return on investment	208%

Figure 4-5
Company S Cost Justification

COSTS C-Computer	One Time	Recurring	Comments
Hardware and software	$ 80,000	0	Company S has no computer. This covers the purchase of microcomputers and software.
Systems and programming	60,000	40,000	This reflects the addition of a data processing person to operate the computer, install the software, make additions to it, etc.

B-Data	One Time	Recurring	Comments
Inventory records	65,000	15,000	One-time costs are equipment and people. Recurring costs cover a half-time cycle counter.
Bills of material	—	—	The small amount of work needed to get bill accuracy will be done by people on the exempt payroll.
Routings	100,000	15,000	Company S has no routings and no standards. An outside industrial engineering firm will be used to help create the routings and standards, and a half-time person will be required to maintain them.

A-People	One Time	Recurring	Comments
Project team	56,250	—	
Outside education	30,000	5,000	
Inside education	30,000	8,000	
Professional guidance	28,000	3,000	
Total	$449,250	$86,000	

BENEFITS Function	Current	% Improvement	Annual Benefits
Sales	$10,000,000	10% @ 10%	$100,000
Direct labor productivity	1,000,000	10%	100,000
Purchase cost	3,000,000	3%	90,000
Inventories	2,000,000	30% @ 20%	120,000
Obsolescence	150,000	50%	75,000
Quality (scrap)	200,000	50%	100,000
Premium freight	50,000	50%	25,000
Other	—	—	—
Gross annual benefits			$610,000
Subtracting: recurring costs			−86,000
Net annual benefits			$524,000
			divided by 12
Cost of one-month delay			$ 43,666
Payback period			10.3 months
Return on investment			116%

systems will begin to break down. The answer, they believe, is MRP II. But how can they justify it based on dollars and cents? What will be the benefits?

One approach is to project how large the company will be at some point in the future, based on anticipated growth rates, and to estimate the penalties of operating in that environment with today's systems. These penalties would be the costs from poor customer service, low productivity, poor purchase cost performance, excessive inventories, scrap, obsolescence, etc. The elimination of these costs can become the benefit numbers in the cost justification equation.

COMMITMENT

Getting commitment is the first moment of truth in an implementation project. This is when the company turns thumbs-up or thumbs-down on MRP II.

Key people within the company have gone through audit/assessment I and first-cut education, and have done the vision statement and cost/benefit analysis. They should now know:

- What is MRP II?

- Is it right for our company?

- What will it cost?

- What will it save?

- How long will it take?

How do the numbers in the cost justification look? Are they good enough to peg the implementation of MRP II as a very high priority in the company?

There's one final acid test for implementation readiness: Is the company prepared to keep this implementation as a high number-two priority for the next year or two, and to allocate the required amounts of its people's time? If the answer is no, don't go ahead. If it's yes, put it in *writing*.

THE WRITTEN PROJECT CHARTER

Do a formal sign-off on the cost justification. The people who developed and accepted the numbers should sign their names on the cost/benefit study. Together with the vision statement, these documents will form the written project charter. They will spell out what the company will look like following implementation, levels of performance to be achieved, costs and benefits, and time frame.

Why make this process so formal? First, it will stress the importance of the project. Second, the written charter can serve as a beacon, a rallying point during the next year or so of implementation when the tough times come. *And they will come.* Business may get real good, or real bad. Or the government gets on the company's back. Or, perhaps most frightening of all, the enthusiastic and MRP II-knowledgeable general manager is transferred to another division. His successor may not share his perspective on MRP II.

A written charter won't make these problems disappear. But it will make it easier to address them, and to stay the course.

Don't be bashful with this document. Consider doing what some companies have done: Get three or four high-quality copies of this document; get 'em framed; hang one on the wall in the executive conference room, one in the conference room where the project team will be meeting, one in the education and training room, one in the cafeteria, and maybe elsewhere. Let's drive a stake in the ground. Let's make a statement that this implementation is not just another project but rather that we're serious about it and that we're going to do it right.

We've just completed the first four steps on the Proven Path: Audit/ assessment I, first-cut education, vision statement, and cost/benefit analysis. A company at this point has accomplished a number of things. First of all, its key people, typically with help from outside experts, have done a focused assessment of the company's current problems and opportunities, which has pointed them to Manufacturing Resource Planning. Next, these key people received some initial education on MRP II. They've created a vision of the future, estimated costs and benefits, and have made a commitment to implement MRP II, via the Proven Path so that the company can get to Class A quickly.

THE IMPLEMENTERS' CHECKLISTS

At this point, it's time to introduce the concept of Implementers' Checklists. These are documents that detail the major tasks necessary to ensure total compliance with the Proven Path approach.

A company that is able to check yes for each task on each list can be virtually guaranteed of a successful implementation of MRP II. As such, these checklists can be important tools for key implementers—people like project leaders, torchbearers, general managers, and other members of the steering committee and project team.

Beginning here, an Implementers' Checklist will appear at the end of most of the following chapters. The reader may be able to expand his utility by adding tasks, as appropriate. However, I recommend against the deletion of tasks from any of the checklists. To do so would weaken their ability to help monitor compliance with the Proven Path.

IMPLEMENTERS' CHECKLIST

Functions: Audit/Assessment I, First-cut Education, Vision Statement, Cost Justification, & Commitment

	Complete	
Task	YES	NO
1. Audit/assessment I conducted with participation by top management, operating management, and outside consultants with Class A experience in MRP II, JIT/TQC, and/or DRP.	____	____
2. The general manager and key staff members have attended first-cut education.	____	____
3. All key operating managers (department heads) have attended first-cut education.	____	____
4. Vision statement prepared and accepted by top management and operating management from all involved functions.	____	____
5. Cost justification prepared on a joint venture basis, with both top management and operating management from all involved functions participating.	____	____
6. Cost justification approved by general manager and all other necessary individuals.	____	____
7. Manufacturing Resource Planning established as a very high priority within the entire organization.	____	____
8. Written project charter created and formally signed off by all executives and managers participating in the justification process.	____	____

Chapter 5

Project Launch Part II

Once a commitment to implement MRP II is made, it's time to get organized for the project. New groups will need to be created, as well as one or more temporary positions.

PROJECT LEADER

The project leader will head up the MRP II project team, and spearhead the implementation at the operational level. Let's examine some of the requirements of this position.

Requirement 1: The project leader should be full time. Having a full-time project leader is one way to break through the catch-22, as discussed in chapter 2, and get to Class A within two years.

Except in very small organizations (those with about 100 or fewer employees), it's essential to free a key person from all operational responsibilities. If this doesn't happen, that part-time project leader/part-time operating person will often have to spend time on priority number one (running the business) at the expense of priority number two (making progress on MRP II). The result: Delays, a stretched-out implementation, and sharply reduced odds for success.

Figure 5-1
The Proven Path

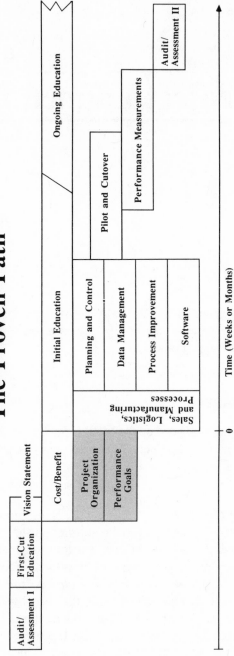

Audit/ Assessment I

First-Cut Education

Vision Statement

Cost/Benefit

Project Organization

Performance Goals

Initial Education

Sales, Logistics, and Manufacturing Processes

Planning and Control

Data Management

Process Improvement

Software

Ongoing Education

Pilot and Cutover

Performance Measurements

Audit/ Assessment II

Time (Weeks or Months)

0

Requirement 2: The project leader should be someone from within the company. Resist the temptation to hire an MRP II expert from outside to be the project leader. There are several important reasons:

1. MRP II isn't complicated, so it won't take long for the insider to learn all he needs to know about MRP II, even though that person may have no background in materials management, data processing, etc.

2. It will take the outsider (a project leader from outside the company who knows MRP II) far longer to learn about the company: Its products, its processes, and its people. The project leader must know these things, because implementing MRP II successfully means changing the way the business will be run. This requires knowing how the business is being run today.

3. While it will take a long time for the outsider to learn the products, the processes, and the people—it will take even longer for the people to learn the outsider. The outside expert brings with him little credibility, little trust, and probably little rapport. He may be a terrific person, but he is fundamentally an unknown quantity to the people inside the company.

This approach can often result in the insiders sitting back, reluctant to get involved, and prepared to watch the new guy "do a wheelie." Their attitude: "MRP II? Oh, that's Charlie's job. He's that new guy the company hired to install MRP II. He's taking care of that." This results in MRP II no longer being an operational effort to change the way the business is run. Rather, it becomes another systems project headed up by an outsider, and the odds for success drop sharply.

Requirement 3: The project leader should have an operational background. He should come from an operating department within the company—a department involved in a key function regarding the products: Design, sales, production, purchasing, planning. I recommend against selecting the project leader from the data processing department unless that person also has recent operating experience within the company.

One reason is that, typically, a systems person hasn't been directly involved in the challenging business of getting product shipped, week after week, month after month. He hasn't "been there," even though he may have been working longer hours than the operational folks. Another problem with selecting a data processing person to head up the entire project is that it sends the wrong signal throughout the company. It says: "This is a computer project." Obviously, it's not. It's a line management activity, involving virtually all areas of the business.

Requirement 4: The project leader should be the best available person for the job from within the ranks of the operating managers of the business—the department heads. (Or maybe even higher in the organization. Over the past few years, we've seen some companies appoint a vice president as the full time project leader.) Bite the bullet, and relieve one of your very best managers from all operating responsibilities, and appoint him project leader. It's that important.

In any given company, there's a wide variety of candidates:

- Production manager.

- Purchasing manager.

- Sales administration manager.

- Production & inventory control manager.

- Customer service manager.

- Product engineering manager.

- Manufacturing engineering manager.

- Materials manager.

- Distribution manager.

One of the best background project leaders I've ever seen was in a machine tool company. The project leader had been the assembly superintendent. Of all the people in a typical machine tool company, perhaps the assembly superintendent understands the problems best.[1]

Often, senior executives are reluctant to assign that excellent operating manager totally to MRP II. While they realize the critical impor-

---

[1] Assembly superintendents frequently are heard to say things like: "We don't have the parts. Give us the parts and we'll make the product." They tend to say this with greater frequency and volume near the end of the month.

tance of MRP II and the need for a heavyweight to manage it, they're hesitant. Perhaps they're concerned, understandably, about the impact on priority number one (running the business).

Imagine the following conversation between a general manager and myself:

GENERAL MANAGER (GM): We can't afford to free up any of our operating managers to be the full-time project leader. We just don't have enough management depth. We'll have to hire the project leader from outside.

TOM WALLACE (TW): Oh, really? Suppose one of your key managers was to get run over by a train tomorrow. Are you telling me that your company would be in big trouble?

GM: Oh, no, not at all.

TW: What would you do in that case?

GM: We'd have to hire the replacement from outside the company. As I said, we don't have much bench strength.

TW: Great. Make believe your best manager just got run over by a train. Make him the full-time project leader. And then, if absolutely necessary, use an outside hire to fill the operating job that he vacated.

Bottom line: If it doesn't hurt to free up the person who'll be your project leader, you probably have the wrong person. Further, as my colleague Pete Skurla points out, if you select the person you can least afford to free up, then you can be sure you've got the right guy. This is an early and important test of true management commitment.

Requirement 5: The project leader should be a veteran—someone who's been with the company for a good while, and has the scar tissue to prove it. People who are quite new to the company are still technically outsiders. They don't know the business or the people. The people don't know them; trust hasn't had time to develop. Companies, other than very young ones, should try to get as their project leader someone who's been on board for about five years or more.

Requirement 6: The project leader should have good people skills, good communication skills, the respect and trust of his peers, and a good track record. In short, someone who's a good person and a good manager. It's important, because the project leader's job is almost entirely involved with people. The important elements are trust, mutual respect, frequent and open communications, and enthusiasm. (See figure 5-2 for a summary of the characteristics of the project leader.)

What does the project leader do? Quite a bit, and I'll discuss some of the details later, after examining the other elements of organization for MRP II. For the time being, however, please refer to figure 5-3 for an outline of the job.

One last question about the project leader: What does the project leader do after MRP II is successfully implemented? After all, his job has probably been filled by someone else.

Well, most of them stay with the company, sometimes returning to their prior job, sometimes moving to a bigger one. It figures. These people are really valuable; they've demonstrated excellent people and organizational skills as project leader, and they certainly know the set of tools being used to manage the day-to-day business.

In some cases, they become deeply involved with Just-in-Time and Total Quality Control initiatives in their company. In other cases, they return to their prior jobs, because their jobs have been filled with a temporary for that one- to two-year period.

How so? Through the use of temporaries, and there are several possibilities here. First there's a wealth of talented, vigorous ex-managers in North America who've received early retirement from their long-term employers. Many of them are delighted to get back into the saddle for a year or two. Win-win.

Secondly, some organizations with bench strength have moved people up temporarily for the duration of the project. For example, the number two person in the customer service department may become the acting manager, filling the job vacated by the newly appointed project leader.

Figure 5-2
Project Leader Characteristics

- Full time on the project.
- Assigned from within the company, not hired from outside.
- An operating person—someone who has been deeply involved in making shipments and/or other fundamental aspects of running the business.
- Heavyweight, not a lightweight.
- A veteran with the company, not a rookie.
- A good manager and a respected person within the company.

When the project's over, everyone returns to their original jobs. The junior people get good experience and a chance to prove themselves; the project leader has a job to return to. Here also, win-win.

In a company with multiple divisions, it's not unusual for the ex-project leader at division A to move to division B as that division begins implementation. But a word of caution: This person should not be the project leader at division B *because he is an outsider*. Rather, he should fill an operating job there, perhaps the one vacated by the person tapped to be the project leader.

When offering the project leader's job to your first choice, make it a real offer. Make it clear that he can accept it or turn it down, and that his career won't be impacted negatively if it's the latter. Further, I'd like to see some career planning going on at that point, spelling out plans for him after the project is completed.

PROJECT TEAM

The next step in getting organized is to establish the MRP II project team. This is the group responsible for implementing the system at the operational level. Its jobs include:

- Establishing the MRP II project schedule.

- Reporting actual performance against the schedule.

- Identifying problems and obstacles to successful implementation.

- Activating ad hoc groups called spin-off task forces (discussed later in this chapter) to solve these problems.

- Making decisions, as appropriate, regarding priorities, resource reallocation, etc.

- Making recommendations, when necessary, to the executive steering committee (discussed later in this chapter).

- Doing whatever is required to permit a smooth, rapid and success-ful implementation of MRP II at the operational level of the business.

The project team consists of relatively few full-time members. Typically, they are the project leader, perhaps one or several assistant project

Figure 5-3
Project Leader Job Outline

- Chairs the MRP II project team.
- Is a member of the MRP II executive steering committee.
- Oversees the MRP II educational process—both outside and inside.
- Coordinates the preparation of the MRP II project schedule, obtaining concurrence and commitment from all involved parties..
- Updates the project schedule each week and highlights jobs behind schedule.
- Counsels with departments and individuals who are behind schedule, and attempts to help them get back on schedule.
- Reports serious behind-schedule situations to the executive steering committee, and makes recommendations for their solution.
- Reschedules the project as necessary, and only when directed by the executive steering committee.
- Works closely with the outside consultant, routinely keeping that person advised of progress and problems.

The essence of the project leader's job is to remove obstacles and to support the people doing the work of implementing MRP II:

Foremen	Systems People
Buyers	Marketing People
Engineers	Warehouse People
Planners	Executives
Accountants	Etc.

---

leaders (to support the project leader, coordinate education, write procedures, provide support to other departments, etc.), and often one or several systems people.

Most of the members of the project team are part-time members. They are the department heads—the operating managers of the business. Below is an example of a project team from sample Company T (as described in chapter 4: 800 people, one location, fabrication and assembly, make-to-order product, etc.).

This group totals 15 people, which is big enough to handle the job but not too large to execute responsibilities effectively. Some of you may question how effective a group of 15 people can be. Well, actual experience has shown that an MRP II project team of 15, or even 20, can function very well—provided that the meetings are well structured and well managed. Stay tuned.

Full-time Members	*Part-time Members*
Project leader	Cost accounting manager
Assistant project leader	Customer service manager[2]
Systems analyst	Data processing manager
	Demand manager
	Distribution manager
	General accounting manager
	Human resources manager
	Manufacturing engineering manager
	Production superintendent
	Product engineering manager
	Production control manager
	Purchasing manager
	Quality control manager

Do you have a structured Total Quality Control project (or other major improvement initiative) underway at the same time as MRP II? If so, be careful. These projects should not be viewed as competing, but rather complementary; they support, reinforce, and benefit each other. Ideally, the TQC project leader would be a member of the MRP II project team and vice versa.

The project team meets once or twice a week for about an hour. When done properly, meetings are crisp and to the point. A typical meeting would consist of:

1. Feedback on the status of the project schedule—what tasks have been completed in the past week, what tasks have been started in the past week, what's behind schedule.

2. A review of an interim report from a task force that has been addressing a specific problem.

3. A decision on the priority of a requested enhancement to the software.

---

[2] I'm referring here to the manager of the inside sales and order entry organization. Other titles for this position include inside sales manager, sales administration manager, and marketing services manager.

4. Identification of a potential or real problem. Perhaps the creation of another task force to address the problem.

Please note: No education is being done here, not a lot of consensus building, not much getting into the nitty-gritty. These things are all essential but should be minimized in a project management meeting such as this. Rather, they should be addressed in a series of business meetings, and we'll cover those in the next chapter. The message regarding project team meetings: Keep 'em brief. Remember, the managers still have a business to run, plus other things to do to get MRP II implemented.

UPWARD DELEGATION

Brevity is one important characteristic of the project team meetings. Another is that they be mandatory. The members of the project team need to attend each meeting.

Except . . . what about priority number one? What about running the business? Situations just might arise when it's more important for a manager to be somewhere else. For example, the plant manager may be needed on the plant floor to solve a critical production problem; the customer service manager may need to meet with an important new customer who's come in to see the plant; the purchasing manager may have to visit a problem supplier who's providing some critical items.

Some companies have used a technique called upward delegation very effectively. If, at any time, a given project team member has a higher priority than attending a project team meeting, that's fine. No problem. All he has to do is make certain his designated alternate will be there in his place. Who's the designated alternate? It's his boss . . . the vice president of manufacturing or marketing or materials per the above examples. The boss covers for the department head. In this way, priority number one is taken care of by keeping the project team meetings populated by people who can make decisions.

THE EXECUTIVE STEERING COMMITTEE

The executive steering committee consists primarily of the top management group in the company. Its mission is to ensure a successful implementation. The project leader cannot do this; the project team can't; only the top management group can ensure success.

To do this, the executive steering committee meets once or twice a month for about an hour. Its members include the general manager, the vice presidents, and one additional person—the full-time project leader. The project leader acts as the link between the executive steering committee and the project team.

The main order of business at the steering committee meetings is a review of the project's status. It's the project leader's responsibility to report progress relative to the schedule, specifically where they're behind. He explains the seriousness of schedule delays, reviews tasks on the critical path, outlines plans to get the project back on schedule, identifies additional resources required, etc.

The steering committee's job is to review these situations and make the tough decisions. In the case of a serious schedule slippage on the critical path, the steering committee needs to consider the following questions (not necessarily in the sequence listed):

1. Can resources already existing within the company be re-allocated and applied to the project? (Remember the three knobs principle discussed in chapter 2? This represents turning up the resource knob.)

2. Is it possible to acquire additional resources from outside the company? (The resource knob.) If so, how much will that cost versus the cost of a number of months of delay?

3. Is all the work called for by the project schedule really necessary? Would it be possible to reduce somewhat the amount of work without harming the chances for success with MRP II? (The work knob.)

4. Will it be necessary to reschedule a portion of the project or, worst case, the entire project? (The time knob.)

Only the executive steering committee can authorize a delay in the project. These are the only people with the visibility, the control, and the leverage to make such a decision. They are the ones ultimately accountable.[3]

In addition to schedule slippage, the executive steering committee

---

[3] Here's another place where the rubber meets the road: The wrong signals are sent if repeated slippage is accepted. In many cases, a reschedule out is the easy choice; the tough one is for the company to roll up its collective sleeves, work hard, and get back on schedule.

may have to address other difficult issues: Unforeseen obstacles, problem individuals in key positions, difficulties with the software supplier, etc.

The Torchbearer

The term torchbearer refers very specifically to that executive with assigned top-level responsibility for MRP II. The role of the torchbearer[4] is to be the top-management focal point for the entire project. Typically, he chairs the meetings of the executive steering committee.

Who should be the torchbearer? Ideally, the general manager, and that's very common today. Sometimes that's not possible because of time pressures, travel, or whatever. If so, take your pick from any of the vice presidents. Most often, it's the VP of finance or the VP of manufacturing. The key ingredients are enthusiasm for MRP II and a willingness to devote some additional time to it.

Often, the project leader will be assigned to report directly to the torchbearer. This could happen despite a different reporting relationship prior to the MRP II project. For example, the project leader may have been purchasing manager and, as such, had reported to the VP of manufacturing. Now, as project leader, he reports to the torchbearer, who may be the general manager, or perhaps the vice president of marketing.

What else does the torchbearer do? He shows the top management flag, serves as an executive sounding board for the project team, and perhaps provides some top-level muscle in dealings with suppliers. He rallies support from other executives as required. He's the top management conscience for the project.

Being a torchbearer isn't a terribly time-consuming function, but it can be very, very important. The best person for the job, almost invariably, is the general manager.

Special Situations

What I've described here—one steering committee and one project team—is the standard organizational arrangement for an average-sized company, say from about 200 to 1,200 people. It's a two-group structure. (See figure 5-4.)

---

[4] Often called champion or sponsor. Take your pick of any of the three.

Figure 5-4

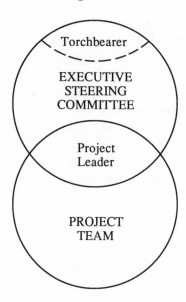

This arrangement doesn't always apply. Take a smaller company, less than 200 people. In many companies of this size, the department heads report directly to the general manager. Thus, there is no need for two separate groups; the steering committee and the project team can be merged into one.

In larger companies, for example multiplant organizations, there's yet another approach. The first thing to ask is: "Do we need a project team at each plant?"

This is best answered with another question: "Well, who's going to make it work at, for example, Plant 3?"

Answer: "The guys and gals who work at Plant 3." Therefore, you'd better have a project team at Plant 3. And also at Plants 1 and 2.[5]

Next question: "Do we need a full-time project leader at each plant?"

Answer: "Yes, if they're large plants and/or if they have a fairly full range of functions: Sales, accounting, product engineering, purchasing, as well as the traditional manufacturing activities. In other cases, the

---

[5] At small plants, with few functions, they're sometimes called "mini-teams"—made up of only a few people, including the plant manager.

project leader might be a part-timer, devoting about halftime to the project."

See figure 5-5 for how this arrangement ties together. You can see that the steering committee is in place, as is the project team at the general office. This project team would include people from all the key general office departments: Marketing and sales, purchasing, finance and accounting, human resources, R & D/product engineering, and others. It would also include plant people, if there were a plant located at or near the general office. The remote plants, in this example all three of them, each have their own team and project leader. The project leader is also a member of the project team at the general office, although typically he will not attend each meeting there, but rather a meeting once or twice per month.

SPIN-OFF TASK FORCES

Spin-off task forces are the ad hoc groups I referred to earlier. They represent a key tool to keep the project team from getting bogged down in a lot of detail.

Figure 5-5

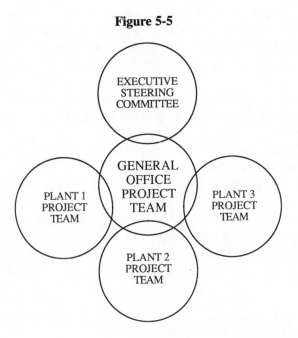

A spin-off task force is typically created to address a specific issue. The issue could be relatively major (e.g., software selection, structuring modular bills of material, deciding how to master schedule satellite plants) or less so (floor-stock inventory control, engineering change procedures, etc.). The spin-off task force is given a specific amount of time—a week or so for a lesser issue, perhaps a bit longer for those more significant. Its job is to research the issue, formulate alternative solutions, and report back to the project team with recommendations.

Spin-off task forces:

• Are created by the project team.

• Are temporary—lasting for only several days, several weeks or, at most, several months.

• Normally involve no more than one member of the project team.[6]

• Are cross-functional, involving people from more than one department. (If all task force members are from within a given department, then the problem must exist totally within that department. In that case, why have a task force? It should simply be the responsibility of the department manager and his people to get the problem fixed.)

• Make their recommendations to the project team, then go out of existence.

Upon receiving a spin-off task force's report, the project team may:

• Accept the task force's recommended solutions.

• Adopt one of the different alternatives identified by the task force.

• Forward the matter to the executive steering committee, with a recommendation, if it requires their approval (e.g., the software decision).

• Disagree with the task force's report, and re-activate the task force with additional instructions.

---

[6] Or maybe none. More and more companies are pushing decision making and accountability farther down in the organization. If there is to be a project team member on the spin-off task force, he needn't be the task force leader but could mainly serve as the contact point with the project team.

Once the decision is made as to what to do, then people must be assigned to do it. This may include one or more members of the spin-off task force, or it may not. The task force's job is to *develop* the solution. The steps to implement the solution should be integrated into the project schedule and carried out by people as a part of their departmental activities.

Back in chapter 3, I discussed time wasters such as documenting the current system or designing the new system. The organizational format that I'm recommending here—executive steering committee, project team, and spin-off task forces—is part of what's needed to ensure that the details of MRP II will fit the business. The other part is education, and that's coming up in the next chapter.

Spin-off task forces are win-win. They reduce time pressures on the busy department heads, involve other people within the organization, and, most of the time, the task force sees its recommendations being put into practice. George Bevis, former senior vice president and torchbearer at the Tennant Company, utilized the concept very successfully during Tennant's Class A implementation of MRP II. George says, "Spin-off task forces work so well, they must be illegal, immoral, or fattening."

PROFESSIONAL GUIDANCE

MRP II is not an extension of past experience. For those who've never done it before, it's a whole new ball game. And most companies don't have anyone on board who has ever done it before—successfully.

Companies implementing MRP II need some help from an *experienced, qualified* professional in the field. They're sailing into uncharted (for them) waters; they need some navigation help to avoid the rocks and shoals. They need access to *someone who's been there.*

Note the use of the words *experienced* and *qualified* and *someone who's been there.* This refers to *meaningful Class A* experience. The key question is: Where has this person made it work? Was this person involved, in a significant way, in at least one Class A implementation? In other words, has this person truly been there?

Some companies recognize the need for professional guidance but make the mistake of retaining someone without Class A credentials. They're no better off than before, because they're receiving advice on how to do it from a person who has not yet done it successfully.

Before deciding on a specific consultant, find out where he got his Class A experience. Then contact the company or companies given as references and establish:

1. Are they Class A?

2. Did the prospective consultant serve in a key role in the implementation?

If the answer to either question is no, then run, don't walk, the other way! Find someone who has Class A MRP II credentials. Happily, there are many more consultants today with Class A experience than 10 or 20 years ago. Use one of them. To do otherwise means that the company will be paying for the inexperienced outsider's on-the-job training and, at the same time, won't be getting the expert advice it needs so badly.

The consultant supports the general manager, the torchbearer (if other than the GM), the project leader, and other members of the executive steering committee and the project team. In addition to giving advice on specific issues, the outside professional also:

• Serves as a conscience to top management. This is perhaps the most important job for the consultant. In all the many MRP II implementations I've been involved in over the last 18 years, I can't remember even one where I didn't have to have a heart-to-heart talk with the general manager. I frequently have found myself saying things like, "Lee, your vice president of manufacturing is becoming a problem on this implementation. Let's talk about how we might help him to get on board." Or, even more critical, "Harry, what you're doing is sending some very mixed messages to the troops. Here's what I recommend you do instead." These kinds of things are often difficult or impossible for people within the company to do.

• Helps people focus on the right priorities and, hence, keep the project on the right track. Example: "I'm concerned about the sequence of some of the tasks on your project schedule. It seems to me that the cart may be ahead of the horse in some of these steps. Let's take a look."

• Serves as a sounding board, perhaps helping to resolve issues of disagreement among several people or groups.

• Coaches the top management group through its early sales & operations planning meetings.

• Asks questions that force people to address the tough issues. Example: "Are your inventories really 95-percent accurate overall? What about the floor stock? How about your work-in-process counts? How good are your production-order close-out procedures? What about your open purchase orders?" In other words, he "shoots bullets" at the project; it's the job of the project team and the steering committee to do the bulletproofing.

How much consulting is the right amount? How often should you see your consultant?

Answer: Key issues here are results and ownership. The right amount of consulting, of the right kind, can often make the difference between success and failure. Too much consulting, of whatever quality, is almost always counterproductive to a successful implementation.

Why? Because frequently the consultants take over to one degree or another. They can become deeply involved in the implementation process, including the decision-making aspects of it. And that's exactly the wrong way to do it. It inhibits the development of essential ingredients for success: Ownership of the system and line accountability for results.

In summary, the consultant should be an adviser, not a doer. For an average-sized company, say between 200 and 1,200 people, about one to three days every month or two should be fine once the project gets rolling.[7]

What happens during these consulting visits?

Answer: A typical consulting day could take this format:

8:00   Preliminary meeting with general manager, torchbearer, and project leader. Purpose: Identify special problems, firm up the agenda for 9:30 to 3:30.

---

[7] There are some cases where more consulting involvement may be needed. Audit/ assessments will probably require a bit more consulting involvement for a short period. Second, larger companies will most likely need more outside support. Third, consultants can sometimes be used to "turn up the resource knob," when a company's people have a severe work-load problem.

In this case, the consultants might help with things like procedure writing, bill of material restructuring, and developing specs for software. However, they should not be decision makers, nor should they lead the internal business meetings where the details of MRP II operation within the company are hammered out (see chapter 6). Line accountability for results must be maintained.

8:30–9:30 Project team meeting. Purpose: Get updated, probe for problems.

9:30–3:30 Meetings with individuals and smaller groups to focus on specific issues and problems.

3:30–4:00 Solitary time for consultant to review notes, collect thoughts, formulate recommendations, etc.

4:00–5:00 Wrap-up meeting with executive steering committee.[8] Purpose: Consultant updates members on his findings, makes recommendations, etc.

In between visits, the consultant must be easily reachable by telephone. The consultant needs to be a *routinely available* resource for information and recommendations . . . but visits the plant in person only once or twice each month or two.

PERFORMANCE GOALS

This step flows directly from the work done in the audit/assessment, vision statement and cost/benefit analysis. It is more detailed than those prior steps. It defines specific and detailed performance targets that the company is committing itself to reach, and that it will begin to measure soon to ensure that it's getting the bang for the buck. These targets are usually expressed in operational, not financial, terms and should link directly back to the financial benefits specified in the cost/benefit analysis. Examples:

For our make-to-stock product lines, we will ship 99 percent of our customers' orders complete, within twenty four hours of order receipt. Benefit: SALES INCREASE.

For our make-to-order products, we will ship 98 percent of our customers' orders on time, per our original promise to them. Benefit: SALES INCREASE.

For all our products, we will reduce the combined cycle time to purchase and manufacture by a 50-percent minimum. Benefit: SALES INCREASE.

---

[8] It's preferable, but not essential, for all members of the steering committee to be present for this wrap-up meeting. At an absolute minimum, the general manager, torchbearer, and project leader must be present. If not, it's unlikely that this session—and the entire day, for that matter—will have real value.

We will reduce material and component shortages by at least 90 percent. Benefit: DIRECT LABOR PRODUCTIVITY.

We will reduce unplanned overtime (less than one-week advance notice) by 75 percent. Benefit: DIRECT LABOR PRODUCTIVITY.

We will establish supplier partnerships, long-term supplier contracts, and supplier scheduling covering 80 percent or more of our purchased volume within the next 18 months. Benefit: PURCHASE COST REDUC-TION.

We could go on and on, but I'm sure by now you have the idea. A quantified set of performance goals can serve as benchmarks down the road. After implementation, actual results can be compared to those projected here. Is the company getting the benefits? If not, why not? The people can then find out what's wrong, fix it, and start getting the benefits they targeted.

Please note: *Each financial benefit in the cost/benefit analysis should be backed by one or more operational performance measures,* such as the ones above.

The key players in developing performance measurements are essentially the same folks who've been involved in the prior steps: Top management and operating management, perhaps with a little help from their friends elsewhere in the company.

This chapter and the previous one have covered four key steps on the Proven Path following first-cut education. They are the vision statement, cost/benefit analysis, project organization and performance goals. Here's an important point, which can work in your favor: It's often possible for these four steps to be accomplished by the same people in the same several meetings. This is good, since there is urgency to get started and time is of the essence.

IMPLEMENTERS' CHECKLIST

Function: Project Organization and Responsibilities

Task	Complete	
	YES	NO
1. Full-time project leader selected from a key management role in an operating department within the company.	_____	_____
2. Torchbearer identified and formally appointed.	_____	_____
3. Project team formed, consisting mainly of operating managers of all involved departments.	_____	_____
4. Executive steering committee formed, consisting of the general manager, all staff members, and the project leader.	_____	_____
5. Project team meeting at least once per week.	_____	_____
6. Executive steering committee meeting at least once per month.	_____	_____
7. Outside consultant, with Class A MRP II experience, retained and on-site approximately one or two days every month or two.	_____	_____
8. Detailed performance goals established, linking directly back to each of the benefits specified in the cost/benefit analysis.	_____	_____

Chapter 6

Initial Education

It's fascinating to look at how education for MRP and MRP II has been viewed over the past 25 years. Quite an evolution has taken place.

At the beginning, in what could be called the Dark Ages, education was perceived as unnecessary. The implication was that the users would figure it out on the fly. The relatively few early successes were, not surprisingly, in companies where the users were deeply involved in the design of the system and, hence, became educated as part of that process.

The Dark Ages were followed by the How Not Why era. Attention was focused on telling people *how* to do things but not *why* certain things needed to be done. This approach may work in certain parts of the world, but its track record in North America proved to be poor indeed.

Next came the age of Give 'Em the Facts. With it came the recognition that people needed to see the big picture, that they needed to understand the principles and concepts, as well as the mechanics.

Was this new awareness a step forward? Yes. Did it help to improve the success rate? You bet. Was it the total answer? Not by a long shot.

OBJECTIVES OF EDUCATION FOR MRP II

Today, education for MRP II is seen as having a far broader mission. It's recognized as having not one but two critically important objectives:

1. *Fact Transfer.* This takes place when people learn the *whats, whys,* and *hows.* It's essential, but, by itself, it's not nearly enough.

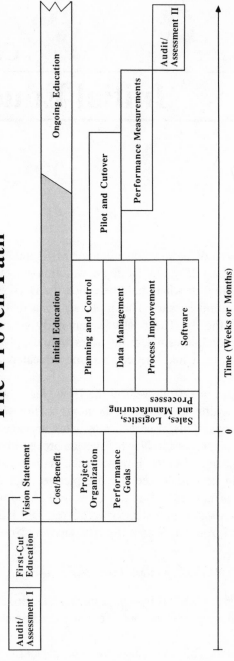

Figure 6-1
The Proven Path

2. *Behavior Change.* This occurs when people who have lived in the world of the informal system become convinced of the need to do their jobs differently. It's when they truly understand why and how they should use a formal system as a team to run the business more professionally and how it will benefit them.

Some examples. *Fact transfer* occurs when the marketing and sales people learn how demand management and master scheduling operate, how the master schedule should be used as the source of customer order promising, how to calculate the available-to-promise quantity.

Behavior change takes place when the folks in marketing and sales participate willingly in the demand management process because they recognize it as the way to give better and faster service to their customers, increase sales volume, and make the company more competitive.

Fact transfer happens when the production manager learns about shop floor control and how the plant floor schedules can be used by foremen to manage their departments more efficiently. *Behavior change* is when the production manager banishes hot lists from the plant floor because he's convinced that the formal system can and will work.

Fact transfer is the engineers learning about the engineering-change control capabilities within material requirements planning. *Behavior change* is the engineers communicating early and often with material planners about new products and pending engineering changes because they understand how this will help drastically to reduce obsolescence, disruptions to production, and late shipments to customers.

Behavior change is central to a successful implementation of Manufacturing Resource Planning. It's also an awesome task—to enable hundreds or perhaps thousands of people to change the way they do their jobs.

The mission of the MRP II education program is, therefore, of enormous importance. It involves not only fact transfer, by itself not a small task, but far more important, behavior change. One can speculate about the odds for success at a company using an off-the-wall, half-baked approach to education.

A key element in the Proven Path, perhaps the most important of all, is effective education. This is synonymous with managing the process of change. Behavior change is a process that leads people to believe in this new set of tools, this new set of values, this new way of managing a manufacturing company.

Further, people acquire ownership of it. It becomes theirs; it becomes the way we're going to run the business. Executing the process of behavior change, (i.e., education for MRP II) is a management issue, not a technical one. The results of this process are teams of people who believe in this new way to run the business and who are prepared to change the way they do their jobs to make it happen.

CRITERIA FOR A PROGRAM TO ACCOMPLISH BEHAVIOR CHANGE

Following are the criteria for this process of MRP II education[1] that will achieve the primary objective of behavior change widely throughout the company. (See figure 6-2 for a summary of these criteria.)

1. *Active, visible and informed top management leadership and participation.*

The need to involve top management deeply in this change process is absolute. This group is the most important of all, and within this group, the general manager is the most important person. Failure to educate top management, and most specifically the general manager, is probably the single most significant cause why companies do not get beyond Class C. Why? For several reasons, one being the law of organizational gravity. Change must cascade down the organization chart; it doesn't flow

Figure 6-2
Criteria for a Program to Accomplish Behavior Change

1. Active top management leadership and participation.
2. Line accountability for change.
3. Total immersion for key people.
4. Total coverage throughout the company.
5. Continuing reinforcement.
6. Instructor credibility.
7. Peer confirmation.
8. Enthusiasm.

[1] Or education for other major improvement initiatives within the company. Several years ago I attended a class conducted by one of the well-known quality gurus. I learned there are great similarities between implementing MRP II and implementing Total Quality Control. The same point applies to Just-in-Time and Distribution Resource Planning. Therefore the points to be covered here apply virtually 100 percent to implementing any of these very important capabilities.

uphill. Leadership, by informed and knowledgeable senior management people, including the general manager, is essential.

Another reason: The risk factor. How could a company possibly succeed in acquiring a superior set of tools to manage the business when the senior managers of the business don't understand the tools and how to use them? One well-intentioned decision by an uninformed general manager can kill an otherwise solid MRP II system. An example: The general manager says, "Business is great! Put all those new orders into the master schedule. So what if it gets overloaded? That'll motivate the troops." There goes the integrity of the master production schedule, and, hence, the effectiveness of MRP II.

Another example: "Business is lousy! We have to cut indirect payroll expense. Lay off the cycle counter." There goes the integrity of the inventory records, and, hence, the effectiveness of MRP II.

Okay so far? Now the next question to address is how to convince top management, specifically the general manager (GM), to get educated. In many companies, this is no problem. The GM is open-minded, and more than willing to take several days out of a busy schedule to go to a class on MRP II.

This is particularly true when audit/assessment I is done at the first step in the entire process. Even where there may have been initial reluctance towards education on the part of the GM and others, it tends to evaporate during the wrap-up phase of audit/assessment I. (See chapter 4.)

In some companies, unfortunately, this is not so. The general manager is totally uninterested in MRP II, and won't even authorize an audit/assessment. Further, he refuses to take the time to learn about MRP II. Common objections:

I don't need to know that. That's for the guys and gals in the back room.

I know it all already. I went to a seminar by our computer hardware supplier three years ago.

I'll support the system. I'm committed. I'll sign the appropriations requests. I don't need to do any more than that. [Author's note: Support isn't good enough. Neither is commitment. What's absolutely necessary is *informed leadership* by the general manager. Note the use of word "informed"; this comes about through education.]

I'm too busy.

And on and on. The reluctance by GMs to get educated often falls into one of two categories:

- Lack of understanding (they either think they know all about it, or they don't think they need to know about it at all).
- Lack of comfort with the notion of needing education.

The first category—lack of understanding—can usually be addressed by logic. Articles, books, videotapes, and oral presentations have been used with success. Perhaps the most effective approach, besides audit/assessment, is what's called an Executive Briefing. This is a presentation by a qualified MRP II professional, lasting for several hours,[2] to the general manager and his staff. This is not education but rather an introduction to MRP II. Its mission: Consciousness raising, once again. It enables the GM and others to see that important connection between their problems/opportunities on the one hand and MRP II as the solution on the other.

The second category—discomfort with the idea of education—is often not amenable to logic. It's emotional, and can run deep. Here are three ways that have been successful:

a. *Peer input.* Put the reluctant general manager in touch with other GMs who have been through both MRP II education and a successful implementation. Their input can be sufficiently reassuring to defuse the issue.

b. *The trusted lieutenant.* Send one or several of the reluctant general manager's most-trusted vice presidents to a top management MRP II class. It is hoped their subsequent recommendation will be something like this: "Boss, you have to get some education on MRP II if we're going to make this thing work. Take our word for it—we can't do it without you."

c. *The safety glasses approach.* Imagine this dialogue between the reluctant general manager and another person, perhaps the torchbearer.

---

[2] This consumes less time and, hence, costs less than an audit/assessment. It is also less desirable, in that it does only a fraction of what is accomplished in an audit/assessment. However, when an audit/assessment isn't possible, it's usually the next best choice.

TORCHBEARER (TB): Boss, when you go out on the plant floor, do you wear safety glasses?

GENERAL MANAGER (GM): Of course.

TB: Why? Are you afraid of getting metal in your eye?

GM (chuckling): No, of course not. I don't get my head that close to the machinery. The reason I wear safety glasses on the plant floor is that to do otherwise would send out the wrong signal. It would say that wearing safety glasses wasn't important. It would make it difficult for the managers and supervisors to enforce the rule that everyone must wear safety glasses.

TB: Well, boss, what kind of signal are you going to send out if you refuse to go through the MRP II education? We'll be asking many of our people to devote many of their hours to getting educated on MRP II. Without you setting the example, that'll be a whole lot harder.

If a general manager won't go (to get educated on MRP II), then the company shouldn't go ahead with a company-wide implementation. It will probably not succeed. Far better not to attempt it, than to attempt it in the face of such long odds. What should you do in this case? Well, your best bet may be to do a Quick-Slice MRP implementation, and we'll cover that in detail in chapters 11 and 12.

2. *Line accountability for change.*

Remember the ABCs of MRP II? The A item, the most important element, is the people. It's people who'll make it work.

Education is fundamental to making it happen. It's teaching the people how to use the tools, and getting them to believe they can work with the tools as a team. Since it's so fundamental to success, an education program must be structured so that a specific group of key managers can be held accountable for properly educating the people. The process of changing how the business is run must not be delegated to the training department, the personnel department, a few full-time people on the project team, or, worst of all, outsiders. To attempt to do so seriously weakens accountability for effective education and, hence, sharply reduces the odds for success.

In order to make possible ownership and behavior change, the process of change must be managed and led by a key group of people with the following characteristics:

• They must be held accountable for the success of the change process, hence, the success of MRP II at the operational level of the business.

• They must know, as a group, how the business is being run today.

• They must have the authority to make changes in how the business is run.

Who are these people? They're the department heads, the operating managers of the business. Who else could they be? Only these operating managers can legitimately be held accountable for success in their areas, be intimately knowledgeable with how the business is being run today in their departments, and have the authority to make changes.

3. *Total immersion for key people.*

These managers, these key people who'll facilitate and manage this process of change, first need to go through the change process themselves. They'll need more help with this, since they're the first group in the company to go through the process. What they need is total immersion—an intensive, in-depth educational experience to equip them to be change agents. Obviously, it's essential that top management understand this need, and enable it to happen.

4. *Total coverage throughout the company.*

The question arises: "Who in a typical company needs MRP II education?" Answer: Darn near everybody. Education has to be widespread because of the need for behavior change so widely throughout the company.

What's needed is to educate the critical mass to achieve a high level of MRP II knowledgeability and enthusiasm throughout the entire organization. When that occurs, the result is not unlike a chemical reaction. MRP II becomes the way we do it around here—the way we run the business.

The critical mass in most companies means 80 percent—*minimum*—of all the people in the company prior to going on the air with MRP, with the balance being educated shortly thereafter. That's *all* the people—from the folks in mahogany row to the guys and gals on the plant floor running the equipment and working on the line. It also includes the people in the middle—the managers, the supervisors, the buyers, the sales people, etc. An excellent way of focusing on the need for widespread education is depicted graphically in figure 6-3.

Figure 6-3
Before MRP II Education

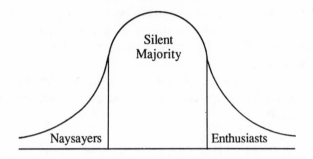

There's a small group of people who believe in MRP II, who are enthusiastic, and who want to get going. There's also a small percentage of naysayers, people who don't believe MRP II will work and who are vocally against it. Most folks are in the middle—arms folded, sitting back, not saying much, and not expecting much. They're thinking, "Here we go again—another management fad that'll blow over before long."

Here's what needs to happen:

Figure 6-4
After MRP II Education

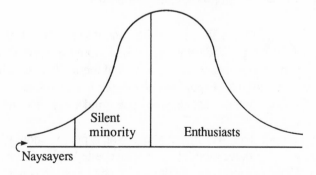

That's the mission: Get a majority of the people enthusiastically on board, reduce the folded-arm set into a minority, and minimize the ranks of the prophets of doom and gloom.

Yes, but (you may be saying to yourself) . . . is it really necessary to educate folks such as group leaders, setup people, machine operators? You bet it is. Here's one example why:

Harry, an excellent machine operator and a hard worker, has been with the company for 12 years. There's been a large queue of work-in-process jobs at Harry's machine during all of those years, except for a time during the early 1980s when business was really bad. Harry got laid off for a while.

Harry's come to associate, perhaps subconsciously, large queues with job security and shrinking queues with reduced business and the possibility of a layoff.

QUESTION: As MRP II is implemented, what should happen to the queues?

ANSWER: Go down.

QUESTION: When Harry sees the queues dropping, what might he tend to do?

ANSWER: Slow down.

QUESTION: What will Harry's coworkers tend to do?

ANSWER: Slow down.

QUESTION: What happens then?

ANSWER: Output drops, queues don't get smaller, shop floor control doesn't work as well as it should, and so on.

QUESTION: What's the solution?

ANSWER: Simple. Tell 'em about MRP II. Tell 'em what's coming and why. Tell 'em how it will affect them and their jobs.

Telling 'em about it is called education, and it's essential. If you don't tell them what's coming and why, they'll hear about it anyway and will probably assume the worst. Even if you do tell them what and why, they may not believe it all. Our experience, however, has been that most folks in most companies will at least keep an open mind and give it the benefit of the doubt.

The best advice I've ever heard about which people should be educated comes from Walter Goddard, who succeeded Ollie as the head of the Oliver Wight organization. Walt says, "The question is not 'who to include' in this change process. Rather, it's 'who to exclude.' " Yes, indeed! Companies should start with the assumption that they'll involve everyone, and then ask themselves whom to leave out. One might say, "Well, we really don't need to educate the folks who cut the grass and shovel the snow. And I guess we could exclude those who answer the phones. But do we really want to do that? That could be interpreted that we don't feel these people are important, but that's not true. Everyone who works here is important."

Total coverage means *mandatory*. Education for MRP II can be optional under only one condition—if success with MRP II is considered as optional. On the other hand, if the company's committed to making it work, then it can't be left up to individuals to decide whether or not they'll get educated on MRP II. Education is a process with the objectives of behavior change, teamwork, ownership. The process can't succeed with spotty, sporadic, random participation.

5. Continuing reinforcement.

Ollie Wight said it well: "Grease-gun education doesn't work." He was referring to the one-shot, quick-hit educational approaches tried so often without lasting results. Retention of the facts is poor, and that's the least of it. It's difficult to get down to the details of how MRP II will work within the company; ownership and, hence, behavior change is almost impossible to get in this environment. What's needed is a process that occurs over an extended period of time. People can learn some things about MRP II, go back and do their jobs, think about what they've learned, let it sink in, evaluate it in the light of how they do their jobs, formulate questions, and then ask those questions at the next session.

Repetition is important. When my kids were in grade school, in addition to readin' and 'rithmetic, they also took 'ritin'. Writing in this context means grammar, spelling, punctuation, composition. When they got to high school, they took freshman English, which dealt with grammar, spelling, etc. Upon arriving at college, believe it or not, one of the first courses they took was English 101: Grammar and Composition. They took the same subject matter over and over again. Why? Because the ability to speak and write well is so important. Likewise, MRP II is important; people will need to change the way they do their jobs and run the business. Before that can happen, they'll need to acquire ownership of it. To do that, in most cases, means that they'll have to learn about it more than once. In short, reinforcement facilitates ownership; owner-ship leads directly to behavior change.

In this process of facilitating behavior change, two-way communica-tions are essential. Putting 200 people in a hall and talking at them about MRP II may constitute exposure, but not education. The essence of MRP II education is dialogue—where people discuss, ask questions, and get answers, focus on issues, get specific. It must be involving ("This stuff is interesting") and reassuring ("I'm beginning to see how we can make this work for us").

People asking questions means people getting believable answers, and this leads us to the next criterion.

6. Instructor credibility.

Education for MRP II comes in two formats—outside and inside. Both are necessary. It's essential that some key people go to live outside classes, to start to become the company's experts on MRP II. It's essential that the instructors of these outside classes already be experts, that they've been deeply involved in successful implementations, that they can speak from firsthand experience. If not, credibility will suffer, and behavior change for their key people may never get started.

Since it's obviously not practical to send everyone to outside classes,[3] education within the company is also necessary. The leaders of these sessions must not only know about MRP II; they must be experts on the company—its products, its processes, its people, its customers, its suppliers, etc. If not, credibility will suffer and behavior change by the critical mass may never happen.

7. Peer confirmation.

It's likely that the president in a given company feels that he has no peer within that company. Not only is no one on an equal footing, perhaps he feels that no one really understands the problems, the chal-lenges, the requirements of the job.

Interestingly, the vice president of marketing (or finance or engineer-

---

[3] Even if it were practical, it wouldn't be a good idea because it wouldn't be as effective.

ing or whatever) may feel exactly the same way—that he has no peer within the company when it comes to his job. And so might the purchasing manager feel that way, and the assembly superintendent, and others.

Peer confirmation is essential to build confidence in success, so that the process of acquiring ownership can take place. The education program must support this, with a mix of both outside and inside sessions. Outside classes enable key people in similar jobs at different companies to talk, share experiences, compare notes, and use each other as a sounding board.

Inside sessions are often grouped departmentally.[4] When a number of people in similar jobs are in the same class, peer confirmation, hence ownership, hence behavior change are facilitated. The foremen can talk to other foremen, hear them ask questions, hear the answers coming back from their boss (who's been to one or more outside classes). This process is reassuring. It lowers the level of uncertainty and anxiety; it raises the level of confidence in success; it builds ownership. It enables people to see the need to change the way they do their jobs.

Let's go back to outside classes for a moment. They make another major contribution, in that they get at the uniqueness syndrome. One of the things heard from time to time is: "We're unique. We're different. MRP II won't work for us." Almost invariably, this comes from people who've not yet received proper MRP II education.

One of the key missions of outside education is to help people work through the uniqueness syndrome, to begin to see MRP II as a generalized set of tools that has virtually universal application potential. This is best done at a public class with people from a variety of companies, with different products, in different types of industries.

Private classes, held specifically for people from one company, have been shown to work and to yield positive results when done correctly. They require high-quality instructors, with Class A credentials, of course. Further, they require homework to be done up front, in terms of customizing and tailoring the sessions. In many cases, private classes make possible the discussion of sensitive and strategic issues, which, of course, can't be done at a public class.

---

[4] But not all of them. Some of the earlier, less-detailed sessions should include people from a variety of departments. This encourages communication across department boundaries and helps to break down barriers.

However, private classes should not be attempted in companies with a high degree of the we're-unique syndrome. Nor in companies with heavy politics, because people will be reluctant to open up, to ask questions that might imply that they're not doing things perfectly already.

8. Enthusiasm.

Remember the catch-22 of MRP II? It's a lot of work; we have to do it ourselves; it's not the number one priority. Widespread enthusiasm is one of the key elements needed to break through the catch-22.

Enthusiasm comes about when people begin mentally matching their problems (late shipments, massive expediting, excessive overtime, material shortages, finger pointing, funny numbers, and on and on) with MRP II as the solution. The kind of enthusiasm we're talking about here doesn't necessarily mean the flag-waving, rah-rah variety. More important is a solid conviction that might go like this:

> MRP II makes sense. It's valid for our business. If we do it right, we can solve many of the problems that have been nagging us for years. We, as a company, can become more competitive, more secure, more prosperous—and we can have more fun in the process.

Enthusiasm is contagious.[5] Most successful MRP II implementations happen without hiring lots of extra people. It's the people already on board who fix the inventory records, the bills, the routings; do the education; solve the problems and knock down the roadblocks—and all the while they're making shipments and running the business as well or better than before. Here's Ollie again: "Those who've been through a Class A MRP II installation repeatedly use the phrase 'a sense of mission.' To those who haven't, that may sound like an overstatement. It isn't."

THE CHANGE PROCESS

Thus far we've looked at the *objectives* of MRP II education, the most important by far being behavior change, and also the necessary *criteria* for such a program. Now let's look at the *process* itself, a process that

---

[5] A warning: the ho-hum syndrome is also contagious. If you don't go through this change process correctly, you'll probably get the opposite of enthusiasm.

will meet the above criteria and enable behavior change to happen. In other words, this process has to bring people to see the need and benefits from running the business differently and, hence, of the need and benefits from doing their jobs differently.

There are two major aspects to this change process. First, create the team of experts, and second, reach the critical mass of people within the company.

CREATE THE TEAM OF EXPERTS

The future team of experts has already been identified—the department heads, the operating managers of the business. The good news here is that these folks are already halfway there to becoming the team of experts. They're already experts in how the business is being run today. What remains is for them to become experts in how the business will be run in the future, using the new set of tools called MRP II.

Let's now take a look at how it happens—at how the operating management group within a company becomes a team of experts to facilitate and manage the change process.

Very simply, these people themselves go through the process of change via the following steps:

1. *Outside classes.*

It's essential for this future team of experts to get away from the plant or office for an in-depth educational experience on MRP II. (See criterion 3.)

In such a class, there should be a variety of job functions represented—production managers, engineers, marketers, accountants, materials people, etc. (See criterion 7.)

Of course, these outside classes must be taught by MRP II professionals, people who have a solid track record of participating in successful Class A implementations of MRP II. These instructors not only need to be able to communicate the principles, techniques, and mechanics of MRP II but also to illustrate the *results*, the benefits that companies have realized from MRP II.

Here's some good news. Virtually all the members of the future team of experts have already been to outside classes, as a part of first-cut education (see chapter 4). A number of them will need to attend one or several specialty classes, and perhaps a few haven't been to class at all yet and, hence, will need to go. (Similarly, most of the top management group has already received most of its outside education, again via the first-cut process.)

2. *A series of business meetings.*

Next on the agenda for the team of experts is to go through a series of business meetings. The objectives here are:

• To continue to enhance the change process begun in the outside classes.

• To equip these operating managers with the tools to reach the critical mass.

• To develop detailed definitions of how the company's sales, logistics, and manufacturing processes will look after MRP II has been implemented.

Important: Please note that these are decision-making meetings. They are not show-and-tell; they're not Saturday-night-at-the-movies. More on this in a moment.

Doing this properly requires a substantial amount of time, perhaps 30 or 40 business meetings of about two hours each, spread over several months. Not nearly as much time would be required here if the only objective were fact transfer. However, since the main objective is behavior change, project team members—the team of experts—should be prepared for a substantial time commitment. (See criteria 3 and 5.)

Since we refer to these sessions as a series of business meetings, the question arises: "Does any education take place at these meetings?" Yes, indeed. Education is essential, as a means to the goal of making behavior change happen.

It needs to occur at three levels:

• Principles, concepts, and techniques.

• Application.

• Training.

Principles, concepts, and techniques relate to the defined body of knowledge that we call Manufacturing Resource Planning—the various

Figure 6-5
MRP II Training and Education

	Training	*Education*
Focus	Details and specific aspects of the software	Principles, concepts, and techniques, and their application to the business
Emphasis	Technical	Managerial
Will determine	How you operate the system	How well you manage the business

functions, how they tie together, the need for feedback, the details of how planned orders are created, how the available-to-promise quantity is calculated, the mechanics of the dispatch list, etc.

The next level involves the *application* of those principles, concepts, and techniques into the individual company. It gets at the details of how we're going to make this set of tools work for us.

Training is not synonymous with education. Rather, it's a subset of education. . . . Training is heavily software dependent. It involves things like how to interpret the master schedule report, what keys to hit on the CRT to release a production order, how to record an inventory transaction, etc. (See figure 6-5.)

A key point: Don't train before you educate. People need to know what and why before they're taught how. Education should occur either prior to, or simultaneously with, training.

The series of business meetings should function at all three levels. However, it may not be possible to do all of the training at this point. This would be so if, for example, new software were required but not yet selected. In such a case, the software aspects of training must be done later, after the new software package had been chosen. In any case, don't delay education while waiting for all the training materials to be available. (See figure 6-6 for an outline of a typical session.)

Figure 6-6
Typical Agenda for a Business Meeting

1. Fact transfer
2. Summary of key points
3. Discussion of application
4. Reach consensus
5. Identify assignments
6. Document decisions

The overall agenda for these business meetings needs to be provided by the educational materials themselves. A variety of media are possible candidates. Today, however, companies serious about MRP II invariably use professionally developed videotape courses, supplemented by extensive printed material.

Some of the educational material presented to the future (and rapidly developing) team of experts will contain specific topics, which are new to them. However, much of it should be material to which they've already been exposed. These are key people, and they'll need to hear a number of things more than once. (See criterion 5.)

The heart of these business meetings is that approximately three-fourths of the time is devoted to discussion. This is where the key people focus on *application*, on how the tools of MRP II will be used within the company to run the business. (See figure 6-7.)

Let's get our minds completely out of implementing MRP II for a moment, and talk about a business meeting to explore a specific problem. Let's say our company is experiencing a 10 percent sales decrease in the western region. What's the first thing we'd cover in the meeting? Probably, the person leading the meeting would present the background data, in some degree of detail (fact transfer). Then, he would condense the detail into the one or several most important points (summary of key points). Next, the group would explore alternative solutions to the problem, and identify which of the company's resources could be applied to solve the problem of the sales decline (discussion on application). The group would strive for agreement, ideally but not necessarily unanimous, as to the best course of action (reach consensus). Then they'd lay out the game plan and decide who's going to do what (identify assignments). One of the assignments would be for one or more of the attendees to write up the decisions and action plan developed at the meeting (document decisions).

The business meetings for MRP II implementation are much the

Figure 6-7
Business Meeting Time Allocation

Activity	Purpose	Ratio of Total Time Spent
Presentation of educational materials	Fact transfer	$\frac{1}{4}$
Discussion	Behavior change	$\frac{3}{4}$

same. The educational materials cover the fact transfer, enabling the meeting leaders to function effectively without having to become proficient classroom instructors. The meeting leader, who is not expected to know everything, does summarize the key points, and helps to focus the group toward the important areas to be discussed: How are we going to apply these specific tools to run the business better? Consensus is an important goal in these sessions, the outcome of which is often uncertain going in. Frequently, specific assignments are made to work on an issue that surfaced in the meeting. To me, that sounds a lot more like the business meeting to solve the sales problem than it does an education-and-training session.

It's in these business meetings where, for example, the production manager might say:

"Okay, I understand about shop floor control and dispatch lists." [Author's note: He understands the principles, concepts and techniques.] "But how are we going to make it work back in department 15? Man, that's a whole different world back there."

The production manager in this case, and the company, in a larger sense, need an answer. How are we going to schedule department 15 using the tools contained within MRP II? Perhaps the answer can be obtained right in the same session, following some discussion. Perhaps it needs some research, and the answer might not be forthcoming until the following week. Perhaps it's a very sticky issue. Input from the consultant may be sought, either at his next visit or via the telephone. Alternatively, a spin-off task force may be required, perhaps with the production manager as the leader. This is the right way to design the system.

It's what my colleague, Bill Hartman, calls bulletproofing MRP II. People need to have opportunities to "take potshots" at MRP II, to try to shoot holes in it. That's what the production manager just did. Giving people answers that make sense helps to bulletproof MRP II. Making necessary changes to how the system will be used is further bulletproofing. Bulletproofing isn't instantaneous. It's not like turning on a light switch. It's a gradual process, the result of responding to people's questions and being sensitive to their concerns.

Bulletproofing doesn't happen if answers to questions aren't valid or if essential changes are not recognized. In that case, MRP II has just had a hole shot in it. Holes in MRP II mean that ownership won't take place, and, therefore, behavior change won't happen.

Most people need to:

• Understand it.

• Think about it.

• Talk to each other about it.

• Ask questions about it (take potshots) and get answers.

• Hear their peers ask questions about it (take potshots), and get answers.

• See how it will help them and help the company before they'll willingly and enthusiastically proceed to change the way they do their jobs.

A word about enthusiasm. (See criterion 8.) During this series of business meetings, enthusiasm should noticeably start to build. Enthusiasm is the visual signal that the change process is happening. If that signal isn't forthcoming, then the change process is probably not happening. Stop right there. Fix what's not being done properly before moving forward.

Who's the best person to run these business meetings for the team of experts? Probably the project leader, at the outset. He has more time to devote to getting ready to lead each meeting and subsequently getting answers to questions. Some companies have varied this approach somewhat, with fine results. What they've done is to have the project leader initially run the meetings, lead the discussions, etc. However, after several weeks, as enthusiasm noticeably starts to build, the meetings can start to be run by others in the group. This gets the managers accustomed to running these kinds of meetings before they start leading the sessions for their own departments.

The important step of documenting decisions is often handled by the project leader, and we'll discuss that more in the next chapter when we cover the defining of sales, logistics, and manufacturing processes.

(For a recap of what we've covered for the team of experts, see figure 6-8.)

REACH THE CRITICAL MASS

Here's where the company begins to leverage on the time invested in creating the team of experts. The next step is for the experts to reach the critical mass, the majority of people within the company who become

Figure 6-8
Creating the Team of Experts

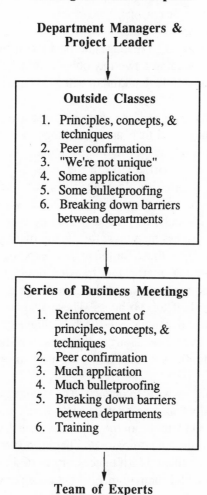

Department Managers &
Project Leader

Outside Classes

1. Principles, concepts, &
   techniques
2. Peer confirmation
3. "We're not unique"
4. Some application
5. Some bulletproofing
6. Breaking down barriers
   between departments

Series of Business Meetings

1. Reinforcement of
   principles, concepts, &
   techniques
2. Peer confirmation
3. Much application
4. Much bulletproofing
5. Breaking down barriers
   between departments
6. Training

Team of Experts

knowledgeable and enthusiastic about MRP II and who see the need and benefits from changing the way they do their jobs.

How is this accomplished? Very simply, by a series of business meetings. These meetings are conducted by the members of the team of experts (see criterion 6) for all the people within their respective departments (see criteria 2 and 4.) (Figure 6-7 depicts this process graphically.)

All the other people in the company? Yes. Including top management? Definitely. Even though they went to an outside class on MRP II? Yes, indeed, for a number of reasons, but primarily because for MRP II to succeed, they will need to change the way they do their jobs in many respects. They will need to manage the business differently than they have in the past. Attending a two-day outside class on MRP II is rarely sufficient to make possible that kind of behavior change on a permanent basis.

Top management people, like everyone else, need repetition and reinforcement. They need to hear some things more than once (criterion). They need to get deeper into application than they were able to in the outside classes, particularly in the areas of sales & operations planning, rough-cut capacity planning, and master scheduling. It's essential that they see how these tools will work within the company (criterion 8). Additionally, they need to lead by example (criterion 1).

This series of business meetings, for the top management group and others, is very similar to those for the team of experts. The same format is employed (about one-quarter fact transfer, three-quarters discussion and decisions); and the duration of these meetings generally should be about one and one-half to two hours. These also are decision-making meetings, and those decisions need to be documented and communicated. Some may trigger revisions to the sales, logistics, and manufacturing process definitions created in the business meetings for the team of experts.

A key difference is with frequency. The meetings for the team of experts are normally held every day because there's urgency to get these folks up to speed. Only then can they nail down the details of how MRP II will be used within the company and begin to spread the word. An accelerated schedule like this isn't necessary or desirable for the rest of the people. It's better for them to meet about once per week, learn some new things, discuss them with their coworkers (criterion 7), shoot some bullets at MRP II, get some answers, etc. Then they go back to their jobs, think about what they learned, and match it up to what they're currently doing. As they're doing their jobs during the rest of the week, they can shoot some more bullets (mental, not verbal) at MRP II. In some cases, they can do their own bulletproofing, internally, as they mentally formulate the solution to the problem that just occurred to them. In other cases, not so. They think of the problem but not the solution.

Figure 6-9
Creating the Critical Mass

Department Managers &
Project Leader

Outside Classes

1. Principles, concepts, & techniques
2. Peer confirmation
3. "We're not unique"
4. Some application
5. Some bulletproofing
6. Breaking down barriers between departments

Series of Business Meetings

1. Reinforcement of principles, concepts, & techniques
2. Peer confirmation
3. Much application
4. Much bulletproofing
5. Breaking down barriers between departments
6. Training

Team of Experts

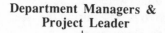

Series of Business Meetings

1. Principles, concepts, & techniques
2. Peer confirmation
3. Application
4. Bulletproofing
5. Breaking down barriers between departments
6. Training

All
the People
in the
Company

**Critical Mass of enthusiastic
and MRP II knowledgeable people,
ready and willing to change the way
they do their jobs**

Hence, the first agenda item for each business meeting should be Questions and Answers from the Last Meeting. This includes answers to questions raised but unanswered at the last week's session and also questions that occurred to people during the week. Here, also, they must be given an answer, either right away or at a subsequent session or as the result of a larger effort involving a spin-off task force. Bulletproofing.

Certain groups don't need to meet nearly as often as once per week. One good example is the direct labor people. A few sessions of about one hour each, spread over some months, has been shown to work very well (criterion 4). These people need to know about MRP II and how it'll affect them and the way they do their jobs. However, in most companies, they simply don't need to know as much about MRP II as others.

The principle of need-to-know is a key element in developing an internal education program to support this series of business meetings. Need-to-know operates at two levels: Company characteristics and job functions.

Company characteristics involve such things as having make-to-stock products, make-to-order products with many options, custom-engineered products, or a distribution network for finished goods, all of which are addressed by the defined body of knowledge called MRP II. The inside education program needs to be sensitive to these characteristics. There are few things worse than forcing people to learn a solution to a problem they don't have. What *is* worse is not giving them the solution to a problem they do have.

The second element of need-to-know reflects the different functions within a company, which call for different depths of education and discussion. This gets us back to reinforcement—the concept that people need to hear the important things more than once. Well, what's very important to people in one department may be less so to those in another department.

For example, the vice president of marketing does not need to know a great deal about the mechanics of generating the supplier schedule. He does need to know that this tool exists, that it's valid, and that it's derived via a rack-and-pinion relationship from material requirements planning, the master schedule, and the sales & operations plan.

However, the plant foremen and plant schedulers need to know more about the supplier schedules than the VP of marketing. This is because they're dependent on availability of purchased material to support their shop schedules, and they need the confidence to know that the tool being used is valid. Conversely, the VP of marketing and other executives will need to know more about sales & operations planning than the foremen. Sales & operations planning is their responsibility; it's their part of the ship.

The supplier schedulers and buyers need to know more about the supplier schedule than the foremen. It's their tool; they'll be living with it every day. They'll need more education, more discussion, more bulletproofing on this topic than anyone else.

One last point regarding the principle of need-to-know—the educational materials must lend themselves to need-to-know. They must be comprehensive and detailed. Providing only overview material can frustrate the people; their reaction will most likely be: "Where's the beef?" The materials should be tailored to reflect company characteristics and to support the differing levels of depth required by the various departments and job functions.

How does one know if it's working, this process of change? The test to apply as the sessions proceed is *enthusiasm* (criterion 8). If enthusiasm, teamwork, a sense of mission, and a sense of ownership are not visibly increasing during this process, then stop the process and fix it. Ask: "What's missing? What's not being done properly? Which of the eight criteria are being violated? Is bulletproofing working, or are people *not* getting answers?" (That means holes in MRP II, and not many people want to get aboard a leaking ship.)

A MINI CASE STUDY

Company CS (the name has been disguised to protect the successful) sent about a dozen of its senior executives to an outside top management class on MRP II. All but one became convinced that MRP II was essential for the continued growth and prosperity of the business because it would enable them to solve many of their problems with customer service, productivity, and high inventory levels.

The one exception was the CEO. His response after attending was less than completely enthusiastic. He was not anti-MRP II, but rather he was lukewarm. This caused great concern to Sam, the project leader, who said the following to your friendly author.

SAM: "Tom, I'm really concerned about our CEO. He's very neutral toward MRP II. With that mind set, I don't think we can succeed."

FRIENDLY AUTHOR (FA): "I think you're right. What do you plan to do about it?"

SAM: "We're going to start the inside business meetings for top management next month. If that doesn't turn our CEO around, I'm going to recommend that we pull the plug on the entire project."

FA: "Sam, I don't think it'll come to that. But if it does, I'll back you up 100 percent."

Company CS started the series of MRP II business meetings for its top management, with the CEO in attendance. After a half dozen or so sessions, the lukewarm CEO got the fire lit. He was able to see that MRP II, implemented properly, could enable him and his people to solve many of their nagging problems. He did, among other things, the following:

1. Sent a memo to each one of his nine plant managers, directing them to send him a report each week listing any unauthorized absences from the internal MRP II education sessions.

2. He then sent a personal letter to each person so identified. He expressed his concern over their unauthorized absence, asked them to attend the makeup session as soon as possible, and to do everything they could to avoid missing future sessions.

Needless to say, people receiving such a letter would be very unlikely to miss future sessions. So would their fellow foremen and buyers and sales people and schedulers because the word quickly got around.

Within a few years, all nine of company CS's divisions were operating at a Class A level. The key to their success—education. They did it right.

• They educated virtually everyone in the company.

• They educated from top to bottom, from the CEO to the machine operators.

• They educated both outside and inside. (Note: It wasn't until *inside* education that the CEO really got on board. Why? I'm not sure. One cause could be the need for reinforcement, the need to hear some things more than once. Or perhaps it was getting down to specifics. Some folks really can't get the fire lit until they can see in specific terms how MRP II's going to be used in the company.)

• Education became mandatory, thanks to the CEO and the repeated education he received. Consequently, success also became mandatory. And succeed they did.

IMPLEMENTERS' CHECKLIST

Function: Initial Education

Task	Complete	
	YES	NO
1. All members of executive steering committee, including general manager, attend outside MRP II class.	____	____
2. All members of project team attend outside MRP II class.	____	____
3. Series of business meetings conducted for operating managers, completing the total immersion process and resulting in the team of experts.	____	____
4. Series of business meetings conducted by the team of experts for all persons within the company, including the general manager and staff.	____	____
5. Enthusiasm, teamwork and a sense of ownership becoming visible throughout the company.	____	____

Chapter 7

Process Definition and Improvement

DEFINING SALES, LOGISTICS[1] AND MANUFACTURING PROCESSES

This step ensures that the implementation will be consistent with the vision statement. It adds essential detail to the vision statement and creates the detailed schedule necessary for effective project management.

PROCESS DEFINITION

There are two parts to this step. First, it spells out the details of what's going to be done, how it's to be done, and who's going to do it. It answers questions such as:

Where do we meet the customer today and should we be doing it differently? Should we be design-to-order, make-to-order, finish-to-order, or make-to-stock? Would a change here make us more competitive in the marketplace?

Specifically, how are we going to promise customer orders? Will the people in inside sales have direct access to the available-to-promise information, and if not, how will they assign commitment dates?

[1] Includes both outbound and inbound logistics: the distribution of product to customers and the acquisition of material from suppliers.

119

Figure 7-1
The Proven Path

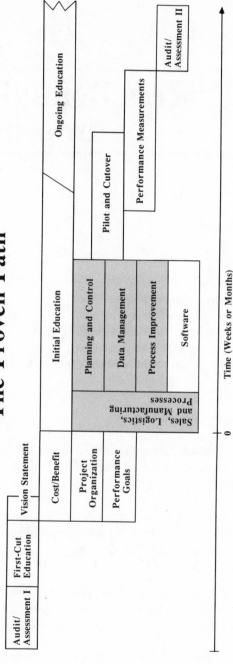

We don't have branch warehouses, but we do have consignment inventories at our stocking reps. Will we need to do a form of DRP on those inventories? If so, will the sales department be responsible for operating the DRP system?

We understand supplier scheduling and how it works. But specifically, how will we do it with our overseas suppliers? And what about our sister divisions within the corporation from whom we buy material; will we provide them with supplier schedules or with something else?

Less than half of our manufacturing processes are job shop, and they're not very complex. Will we need to implement capacity requirements planning and shop floor control? Could we avoid having to implement them by creating cells and moving even closer to 100 percent flow?"

This is an early task for project team people, with a little help from their friends on the steering committee. We've already discussed the forum for this step: the series of business meetings for the department heads covered in the preceding chapter. On the Proven Path display, we break out this definition step separately to emphasize its importance. However, these detailed definitions are largely the output from the series of business meetings, perhaps with some additional refinement and improvements by the manager(s) involved. As a final step, the executive steering committee as a whole should review and authorize these definitions.

This step provides an important linkage function: It flows logically from audit/assessment I, the vision statement, and education, and it serves as a major input into the project schedule. It verifies that the details of the schedule—what actually will be done—are consistent with the vision statement. Figure 7-2, developed by Pete Skurla, depicts this process.

THE PROJECT SCHEDULE

The MRP II project schedule is the basic control tool used to manage the project to a timely and successful conclusion. For a company-wide implementation, it needs to be:

- Aggressive but attainable (i.e., a 12-, 15-, or 18-month schedule).

- Expressed in days or weeks, for at least the short-to-medium term.

Figure 7-2

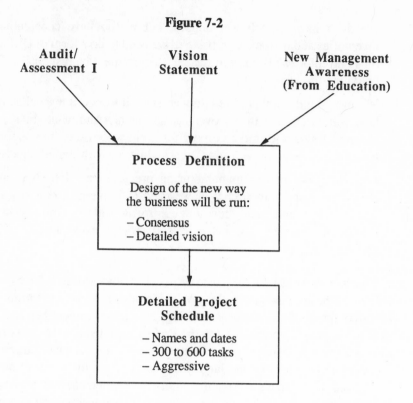

Just as with MRP II, months are too large a time frame for effective scheduling.

• Complete, covering all the tasks through closing the loop and finance and simulation.

• In sufficient detail to manage the project effectively, but not so weighty it overwhelms the people using it. For an average-sized business unit, a project schedule with between 300 and 600 tasks could serve as an effective project management tool.

• Specific in assigning accountability. It should name names, not merely job titles and/or departments.

Creating the project schedule. There needs to be widespread buy in to the project schedule, or it'll be just another piece of paper. It follows, then, that the people who develop the project schedule need to be the same people who'll be held accountable for sticking to it. They're primarily the department managers, and they're on the project team.

The project leader can help the department heads and other project team members develop the project schedule. However, he cannot do it for them or dictate to them what will be done and when.

Here's one good way to approach it:

1. Members of the project team individually review Darryl Landvater's Company-Wide Detailed Implementation Plan (see Appendix C). In this process, they need to add and delete steps where necessary, assign people, make estimates of time, etc. More steps will need to be added than deleted, as the plan is merely a framework from which an individual company's plan is derived and tailored.

2. This information goes to the project leader, who puts it together into a first-cut schedule.

3. This first-cut schedule is given to the project team members for their review, adjustment, etc. During this process, they may wish to consult with their bosses, most of whom are on the executive steering committee.

4. The project team finalizes the project schedule.

5. The project leader presents the schedule to the executive steering committee for their approval.

A process such as this helps to generate consensus, commitment, and willingness to work hard to hit the schedule.

MANAGING THE SCHEDULE—A SCENARIO

Consider the following case. This is a typical example of what could occur in practically any company implementing MRP II using the Proven Path. The project leader (PL) is talking to the manufacturing engineering manager (ME).

PL: "Mike, we've got a problem. Your department is three weeks late on the MRP II project schedule, specifically routing accuracy."

ME: "I know we are, Pat, and I really don't know what to do about it.

We've got all that new equipment back in department 15, and all of my people are tied up on that project."

[Author's comment: This is possibly a case of conflict between priority number two—implement MRP II—and priority number one—run the business.]

PL: "Can I help?"

ME: "Thanks, Pat, but I don't think so. I'll have to talk to my boss. What's the impact of us being behind?"

PL: "With this one, we're on the critical path for shop floor control. Each week late means a one-week delay in the overall implementation of MRP II."

ME: "Ouch, that smarts. When's the next steering committee meeting?"

[Author's comment: Mike knows Pat and the other members of the executive steering committee will be meeting shortly to review performance to the project schedule.]

PL: "Next Tuesday."

ME: "Okay. I'll get back to you."

PL: "Fine. Remember, if I can help in any way . . ."

At this point, from the project leader's point of view, the matter is well on the way to resolution. Here's why:

1. Mike, the manufacturing engineering manager, knows his department's schedule slippage will be reported at the executive steering committee meeting. (Pat, the project leader, has no choice but to report it; that's part of her job.)

2. Mike knows that his boss, the VP of manufacturing, will be in that meeting along with his boss's boss, the general manager.

3. Mike knows his boss doesn't like surprises of this type (who does?).

4. Unless Mike likes to play Russian roulette with his career, he'll get together with his boss prior to the steering committee meeting.

When they meet, they'll discuss how to get back on schedule, identifying alternatives, costs, etc. They may be able to solve the problem themselves. On the other hand, the only possible solution may be expensive and thus require higher-level approval. In that case, the executive steering committee would be the appropriate forum.

Or, worst case, there may be no feasible solution at all. That's when it becomes bullet-biting time for the steering committee. That group, and only that group, authorizes a reschedule of the MRP II project.

One last point before leaving Pat and Mike. Note the project leader's approach: "*We* have a problem," "Can *I* help?", "*We're* on the critical path," etc. One of Robert Townsend's remarks on managers in general certainly applies to MRP II project leaders—a large part of their job is to facilitate, to carry the water bucket[2] for the folks doing the work.

PLANNING AND CONTROL PROCESSES

In a company-wide implementation of MRP II, this is a big step. It contains policy development, the implementation of sales & operations planning, and the intensive testing of master scheduling and material requirements planning. Let's take 'em one at a time.

POLICIES

A handful of key policy statements is required for the successful operation of Manufacturing Resource Planning. Five bedrock policies are the ones that address sales & operations planning, demand management, master production scheduling, material planning, and engineering change.

The sales & operations planning policy should address issues such as who's accountable, who attends the sales & operations planning meetings, who develops the data, frequency of the meetings, meeting content, guidelines for making changes to the sales & operations plan, product families, etc.

The demand management policy focuses on the role of the demand manager and other key sales and marketing people, their communica-

---

[2] Robert Townsend, *Up the Organization* (New York: Alfred A. Knopf, 1978), p.11.

tions requirements to and from the master scheduler, ground rules for forecasting and promising customer orders, and performance measurements.

The master production scheduling policy needs to define the roles of the master scheduler, time fences, who's authorized to change the schedule in time zones, the fact that the MPS must match the production plan and fit within capacity constraints, allowable safety stock and/or hedges, feedback requirements, performance measurements, and others as appropriate.

The material planning policy focuses on guidelines for allowable order quantities, use of safety stock and safety time, where to use scrap and shrinkage factors, ground rules for lead time compression, feedback required from purchasing and plant, feedback to master scheduler, performance measurements, etc.

The engineering change policy should define the various categories of engineering change. Further, for each category, it needs to spell out who's responsible for initiating changes, for establishing effectivity dates, and for implementing and monitoring the changes. Also included here should be guidelines on new product introduction, communications between engineering and planning, performance measurements, etc.

These are four basic policies that most companies need to operate MRP II effectively, but others may be required for specific situations. Developing these policies is essential in the implementation process. The Oliver Wight ABCD Checklist is an excellent source for points to be included in these policies.

This is another case where both the project team and executive steering committee need to be involved. The project team should:

1. Identify the required policies.

2. Create spin-off task forces to develop them.

3. Revise/approve the draft policies.

4. Forward the approved drafts to the executive steering committee.

The steering committee revises/approves the draft policy and the general manager signs it, to go into effect on a given date.

A warning! Make certain the policy does go into effect and is used to run the business. Don't make the mistake of generating pieces of paper with signatures on them (policy statements), claim they're in effect, but continue to run the business the same old way.[3]

Also, as you create these policies and use them, don't feel they're carved in granite. Be prepared to fine-tune the policies as you gain experience. You'll be getting better and better, and your policies will need to reflect this.

SALES & OPERATIONS PLANNING

Here's a key point from an earlier chapter: implementers = users. This applies to sales & operations planning[4] just as with every other MRP II function. Therefore, since top management is accountable for *operating* sales & operations planning, they must be the ones to implement it.

This identifies another mission for the executive steering committee. In addition to their responsibilities for leadership, resource allocation, breaking bottlenecks, etc., this group is responsible for implementing sales & operations planning. They'll need a little help from their friends at the operating level for the necessary numbers on sales, production, inventories, and backlog.[5] They may also need some input regarding product families, etc. But the responsibility is ultimately theirs.

Sales & operations planning should be implemented just as soon as practical—certainly some months before MPS/MRP. There are three reasons for this timing: learning curve, benefits, and message.

As with most things, there's a definite *learning curve* involved with

---

[3] Sometimes it's not possible to put all elements of the new policy into effect before the related new planning tool has been implemented. (Example: Perhaps master scheduling has not been implemented yet on all the products. Therefore the demand management and master scheduling policies can't be applied 100 percent to those products, until they're added into master scheduling.) In these cases, the policies should spell out which pieces of it are effective at what times. As the new planning tools are implemented, the policy can be modified to remove these interim timing references.

[4] For an excellent treatment of this very powerful portion of MRP II, see Dick Ling and Walt Goddard, *Orchestrating Success* (Essex Junction, VT: Oliver Wight Publications, Inc., 1988).

[5] Most companies using S & OP will involve their operating managers. Typically this involvement centers around what's called a Pre-SOP process, a series of preliminary sessions not including top management. It focuses on areas of agreement and disagreement, verifying numbers, identifying alternatives, etc., so that the actual sales & operations planning meeting can be as efficient and focused as possible.

sales & operations planning. The first time probably won't go very well. The second time will be better than the first, the third better than the second, and so on. The catch is there's only one opportunity per month to do sales & operations planning, so it's important to start as soon as possible. You don't need to wait for all the MRP II software to be up and running. Once everyone on the executive steering committee has been through outside education, start to do sales & operations planning.

One of my associates, Andre Martin, was formerly the director of manufacturing and materials management at Abbott Laboratories Canada. Andre says: "It took Abbott Canada nine months to become truly effective in sales & operations planning."

Many companies have experienced positive *benefits* from operating sales & operations planning alone, before MPS/MRP. For perhaps the first time, the top executives in the company are reviewing the performance of sales, production, inventories, and backlogs on a structured and rigorous basis, and making focused decisions about the future. This process by itself can start to make things better.

Last, but not least, is the *message* this sends to other people in the company. Once again, leadership and example are closely intertwined. People throughout the company will be happy to see top management implementing and operating the part of MRP II they're responsible for. They'll feel reassured about that. As a result, morale should rise and enthusiasm build.

Conference Room Pilot

In chapter 9 we'll discuss the pilot approach to implementation. This is a very controlled method of implementing demand management, master scheduling, material requirements planning and, in some cases, plant and supplier scheduling.

There are three types of pilots: the computer pilot, the conference room pilot, and the live pilot. Relating back to our Proven Path diagram, the conference room pilot belongs here—in the planning and control section of implementation. However, we'll defer getting into the details until we can discuss all three pilots together.

DATA MANAGEMENT

It's essential to build a solid foundation of highly accurate numbers *before* demand management, master production scheduling, and material requirements planning go on the air. Accurate numbers *before*, not during or after.

An enormous amount of data is necessary to operate MRP II. Some of it needs to be highly accurate; some doesn't.

Data for MRP II can be divided into two general categories: *forgiving* and *unforgiving*. Forgiving data can be less precise; it doesn't need to be accurate to four decimal places. Unforgiving data is just that—unforgiving. It has little margin for error. If it's not highly accurate, it can harm MRP II quickly, perhaps fatally, and without mercy.

Forgiving data includes lead times, order quantities, safety stocks, standards, demonstrated capacities, and forecasts. Examples of unforgiving data include inventory balances, scheduled receipts, allocations, bills of material, and routings (excluding standards).

The typical company will need to spend far more time, effort, blood-sweat-and-tears, and money to get the unforgiving data accurate. The forgiving data shouldn't be neglected, but kept in its proper perspective. It needs to be reasonable. The unforgiving data needs to be precise.

UNFORGIVING DATA

Inventory Balances

The inventory balances (on-hand balances) in the computer must be 95 percent accurate, at a minimum. Do not attempt to implement master scheduling and MRP without this minimum level of accuracy.

The inventory balance numbers are vitally important because they represent the starting number for material requirements planning. If the balance for an item is not accurate, the planning for it will probably also be incorrect. If the planning is incorrect for a given item, such as a subassembly, then the erroneous planned orders will be exploded into incorrect gross requirements for all of that subassembly's components. Hence, the planning will probably be incorrect for those items also. The result: large amounts of incorrect recommendations coming out of MRP, a loss of confidence by the users, a return to using the hot list, and an unsuccessful implementation of MRP II.

What specifically does 95 percent accuracy mean? Of all the on-hand balance numbers inside the computer, 95 percent should match—on item number, quantity, and location—what is physically in the stockroom or the warehouse.

"But that's impossible!" people say. "What about all the nuts and bolts and shims and washers and screws and so forth? These are tiny little parts, they're inexpensive, and we usually have thousands of any given item in stock. There's no way to get the computer records to match what's actually out there."

Here enters the concept of *counting tolerance*. Items such as fasteners are normally not hand counted but scale counted. (The stock is weighed, and then translated into pieces by a conversion factor.) If, for example, the scale is accurate to plus or minus 2 percent, and/or the parts vary a bit in weight, then it obviously isn't practical to insist on an exact match of the count to the book record. In cases where items are weigh counted (or volume counted, such as liquids in a tank), companies assign a counting tolerance to the item. In the example above, the counting tolerance might be plus or minus 3 percent. Any physical count within plus or minus 3 percent of the computer record would be considered a hit, and the computer record would be accepted as correct.

Given this consideration, let's expand the earlier statement about accuracy: 95 percent of all the on-hand balance numbers inside the computer should match what is physically on the shelf inside the stockroom, *within the counting tolerance*. Don't leave home (i.e., go on the air) without it.

There are a few more things to consider about counting tolerances. The method of handling and counting an item is only one criterion for using counting tolerances. Others include:

1. The *value* of an item. Inexpensive items will tend to have higher tolerances than the expensive ones.

2. The frequency and volume of *usage*. Items used more frequently will be more subject to error.

3. The *lead time*. Shorter lead times can mean higher tolerances.

4. The *criticality* of an item. More critical items require lower tolerances or possibly zero tolerance. For example, items at higher levels in the bill are more likely to be shipment stoppers; therefore, they may have lower tolerances.

The cost of control obviously should not exceed the cost of inaccuracies. The bottom line is the validity of the material plan. The range of tolerances employed should reflect their impact on the company's ability to produce and ship on time. Our experience shows Class A users use tolerances ranging from 0 percent to 5 percent, with none greater than 5 percent.

The question that remains is how a company achieves the necessary degree of inventory accuracy. The answer involves some basic management principles. Provide people with the right tools to do the job, teach people how to use the tools (called education and training, right?), and then hold them accountable for results. Let's take a closer look.

1. *A zero-defects attitude.*

This is the people part of getting and maintaining inventory accuracy. The folks in the stockroom need to understand that inventory record accuracy is important, and, therefore, *they* are important. The points the company must make go like this:

a. MRP II is very important for our future. It will make the company more prosperous and our jobs more secure.

b. Material requirements planning is an essential part of making MRP II work.

c. Inventory record accuracy is an essential part of making material requirements planning work.

d. The people who are responsible for inventory accuracy are important. How well they do their jobs makes a big difference.

2. *Limited access.*

This is the hardware part of getting accuracy. In many companies, limited access means having the area physically secured—fenced and locked. Psychological restrictions—lines on the floor, signs, roped-off areas—have also been proven to be effective.

The warehouses and stockrooms need to be secured but not primarily to keep people out, although that's the effect. The primary reason is to *keep accountability in.* In order to hold the warehouse and stockroom people accountable for inventory accuracy, the company must give them the necessary tools. One of these is the ability to control who goes in and out. That means limiting access exclusively to those who need to be there. Then, the stockroom people can be the "captain of the ship" and may be legitimately held accountable for results.

Let me add a word of caution about implementing limited access. It can be an emotional issue. In the world of the informal system, many manufacturing people (foremen, general foremen, superintendents) spend a lot of time in the stockroom. This isn't because they think the stockroom's a great place to be. They're in the stockroom trying to get components, to make the product, so they can ship it. It's called expediting, and they do it in self-defense.

If, one morning, these people come to work to find the warehouses and stockrooms fenced and locked, the results can be devastating. They've just lost the only means by which they've been able to do their jobs.

Before installing limited access, do three things:

1. *Tell 'em.* Tell people in advance the stockrooms are going to be secured. Don't let it come as a surprise.

2. *Tell 'em why.* It's not theft. It's accountability. It's being done to get the records accurate, so that MRP can work.

3. *Tell 'em Job 1 is service*—service to the production floor, service to the repair department, service to shipping, service to the customer, etc.

In a company implementing MRP II, priority number one is to run the business; priority number two is implementation. In the stockrooms and warehouses, priority number one is service and priority number two is getting the inventory records accurate. (Priority number two is necessary, of course, to do a really good job on priority number one.)

Make certain that everyone, both in and out of the stockrooms, knows these things *in advance.*

3. *A good transaction system.*

This is the software part of the process. The system for recording inventory transactions and updating stock balances should be simple, and should represent reality.

Simple implies easy to understand and easy to use. It means only a few transaction types. Some software packages contain many unnecessary transaction types. After all, what can happen to inventory? It goes into stock and out of it. That's two transaction types. It can go in or out on a planned or unplanned basis. That's four. Add one for a stock-to-stock transfer and perhaps several others for inventory adjustments and miscellaneous activities. There are still probably less than 10 different transaction types that are really needed. Just because the software package has 32 different types of inventory transactions doesn't mean the company needs to use them all to get its money's worth. Using too many unnecessary transaction types makes the system unduly complicated, which makes it harder to operate, which makes it that much more difficult to get and keep the records accurate. Who needs this? Remember, stockroom people will be using these tools, not PhDs in computer science. Keep it simple. Less is more.

The transaction system should also be a valid representation of reality—how things happen in the real world. For example: inventory by location. Many companies stock items in more than one bin in a given stockroom and/or in more than one stockroom. Their transaction systems should have the capability to reflect this.

Another example: quick updates of the records. Inventory transaction processing does not have to be done in real time. However, it should be done fairly frequently and soon after the actual events have taken place. No transaction should have to wait more than 24 hours to be processed. Backflushing[6] won't work well at all with these kinds of delays.

4. *Cycle counting.*

This is the mechanism through which a company gains and maintains inventory record accuracy. Cycle counting has four main objectives:

a. *To discover the causes of errors, so that the causes can be eliminated.* The saying about the rotten apple in the barrel applies here. Get it out of the barrel before it spoils more apples. Put more emphasis on prevention than cure. When an inventory error is discovered, not only fix the record but also eliminate the cause of the error. Was the cause of the error inadequate physical security, a software bug, a bad procedure, or perhaps insufficient training of a stock person? Whenever practical, find the cause of the error and correct it so that it doesn't happen again.

---

[6] This is a technique to reduce component inventory balances by calculating component usage from completed production counts exploded through the bill of material. Also called postdeduct.

b. *To measure results.* Cycle counting needs to answer the question: "How are we doing?" It frequently should generate accuracy percentages, so the people know whether the records are sufficiently accurate. In addition, some companies routinely verify the cycle counting accuracy numbers via independent audits by people from the accounting department, often on a monthly basis. In this way, they verify that the stockroom's inventory records are as good as the stockroom people say they are.

c. *To correct inaccurate records.* When a cycle count does not match the computer record, the item should be recounted. If the results are the same, the on-hand balance in the computer must be adjusted.

d. *To eliminate the annual physical inventory.* This becomes practical after the 95 percent accuracy level has been reached on an item-to-item basis. Although doing away with it is important, it's not primarily because of the expense involved. The problem is that most annual physical inventories make the records *less* accurate, not more. Over the years, their main purpose has been to verify the balance sheet, not to make the records more accurate.

Consider the following scenario in a company implementing MRP II. The stockroom is fenced and locked; the computer hardware and software is operating properly; and the people in the stockroom are educated, trained, motivated, and enthusiastic. Inventory record accuracy is 97.3 percent. (Remember, this is units, not dollars. When the units are 95 percent to 99 percent accurate, the dollars are almost always in the 99 percent plus accuracy range. This is because plus and minus dollar errors cancel each other out; unit errors stand alone.)

It seems to me counterproductive to open the gates to the stockroom one weekend, bring in a bunch of outsiders, and have them running up and down the aisles, climbing up and down the bins, writing down numbers, and putting them into the computer. What happens to inventory accuracy? It drops. What happens to accountability? There's not much left. What happens to the morale of the people in the stockroom? It's gone—it just flew out the open gates.

Avoid taking annual physical inventories once the records are at least 95 percent accurate. Most major accounting firms won't insist on them. They will want to do a spot audit of inventory accuracy, based on a statistically valid sample. They'll probably also want to review the cycle counting procedures, to audit the cycle count results, and to verify the procedures for booking adjustments. That's fine. But there should be no need to take any more complete physical inventories, not even one last one to confirm the records. Having accounting people doing a monthly audit of inventory accuracy (as per paragraph b above) can facilitate the entire process of eliminating the annual physical inventory. This comes about because the accounting folks are involved routinely, and can begin to feel confidence and ownership of the process.

An effective cycle counting system contains certain key characteristics. First of all, it's done *daily*. Counting some parts once per month or once per quarter won't get the job done.

Good cycle counting procedures often contain a *control group*. This is a group of 100 or so parts that are counted every week. The purpose of the control group gets us back to the first objective of cycle counting—discovering the causes of errors. This is far easier to determine with parts counted last week than with those checked last month, last quarter, or last year.

Ease of operation is another requirement of an effective system. It's got to be easy to compare the cycle count to the book record, easy to reconcile discrepancies, and easy to make the adjustment after the error has been confirmed.

Most good cycle counting systems require a *confirming recount*. If the first count is outside the tolerance, that merely indicates the probability of an error. A recount is necessary to confirm the error. With highly accurate records, often it's the cycle count that's wrong, not the record.

Last, a good cycle counting system should *generate and report measures of accuracy*. A percentage figure seems to work best—total hits (good counts) divided by total counts. (Excluded from these figures are counts for the control group; within a few weeks, the control group should be at or near 100 percent.) Report these numbers frequently, perhaps once per week, to the key individuals—stockroom people, project team, steering committee, etc. Post them on bulletin boards or signs where other people can see them.

Get count coverage on all items, and 95 percent minimum accuracy, *before* going live with material requirements planning. In many companies, cycle counting must be accelerated prior to going on the air in order to get that coverage. The company may need to allocate additional resources to make this possible.

Once the stockroom has reached 95 percent inventory record accuracy, don't stop there. That's merely the *minimum* number for running MRP II. Don't be satisfied with less than 98 percent accuracy. Our experience has been that companies that spend all the money and do all the things necessary to get to 95 percent need only dedication, hard work, and good management to get in the 98 percent to 99 percent range. Make sure everyone knows that going from 95 percent to 98 percent is not merely an accuracy increase of 3 percent. It really is a 60 percent reduction in exposure to error, from 5 percent to 2 percent. MRP II will operate a good deal better with only 1 percent or 2 percent of the records wrong than with 4 percent or 5 percent.

There are two other elements involved in inventory status that need to be mentioned: scheduled receipts and allocations. Both elements must be at least 95 percent accurate prior to turning on MRP.

Scheduled Receipts

Scheduled receipts come in two flavors: open production orders and open purchase orders. They need to be accurate on quantity and *order* due date. Note the emphasis on the word order. Material requirements planning doesn't need to know the *operational* due dates and job location of production orders in a job shop. It does need to know when the order is due to be completed, and how many pieces remain on the order. Don't make the mistake of thinking that shop floor control must be implemented first in order to get the numbers necessary for material requirements planning.

Typically, the company must review all scheduled receipts, both production orders and purchase orders, to verify quantity and timing. Then, establish good order close-out procedures to keep residual garbage from building up in the scheduled receipt files.

In some companies, however, the shop orders can represent a real challenge. Typically, these are companies with high speeds and high volumes. In this kind of environment, it's not unusual for one order to catch up with an earlier order for the same item. Scrap reporting can also be a problem. Reported production may be applied against the wrong shop order.

Here's what I call A Tale of Two Companies (with apologies to Charles Dickens). In a certain midwestern city, two companies are operating MRP II quite successfully. They used to be located on the same street (one has since moved a few miles away). That's where the similarity ends. One, company M, makes machine tools. Company M's products are very complex, and the manufacturing processes are low volume and low speed. The people in this company had to work very hard to get their on-hand balances accurate because of the enormous number of parts in their stockrooms. They had far less of a challenge to get shop order accuracy because of the low volumes and low speeds.

Their neighbor, Company E, makes electrical connectors. The product contains far fewer parts than a machine tool. Fewer parts in stock means an easier job in getting accurate on-hand balances. These connectors, however, are made in high volume at high speeds. Company E's people had to work far harder at getting accurate production order data. They had to apply proportionately more of their resources to the shop order accuracy, unlike company M.

The moral of the story: Scratch where it itches. Put the resources where the problems are.

Allocations

Allocation records detail which components have been reserved for which scheduled receipts (production orders). Typically, they're not a major problem. If the company has them already, take a snapshot of the allocation file, then verify and correct the numbers. In the worst case, cancel all the unreleased scheduled receipts and allocations and start over. Also, be sure to fix what's caused the errors: bad bills of material, poor stockroom practices, inadequate procedures, etc. If there are no allocations yet, make certain the software is keeping them straight when the company starts to run material requirements planning.

Bills of Material

The accuracy target for bills of material is even higher than on inventory balances: 98 percent minimum, in terms of item number, unit of measure, quantity per parent item, and the parent item number itself. An error in any of these elements will generate requirements incorrectly.

Incorrect requirements will be generated into the right components or correct requirements into the wrong components or both.

First of all, what does 98 percent bill of material accuracy mean? In other words, how is bill accuracy calculated? Broadly, there are three approaches: the tight method, the loose method, and the middle-of-the-road method.

In examining the tight method, assume the bill of material in figure 7-3 is in the computer:

Figure 7-3

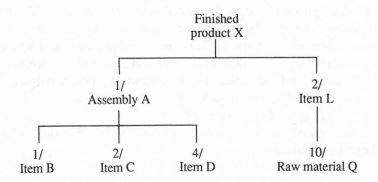

Suppose there's only one incorrect relationship here—assembly A really requires *five* of part D, not four. (Or perhaps it's part D that's not used at all, but, in fact, four of a totally different part is required.) The tight method of calculating bill accuracy would call the entire bill of material for finished product X a miss, zero accuracy. No more than 2 percent of all the products could have misses and still have the bills considered 98 percent accurate.

Is this practical? Sometimes. We've seen it used by companies with relatively simple products, usually with no more than 50 to 100 components per product.

The flip side is the loose method. This goes after each one-to-one relationship, in effect each line on the printed bill of material. Using the example above, the following results would be obtained:

Misses	Hits
D to A	B to A
	C to A
	A to X
	Q to L
	L to X

Accuracy: five hits out of six relationships, for 83 percent accuracy. Most companies would find this method too loose and would probably opt for the middle-of-the-road method. It recognizes hits and misses based on all single-level component relationships to make a given parent. Figure 7-4 uses the same example:

Figure 7-4

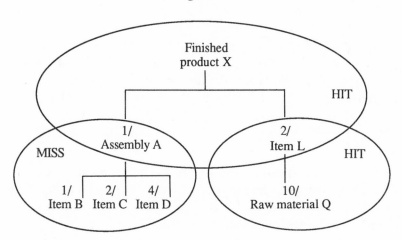

Accuracy: 67 percent. Overall, this approach is used most frequently. Select this method unless there are strong reasons to the contrary, and stick to it. As Walt Goddard points out, consistency is awfully important; if the measurement is consistent, then you can determine if you're improving, plateauing, or backsliding. Again, the overall bottom line is the validity of the material plan.

Once the company's decided how to calculate bill of material accuracy, it'll need to determine the measurement approaches to be used, to both acquire accuracy initially and to monitor it on an ongoing basis. Here are some options:

1. *Floor audit.*

Put some product engineers into the assembly and subassembly areas. Have them compare what's actually being built to the bill of material. They should work closely with not only the foremen but also with the assemblers. Correct errors as they're discovered.

2. *Office/factory review.*

Form a team of engineers, foremen, material planners, and perhaps cost people to review the bills jointly, sitting around a conference table. The question to be asked: "Is this the way we build it?" Again, correct errors as they're found.

3. *Product teardown.*

Take a finished product apart. Compare the parts and pieces on the table with the computer listing and correct the errors. This can be a good approach but may be impractical if the product is a jet airliner. Another shortcoming can be the difficulty in recognizing subassemblies.

4. *Unplanned issues/receipts.*

When production people go back to the stockroom for more parts, is it because they scrapped some or because they didn't get them in the first place? If the latter is the case, there may be a bill error that caused the picking list to be generated incorrectly.

If parts are returned to stock after the assembly of a product, perhaps they shouldn't have gone out to the shop floor in the first place. Again, the picking list may have been wrong because the bill was wrong. Correct the errors as they're discovered.

This can be a good technique to monitor bill of material accuracy on an ongoing basis.

Certainly, some of these methods are inappropriate for some companies. Select one method, or a combination, and get started as soon as possible. Don't go on the air without 98 percent accuracy on all bills because MRP won't work well without accurate bills.

In addition to being accurate, the bills of material need to be complete, properly structured, and integrated.

1. *Completeness.*

Ideally, bills of material should include everything involved in making the product—things like raw materials, fasteners, packing materials, solder and flux, paint, etc. At a minimum, all the important stuff (like raw materials, purchased components, unique packaging materials, etc.) must be in the bills before turning on MRP.

The test is: Is this item a shipment stopper? If the unit in question is truly a standard item (nuts, bolts, paint, rivets, solder) that you can get off the shelf from the supply house down the street, then it's not a shipment stopper. Otherwise, it probably is. Therefore, all the shipment stoppers must be in the bills before you go live. However, don't delay the implementation to get all the nonshipment stoppers on the system. They should be added as soon as it's practical, but don't let them be on the critical path.

2. Structure.

Structure has two meanings. First, bills must be properly structured to show stock points, phantoms, etc.

Second, companies whose products have many options usually need to structure their bills into a modular format. This enables effective forecasting, master scheduling, and customer order promising. Caution: Estimate the work load closely ahead of time. Typically, it takes many man-months of engineering time to develop modular bills. Don't forget the principle of three knobs: the work to be done, the calendar time in which it needs to be done, and the resources available to do it.

3. Integration.

Some companies have a variety of different bill of material files. Engineering has one, but manufacturing has its own. The cost accounting department doesn't like either of those, so it maintains another one to fit its needs.

MRP II represents a company-wide game plan, in units and dollars, so everyone is "singing from the same sheet of music." It's impossible if different departments have different hymnals. After all, the bill of material, along with the routings, represents the network around which MRP II is built. The various bills must be integrated into a single, unified bill that serves the needs of all the different departments[7].

---

[7] This may not be as tough as it sounds. Much of today's software for MRP II allows for flexible retrieval of bill of material information, tailored to the specific needs of each department. This can be done by intelligent coding capabilities within the bill of material (product structure) record.

Routings

Here's another example of why it's easier to implement MRP II in a flow shop: The routings are often not very important. In many cases, they're not needed at all because, you see, in a flow environment the routing is defined by how the equipment is laid out. In a job shop, the routings are not physical; they're informational, and therefore they're essential for you job shoppers.

For those of you who need routings, there's good news and bad news. The bad news is that three key elements are unforgiving; they need to be at least 98 percent accurate. These three elements are the operations to be performed, their sequence, and the work centers at which they'll be done. Their accuracy is extremely important because they'll be used by the computer to locate jobs (in shop floor control) and to apply load (in capacity requirements planning). This is where most companies need to apply a fair amount of time and effort, typically by foremen and manufacturing engineers.

The good news is that the standards, the other key element within the routing, are forgiving. Extreme accuracy of the standards is not necessary for CRP and shop floor control. This is because they convert a variety of units—pieces, pounds, gallons, feet, etc.—into a common unit of measure: standard hours. Errors, plus and minus, tend to cancel each other out. The law of large numbers has an effect. A good rule of thumb for standards is to try for accuracy of plus or minus 10 percent. Even if they're skewed to the high or low side, the efficiency factor can be used to translate the standard hours to clock hours.

Another good rule of thumb: If the standards today are good enough to calculate product costs, payroll, and efficiencies, then they'll be accurate enough for MRP II. Companies that already have standards on a work-center-by-work-center basis typically find that they don't need to spend a great deal of time and effort, and the obviously wrong ones will be fixed. However, most of your time should be spent on the unforgiving elements.

Calculating routing accuracy is fairly straightforward. If, on a given routing, *all* of the operations, sequence numbers, and work centers are correct, that's a hit. Otherwise, it's a miss. The target is to get at least 98 hits out of every 100 routings checked.

Methods for auditing and correcting routings include:

1. *Floor audit.*

Usually one or more manufacturing engineers follows the jobs through the shop, comparing the computer-generated routing to what's actually happening. Here again, talk to the operators, the folks who are making the parts. Virtually every element involves an operator to one degree or another. They know what's happening. A variation here is to check the jobs physically at a given work center. Does each job at a given work center have an operation in its primary routing or alternate that calls for that work center? If not, what's it doing there?

2. *Office/factory review.*

Normally involves foremen and manufacturing engineering people in a group, reviewing the computer-generated routings against their knowledge of the shop and any additional documentation available.

3. *Order close-out.*

As shop orders are completed and closed out, the actual reporting is compared to the computer-generated routing.

Not every method will be practical for every company. Some companies use a combination of several.

Companies that need shop floor control and CRP, but don't have routings and standards by work center, have a big job ahead of them, and can't afford to wait for phase II to begin. They should start just as soon as possible. This part of the project needs to be adequately resourced to do a big job—identify all the work centers, develop routings and standards—without delaying the implementation of the total system. Some companies have had to expand the manufacturing engineering department and/or obtain temporary industrial engineering help from outside the company. This is another case where that cost of a one-month delay number can help a lot with resource allocation/acquisition decisions.

Customer Orders

Last, but certainly not least, customer orders should be accurate. They usually are, and, for that reason, I've listed them last. However, the customer comes first, so we'd better make sure that our customer order files match their purchase orders. Not usually a problem, but at a minimum take a spot check to ensure that everything's okay with what may be the most important set of data in the entire company.

The process of checking is usually simple. Customer service pulls a small sample, maybe 50 or 100 orders, calls the customers and verifies product, quantity, date, and anything else that may be important. If this audit turns up problems, the process may need to be expanded to a complete verification of the entire order file.

FORGIVING DATA

Virtually all forgiving data is made up of item and work center numbers. In these categories, four-decimal-place accuracy isn't necessary. I'm not aware of any MRP initiative that went down the drain because the order quantities were not calculated with sufficient precision[8] or because the demonstrated capacities weren't within plus or minus 2 percent.

Item Data

Item data refers to the other numbers necessary for master production scheduling and material requirements planning. Most of it is static and is stored in the computer's item file. It includes things like lead times, order quantities, safety stock/time, shrinkage factors, scrap or yield factors (stored in the bill of material), etc.

Getting the item data collected and loaded is a necessary step, but it's normally not a big problem. The people doing it should be the same ones who'll be operating these planning systems: the master scheduler(s) and the material planners. They'll need education, time to do the job, and some policy direction.

Wherever practical, use the numbers already available. Review them, make sure they're in the ballpark, and fix the ones that are obviously wrong. If the lead time for an item is too high or too low, change it to a reasonable number; otherwise, leave it alone. If the order quantity for a part is out of line, change it; if not, let it be. If an item routinely experiences some scrap loss in production, add in a scrap or shrinkage factor. Otherwise, leave the factor at zero.

---

[8] Perhaps the reverse is true. Some MRP efforts got hung up on trying to get the order quantities too precise and neglected fundamental, unforgiving data, such as inventories, bills, and routings.

The subject of using the numbers already in place leads to a larger issue. When implementing MRP II, *change only what's absolutely necessary to make it work.* Don't make changes for incremental operational improvement unless they're also necessary for implementation. They'll be plenty of time later, after the system is on the air, to fine-tune the numbers, and to get better and better.

There are two reasons for this—people and diagnosis:

1. Implementing Manufacturing Resource Planning is a time of great change in a company. For most people, change is difficult. Introducing nonessential changes will make the entire implementation process more difficult than it needs to be.

2. Unnecessary changes also complicate the diagnostic process when something goes wrong. The greater the number of things that were changed, the greater the number of things that could be causing the problem. This makes it correspondingly (perhaps even exponentially) harder to find the problem and fix it.

Work Center Data

The information involved here includes things like work center identification, demonstrated capacity, efficiency (or productivity) factors, and desired queues for the job shops.

Review the work center arrangement now being used. Ask whether the machines are grouped correctly into work centers and whether the operator skill groups are established properly. A key factor here—how does each foreman view the equipment and people in his department, in terms of elements to be scheduled and loaded?

Make whatever changes are necessary. The goal is to enable CRP, input/output, and shop dispatching to give the foreman the right information as to work load, priorities, and schedule performance.

Realize that changes in work center identification will mean changes to the routings. A good bit of work may be involved. A computer program can often help in revising routings to reflect new work center assignments.

Start to gather statistics for each work center: demonstrated capacity, efficiency, which may already be available, and planned queue. This last element may represent a dramatic change. For most companies, planned queues will be smaller than they were under the informal system. Many companies determine their queues by considering "the range" and "the pain." Range refers to the variability of job arrival at the work centers; pain means how much it will hurt if the queue for a particular work center disappears, and it runs out of work.

The key players in these decisions are the foremen and the industrial engineers. Usually, the engineers develop the numbers, while the foremen are more involved with the qualitative information, such as grouping equipment for the best work center arrangement, the amount of pain suffered by the center that runs out of work, etc. Foremen buy in is critical here. Therefore, they, and their bosses, must call the shots. They, and their people, are the ones who'll be accountable for making it work.

Forecasts

Yes, Virginia, the sales forecasts fall into the forgiving category. And it's a darn good thing, too, because the forecasts will *never* be super accurate. This may be a tough pill for you long-term manufacturing people to swallow, but that's the way it is.

The reason your sales forecasts will never be highly accurate is that your marketing and sales people cannot predict the future with certainty. Okay? If they could, do you think they'd be working for a living, knocking themselves out 40 plus hours per week trying to get customers to order your product? Of course not. Where would they be if they could foresee the future with certainty? At the racetrack, of course. And if the track's closed? At their brokers.

However, there's a flip side to this. In almost all companies who implement MRP II, forecast accuracy is improved substantially. This is done through more frequent reviews, on a more focused basis, with good communications and measurements. You marketing and sales folks should plan on working hard to improve the accuracy of your forecasts. Everyone, though, should recognize that the law of diminishing return applies here: As forecast accuracy increases, there comes a point where each additional unit of effort does not generate a commensurate unit of greater accuracy.

This is where the forgiving nature of forecasts comes into play. Many companies have found their ability to cope with forecast error increases dramatically as they obtain:

1. *Improved demand management, order promising and master scheduling capabilities.*

As my friend Bill Berry, from the University of North Carolina at Chapel Hill, says so well: "They replace inventory with information." Better information, based on accurate data, with good communications and the intelligent use of time fences, can make a big difference.

2. *Reduced lead times.*

Shorter lead times are one of the most important parts of running a manufacturing business well. The shorter the lead time—to enter the customer orders, to make the product, to buy the material—the less vulnerable a company is to forecast error. Consequently, it's better able to ship what the customers want, when they want it. And isn't that what it's all about?

PROCESS IMPROVEMENT

This step refers to the improvement of physical conversion processes, for the manufacture of products, components, and materials within our plants and our suppliers' plants.

In implementing Just-in-Time and Total Quality Control, this is the major step; process improvement is where JIT/TQC lives. It also plays a substantial role in implementing Quick-Slice MRP, as we'll see later.

In a company-wide MRP II implementation, process improvement is not central. Many companies have implemented MRP II successfully without making substantial improvements to their production processes. And it figures; MRP II enables a company to maximize performance out of its current operating environment. Therefore, for company-wide MRP II, it's possible to skip this step entirely.

But should you skip it totally? Might it not be possible to make some improvements to physical processes during the same time that MRP II's being implemented? I think so. Example: the process of setting up machinery and changing over lines. Frequently, substantial setup reductions can be made easily and at little cost, and can result in sizable drops in inventory and lead times.

Setup reductions are but one example. My advice to you folks who work on the plant floor: Go to work[9] on process improvement as a part of your job in MRP II implementation. A good first step would be to go through some education on JIT/TQC early in the MRP II implementation, to help yourselves get some big bangs from the buck quickly.

IMPLEMENTERS' CHECKLIST

Function: Planning and Control Processes, Data Management, Process Improvement

Task	Complete YES	NO
1. Process definition statements completed for all sales processes to be impacted by MRP II.	——	——
2. Process definition statements completed for all distribution processes to be impacted by MRP II.	——	——
3. Process definition statements completed for all purchasing processes to be impacted by MRP II.	——	——
4. Process definition statements completed for all manufacturing processes to be impacted by MRP II.	——	——
5. Detailed project schedule established by the project team, naming names, in days or weeks, and showing completion of MRP II project in less than two years.	——	——
6. Detailed project schedule being updated at least weekly at project team meetings, with status being reported at each meeting of the executive steering committee.	——	——
7. Sales & operation planning policy written, approved, and being used to run the business.	——	——

[9] Or continue to work on process improvement. Many companies begin JIT and/or TQC activities prior to MRP II. Implementing MRP II is no reason to slack off; rather, it should be an incentive to work even harder on process improvement. The rationale: Think how good it'll be when your improved processes are coupled with a good set of tools for planning and scheduling.

	Complete	
Task	YES	NO
8. Presales & operations planning meetings initiated.	——	——
9. Sales & operations planning meetings initiated.	——	——
10. Master production schedule policy written, approved, and being used to run the business.	——	——
11. Material planning policy written, approved, and being used to run the business.	——	——
12. Engineering change policy written, approved, and being used to run the business.	——	——
13. Inventory record accuracy, including scheduled receipts and allocations, at 95 percent or better.	——	——
14. Bill of material accuracy at 98 percent or better.	——	——
15. Bills of material properly structured, sufficiently complete for MRP, and integrated into one unified bill for the entire company.	——	——
16. Routings (operations, sequence, work centers) at 98 percent or better accuracy.	——	——
17. Item data complete and verified for reasonableness.	——	——
18. Work center data complete and verified for reasonableness.	——	——

Chapter 8

Software

Software for MRP II is like a set of golf clubs. Playing the game competitively requires a reasonably complete set. If Tom Watson went out on the Pro Golf Tour with only a four wood and a sand wedge, he probably wouldn't win a lot of money.

On the other hand, Tom *Wallace* might buy the greatest set of clubs in the world and still couldn't break 100. I don't play golf.[1]

The moral: Software by itself cannot make a company a successful MRP II user. However, the lack of a reasonably complete set of software can keep a company from succeeding.

To Buy or Not to Buy

The first software decision a company normally faces is whether to write its own software or buy an existing package. There are problems with either approach. First, the bad news about writing one's own software:

1. *It takes too long.*

Writing a complete MRP II software package is almost always a multiyear project. As such, it runs counter to all the reasons for an aggressive schedule in light of the cost of a one-month delay. Let's take the case of a company whose one-month delay cost is $100,000. If

---

[1] I probably couldn't break 100 even if I were a golfer, but that's beside the point.

Figure 8-1
The Proven Path

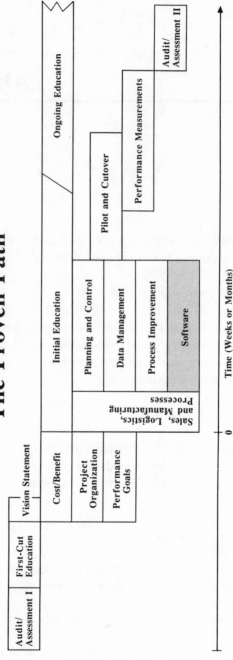

writing its own software would delay the project by no more than two years, the resultant delay cost would equal $2,400,000 (24 months X $100,000 per month). That's an expensive piece of software!

2. *It may not work.*

During the three or four or more years that it will take to write all the software, there'll be a nagging question that can't be answered with certainty: Will it work? One of the key reasons to buy an existing software package is the ability to see it in operation beforehand. Writing one's own software from scratch may result in software that doesn't work—or doesn't *appear* to work. It could turn out that the software's okay, but the people aren't using it correctly. Hence, good results aren't forthcoming. In that scenario, what is likely to get blamed—the software or the management? Nine times out of ten, the finger would be pointed at the software. Using proven software eliminates the possibility of using software as a scapegoat.

3. *It may be too specific to today's business environment.*

Homegrown software for MRP II is usually very specific and very focused on what the company is doing *today*. As such, it may not stand the test of time. Most businesses are dynamic. They change, adapt, grow. One company with which I'm familiar, strictly make-to-stock at the time, implemented MRP II successfully. They used standard software from an outside source. The software properly contained features to support make-to-order master scheduling, as well as make-to-stock. At the time, the company in question needed the latter but not the former. Several years later, however, the company developed an entirely new line of products that were make-to-order. Thanks to having standard software, the software tools were already in place to support the new product line. Things might have been far more difficult if the company had had home-grown software.

Those are some compelling reasons against writing your own software, right? However, don't leap to a decision to buy rather than make. Let's examine some of the problems involved with buying a package:

1. *It will be "incomplete."*

Incompleteness comes in two dimensions: function and fit. As this is written, there is no such thing as a 100 percent functionally complete software package for MRP II. Some are woefully incomplete, others less so. A growing number are relatively but not totally complete in terms of functionality.

Even if a 100 percent complete package were available, some enhancements or modifications would be required to fit it in to a given company.

2. *It may be too complicated.*

Many of the existing software packages are far more complex than need be. They contain a wide variety of options, features, and bells and whistles, many of which are unnecessary and some of which are counterproductive.

Complexity is bad. For the folks in data processing, it makes the programs difficult to install and maintain. It's a poor choice for the users, too, because they are required to spend a lot of time sorting through all the options and deciding which ones to use. Further, it gives them the opportunity to select improper techniques, such as automatic order releasing, automatic rescheduling, finite loading, dynamic lot sizing, etc., which are counterproductive. They inhibit MRP II from working properly.

Last, and probably least in importance, is cost. The more complex software tends to be more expensive. This has led some knowledgeable observers of the MRP II software scene to conclude there is a direct relationship between the cost of software and the time it takes to get it on the air. That relationship is *inverse*. Expensive software tends to be more complex, and complex software is likely to be tougher to install, operate, and maintain.

The situation has improved over the past few years, because of the availability of good MRP II software for mid-sized computers.[2] These machines are becoming more and more common in manufacturing companies, and, in many cases replacing mainframes. In general, MRP II software for mainframes tends to be more complex and more expensive than software for mid-sized machines.

Another recent development in the MRP II software field is the onset of packages that run on personal computers. These machines today are surprisingly powerful. I'm writing this book on an IBM PC-AT, sitting

---

[2] We used to call them minicomputers, but that term seems inappropriate due to the power they possess today.

here on my desk, and it has more speed and storage than the IBM 360/40 mainframe we had at a 1,000-employee manufacturing company where I used to work.

Well, MRP II software is available to run on personal computers, and most of these packages are quite inexpensive. Further, and more important, they tend to be simple and relatively complete in terms of functionality. There may be some real opportunities here for you folks in smaller companies, divisions, plants, etc. (and maybe even for some of you in larger business units). PC-based software for MRP II can mean much lower hardware and software costs.

3. *It may be difficult to interface.*

Tying new software to existing systems can be an enormous job. I'll expand on this topic later.

4. *It will have bugs.*

The odds are extremely high that the sun will rise in the east tomorrow morning. Bet on it. The odds are about the same that there are bugs in any MRP II software package. "Why?" you may be asking, "The software package we're going to buy has been installed in about 1,000 companies. That's 1,000 debugging cycles. There couldn't possibly be any bugs left."

My response is: "Don't count on it." The reason is that these packages are big, many of them containing well over a million lines of program code. Until now, no one has ever processed, through that mass of programs, your specific data with its peculiarities, quirks, etc. There will be bugs in the software.

Bugs can be tough to find and fix, and may require help from the software supplier. If that help isn't forthcoming, the entire MRP II project can be delayed. Therefore, build some wording into the software contract, as airtight as possible, about bugs, responsibility for fixing them, timing, penalties, etc.

A software supplier's refusal to commit to fixing bugs quickly may be a signal they don't have confidence in their product, or the ability to fix it when it doesn't work, or both. In this case, go somewhere else. They're not the only game in town. There are several tested and proven software packages for most hardware.

Some Examples

Let's take the case of two different companies planning to implement MRP II, which I'll call Company 1 and Company 2. Company 1 has no computer and no software. Their choice is clear—they need to buy a package. The killer stroke on writing their own software is the time issue: It simply takes too long.

Company 2 attempted to implement MRP several years ago. They purchased a software package that happened to be functionally fairly complete. The implementation effort, however, like many others, was flawed. It concentrated largely on installing the software, rather than on the people and data.

Company 2 is a C-minus user. Now they want to re-implement MRP II, and this time do it right. It's very unlikely that they'll need new software because they have almost all of it already.

A good way of communicating this situation graphically is by means of a spectrum or a range of possibilities. Company 1 and Company 2 are at opposite ends of the spectrum. (See figure 8-2.)

Company 3, a first-time implementer, has had a computer for many years. Over the years, they developed a number of logistics-related applications on their computer: order entry, inventory transaction processing, shop floor control, bill of material processor, etc. These applications were reasonably well done but never realized their full potential because the company lacked a formal priority planning system that worked. The work they had done in the areas of master scheduling and material planning wasn't adequate to do away with the informal system. Company 3 is in the middle, somewhere in the uncertain zone. (See figure 8-3.)

Company 3 is confronted with a range of alternatives: (a) buy all new software; (b) buy the missing pieces; (c) write the missing pieces

Figure 8-2

Company #1 —Has none—	Company #2 —Has almost all—
BUY NEW SOFTWARE	USE WHAT'S THERE

Figure 8-3

	Company #3 —Has some—	
BUY NEW SOFTWARE	ZONE OF UNCERTAINTY	USE WHAT'S THERE

internally; or (d) some combination of b and c. The correct decision will be based on a number of factors: the quality and completeness of what's already in place, the availability of internal resources, the quality of the outside software available or pieces thereof, etc. The final decision should be based on the shortest distance between company 3's position today and a functionally complete set of software. In short, which alternative will get them there the fastest?

SELECTING SOFTWARE

Okay, suppose a company has looked at their situation closely, and decided they'll need to buy all or most of their MRP II software. They'll need to select a software package, and that leads us to what I call the seven Ps of software selection:

1. *Don't be premature.*

Some companies' first exposure to MRP II is through the software salesman who sells them a package. Often, these people regret having made the purchase after they've gone to class and learned about MRP II.

The right way is to learn about MRP II first, and get the software shortly after the company has made an informed decision and commitment to MRP II.

2. *Don't procrastinate.*

This isn't as contradictory as it sounds. Don't make the mistake of trying to find the perfect software package, or even the best one. That's like searching for the Holy Grail or the perfect wave. There is no best software package.

The correct approach, after learning about MRP II and deciding to do it, is to get a good workable set of software. It's important to move through this selection phase with deliberate haste, so the company can get on with implementing MRP II and start getting paybacks.

3. *Don't pioneer.*

As Walt Goddard pointed out in the foreword, pioneers—people who get too far out in front—often get arrows in their backs. This certainly applies to software for MRP II. Why buy untested, unproven software? Beats the heck out of me. Stay away from brand-new software.

Insist on seeing the package working in a company that operates at a Class A or high B level. (Class A or high B implies that most functions of MRP II are being exercised. Class C companies use the formal system mainly to launch orders.) If the prospective software supplier can't name a Class A or B user of their product, I recommend you don't buy it. Go elsewhere.

However, you may not have much of a choice. Your computer may be one for which no proven software exists. In this case, learn as much as possible about the packages available, and select one that appears simple and easy to modify. Then, plan on having *major problems* with the package; plan to apply *more resources* than normal to making it work; and recognize that the entire MRP II project will probably *take longer and cost more.*

Some companies, when confronted with this problem, make what can be an intelligent choice. They get a new computer, one that has proven software available.

4. *Minimize pain.*

From a systems point of view, some of the most difficult parts of an MRP II project are:

a. Installing the software—just getting it to run on the computer.

b. Interfacing the software with existing applications that will remain following MRP II implementation (payroll, sales analysis, payables, general ledger, etc.).

c. Writing throw-away programs that will be used only once or only for a short period. Often, these are bridges from the old system to the new. This can be difficult emotionally for the folks in data processing.

It's a bit like building a building that one knows will be torn down three weeks later.

However distasteful it may be, though, throwaway programming is almost always necessary. Be prepared to do some, probably more than a little.

Remember, the more complex the software, the tougher it will be to install. Therefore, all things being equal, choose the simpler package.

In some companies, interfacing can be a massive problem, perhaps the single biggest obstacle in the entire implementation. Some projects have literally gone dead in the water when the magnitude of the interfacing job was discovered too late.

Here's a word of warning to the systems folks from someone who used to work there and who's been down the MRP II implementation path many times: Don't underestimate the interfacing task. During the cost justification process, consider the existing applications and the most likely software packages. Try to get a rough-cut estimate of interfacing man-hours (or days, or weeks, or months). When in doubt, lean towards the high side.

Then, when it is time to select the software, choose the route of least *pain*. The ideal here is simple software, easy to interface. Another of my colleagues, John DeVito, points out that the price of a software package is only one element of software costs. John's formula is that the total initial cost of software equals:

Purchase price
+
Modification costs
+
Interface costs
+
Delay costs

The MIS department's challenge is to minimize the total costs.

5. Save the pockets of excellence.

Many companies do some things very well. An example of this would be a company with an excellent shop floor control system but little else.

The computer part of this system may have been programmed in-house, and may contain some essential features for the users.

Let's assume further the MRP II software package selected by this company contains a shop floor control module that's workable, but not as good as the company's current system. This company should not blindly proceed to replace its superior[3] shop floor system with the new, inferior one. That kind of move could severely damage operational performance and user morale.

Save the good stuff. Don't throw the baby out with the bath water.

6. *Beware of plain vanilla.*

Some companies attempt to implement MRP II with the software as is—with no modifications. Their plan is to go back and make the changes after the system is up and running.

Why bother? If the system's working, there's no real need to modify it. Almost invariably, however, the software needs to be modified *before* implementation, just to make it work properly in the first place. What are the chances a given set of software, encompassing all the functions of MRP II, can be implemented properly in a given company without modification? Two chances: slim and none.

When a company buys good software for MRP II, it's going to get somewhere between 75 percent and 95 percent of the lines of program code it'll need to run its business properly.[4] The balance will have to be provided, either by the company's own systems people, the software supplier, a third party, or by the users themselves.[5]

Remember, MRP II implementation is not a backroom computer project. It's a matter of *changing the way the business is run* to allow major improvements in *how well* the business is run.

[3] Superior as far as the users are concerned. It may run less elegantly on the computer.

[4] When practical, try to get closer to 95 percent completeness. Specialized MRP II software packages, tailored for nontraditional industries, are available today. Two examples are packages for aerospace & defense, and for process types of manufacturing.

[5] This can happen when the users are provided with good query language and report-writer software that lets them structure their own reports and screens. Happily, it's become a fairly common occurrence today.

7. Prepare to maintain the software yourselves.

This may be a tough one for some of you systems folks, so fasten your seat belts. Here goes. Most software suppliers offer a maintenance feature with the purchase of their software. For an annual charge, they will send you new releases of their MRP II software package, which contains enhancements and improvements. My advice: Don't buy the maintenance unless absolutely necessary; and if you have to buy it, get yourselves on a track to take over maintenance as soon as possible. Two reasons: control and timing.

Regarding control, consider what we're talking about here. MRP II is a set of planning and execution tools to enable the business to operate far better than before. MRP II, implemented properly, becomes the way we run the business at the operational level. Most MRP II tools are heavily computer supported. Does it seem proper to subcontract to an outside party the maintenance of these tools over the long run? Not to me. You simply can't count on that software supplier providing support for that package over the long pull. With a few exceptions, you can't even count on that software supplier being in business over the long run.

The timing issue gets at when changes are made. Keep in mind, this is the age of Just-in-Time and Total Quality Control. This means continuous improvement; companies not in continuous improvement mode will not survive. As things are improved on the plant floor and elsewhere throughout the company, the MRP II software will often have to be modified to reflect the new operating environment. Here's the question: Do we want to put our company and our drive for continuous improvement on the software supplier's timetable for software enhancements? If I'm the systems guy and manufacturing people are needing software changes to support Just-in-Time, the last thing I want to say is: "Well, let's see—what you're asking for is due from the software supplier in release 8.0, currently promised for late next year." Not acceptable, of course.

Here's what I recommend. One, buy simple software; it'll be much easier to maintain. Two, if the current systems resource isn't sufficiently solid to take on the maintenance task at day 1, beef it up. Three, as soon as possible (maybe day 1), bring that critically important maintenance function in house. Let's be the masters of our own destiny. Let's pack our own chutes.

Managing Requests for Changes

If modifications are going to be necessary, where does a company draw the line? How do they keep from being inundated with requests for changes?

Good question because this can be a real problem. Three elements come into play: education, standard software, and management.

Requests for changes will be minimized if the company does a good job of MRP II education. This will help the users to solve their problems within the overall framework of MRP II. Add to this a set of standard software, relatively complete in terms of functionality.[6] Then, what the users learn about MRP II will be reflected in the software. However, even with excellent education and good software, requests for software modification will still be forthcoming. This is where effective management enters the picture.

Key people, particularly members of the steering committee and project team, need to recognize two principles:

1. *Resist changes.*

The mind-set of these folks should be one of resisting any changes to the software that are not essential for either running the business and/or implementing MRP II. They need to understand that too many changes can delay the project. Thus changes may be very expensive, based on the cost of a one-month delay. Further, they may reduce the odds for real success with MRP II because long, stretched-out implementations are less likely to succeed.

2. *Distinguish between systems that are computer essential and those that are automated manual.*

Systems such as MRP, CRP, and shop floor control are computer essential; they simply cannot be done manually because of the enormous

---

[6] An extremely useful tool is Darryl Landvater and Chris Gray, *MRP II Standard System* (Essex Junction, VT: Oliver Wight Publications, Inc., 1989).

This is not a piece of software. Rather, it is a statement of what constitutes a functionally complete set of software for all elements of MRP II. Many of the more progressive software suppliers have used this document as the high-level systems specifications when designing their MRP II software product.

volume of calculations involved. Ollie had a good way of putting it: "To do material requirements planning manually in most companies would require a staff about the size of the Russian army, plus a year's output from the Eagle pencil factory."

Automated manual systems are ones like payroll, general ledger, billing automating the printing of purchase orders, etc. They can be done manually. Although computerizing these activities may be beneficial, the key is that they can be done effectively without the computer.

Automated manual systems have had great impact in fields such as banking and insurance where the direct labor force, so to speak, is clerical office workers. In manufacturing companies, the big paybacks have come from computer-essential systems, such as the ones that are the subject of this book.

Those are the principles. Here's the procedure:

1. The MIS department is geared up to provide a certain amount of modifications, changes, enhancements, etc. The necessary funds have been budgeted in the cost justification.

2. Requests for modifications are submitted to the MIS department for an evaluation of the amount of work involved. A dividing line of X man-hours of systems/programming time is established to distinguish between major and minor modifications. (Obviously, X will vary from company to company.) The MIS department's evaluation places the requested modification into the major or minor category. (Note: Systems personnel do not decide on the appropriateness or the need for the change. They're free to comment but do not make that decision.)

3. The request then goes to the project team. If the request is for a minor change, the project team decides whether to grant the request (do it soon) or to defer the change to phase III. (Back in chapter 3, I identified phase III as being made up of finance and simulation, plus other elements judged as desirable but not essential for MRP II.)

4. If the request is for a major change, the project team reviews it and makes a decision. The key issue here: Is this change *necessary* in order to run the business and/or for MRP II to work properly? Does the function in question require the computer, or can it be done manually? If the answer is yes to both questions, it's a have-to. It must be done now or at least soon. If it's a nice-to, desirable but not essential, defer it to phase

III. (Sometimes the outside MRP II consultant can be helpful in putting these issues into focus, separating the have-tos from the nice-tos.)

5. At times, there can be a disagreement between the person requesting the change and the project team. In this case, the requester should be able to address the steering committee, presenting the request and the reasons for it. Hence, he has his day in court, and it's up to him to sell the steering committee on the merits of his request.

When handled in this manner, the modification mountain begins to shrink into a manageable molehill.

One last word about changes to the software. The conventional wisdom says: "Make changes on the front end or the back end, but don't make changes to the main internal logic of the programs themselves." I agree, provided it's possible. Sometimes, however, it's the internal logic that's flawed and requires the change. Examples of such problems include computer control over the master schedule, not using the rescheduling assumption in material requirements planning, improper back scheduling logic in shop floor control, etc. The easiest solution to these problems is to choose software with valid logic. When that choice is not possible, it may be necessary to get into the internal guts of the programs and make the necessary changes.[7]

Chapter 9 will address the issue of turning on the first phase of MRP II. (We'll also come back to computer issues in chapter 9 when we discuss the computer pilot.) It's taken a lot of work to get this far— education and training, data integrity and policy statements, software acquisition. But, remember, the clock has been ticking for less than a year.

---

[7] An additional discussion of software maintenance issues can be found in chapter 13.

IMPLEMENTERS' CHECKLIST

Function: Software

Task	Complete	
	YES	NO
1. Decision made to make (write) or buy software for MRP II.	___	___
2. If buying, the software package selected has been seen at one or more user companies operating at a Class A or high Class B level.	___	___
3. The magnitude of the internal systems and programming workload (new programs, interfacing, etc.) has been estimated and provided for in the cost justification.	___	___
4. Procedures to manage requests for changes to the software established and in place.	___	___

Going on the Air—Phase I

Going on the air with a system means turning it on, starting to run it. It's the culmination of a great deal of work done to date.

Back in chapter 3, I discussed the proper implementation sequence:

- Phase I—basic MRP.

- Phase II—closing the loop.

- Phase III—finance and simulation MRP II.

Now it's time to look at going on the air with the phase I tools.

Basic MRP consists of sales & operations planning, demand management, master production scheduling, rough-cut capacity planning, and material requirements planning. Further, in a flow shop, plant scheduling should be implemented here. If a company is implementing distribution resource planning simultaneously with MRP II, it also should be brought up in phase I. (See figure 9-2.)

Recognize that some of the elements of MRP II have already been implemented. Sales & operations planning has been started, as much as several months ago. (See chapter 7.) Supporting systems—bill of material processor, inventory transaction processor, perhaps new sales forecasting software—have, in most cases, already been installed.

Activating master scheduling and material requirements planning is another moment of truth during implementation. Virtually all the company's activities to date have been leading directly to activating MPS/MRP. Turning these on can be tricky, and we need to discuss at length how to do it.

Figure 9-1

The Proven Path

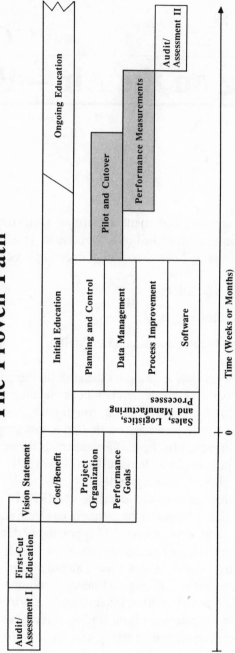

Figure 9-2

Company-Wide MRP II Implementation Phase I

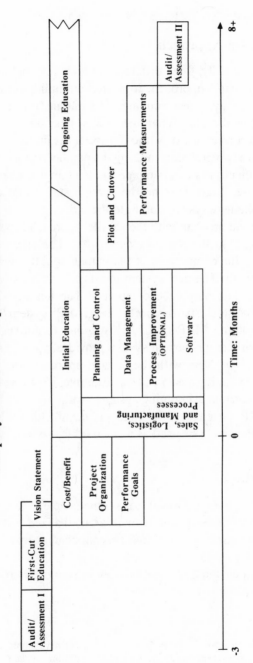

Three Ways to Implement Systems

The Parallel Approach

There are, broadly, three different methods for implementing systems. First, the *parallel* approach. It means continuing to run the old system after the new system is running. The output from the new system is compared to the old. When the new system proves it is consistently giving the correct answers, the old system is dropped.

There are two problems in using the parallel method for MRP. First of all, it's difficult. It's cumbersome to maintain and operate two systems side by side. There may not be enough staff to do all that and still compare the new system output to the old.

The second problem with the parallel approach is perhaps even more compelling than the first: *it's impossible.* The essence of the parallel approach is the comparison of the output from the new system against the old system. The new system in this case is basic MRP. But against *what* should its output be compared? The hot list? The order point system? The stock status report? The HARP[1] system? What's the point of implementing MRP II if it's just going to deliver the same lousy information that the current system provides?

That's the problem with the parallel approach for MRP. For implementing accounting systems, as an example, it's great. It's the way to do it because current accounting systems work.

Pre-MRP systems in the field of manufacturing logistics did not work, so they can't be used as a standard for comparison.

Cold Turkey

The inability to do a parallel leads some people to jump way over to the other side of the fence, and do what's called a *cold-turkey* cutover. I call it "you bet your company," and I recommend against it vigorously and without reservation.

Here's an example of a cold-turkey implementation, as explained by an unenlightened project leader:

---

[1] HARP is an acronym for Half-Assed Requirements Planning. Many people who think they have MRP actually have HARP: monthly time buckets, requirements generated every month or so, etc. It's a primitive order launcher, which does happen to recognize the principle of independent/dependent demand.

We've got MPS and MRP all programmed, tested, and debugged. We're going to run it live over the weekend. On Friday afternoon, we're going to back a pickup truck into the production control office and the computer room, throw all the programs, procedures, forms, etc. into the truck and take 'em down to the incinerator.

This qualifies as burning one's bridges. A cold-turkey implementation carries with it two problems, the first one being that MRP may fail. The volume of output from the first live computer run of MRP may be so great that the users can't handle it all. By the time they work through about a quarter of that output, a week's gone by and then what happens? MRP is run again, and here comes another big pile of output. The result: The users are inundated and your MRP effort has failed.

Folks, that's the least of it. The second problem is far more severe: You may lose your ability to ship product. Some companies who've done a cold turkey have lost their ability to order material and release production. The old system can't help them because they stopped running it some weeks ago, and the data isn't current. MRP isn't helping them; it's overwhelming them.

By the time they realize the seriousness of the problem, they often can't go back to the old system because the inventory balances and other data aren't valid any longer, and it might be a nearly impossible job to reconstruct it.[2]

A company that can't order material and release production will sooner or later lose its ability to ship product. A company that can't ship product will, sooner or later, go out of business.

Some organizations get lucky and muddle through without great difficulty. In other cases, it's far more serious. Although I'm not aware of any company that has actually gone out of business for this reason, there are some who've come close. The people I know who've lived through a cold-turkey cutover never want to do it again. Never. *Don't do it.*

The Pilot Approach

The right way to do it is with a *pilot*. Select a group of products, or one product, or a part of one product—involving no more than several

---

[2] Even those cases when they can go back to the old system are very unfortunate. Why? Because they tried to implement MRP, and it didn't work. Now they're back to running the old system, not MRP, and they'll have to decide what to do now, where to go from here. A most unfortunate situation.

hundred part numbers in all—and do a cold turkey on those. The purpose is to *prove* that MRP works before cutting over all 5,000 or 50,000 or 500,000 items onto the system. The phrase MRP works refers to two things: the technical side (does the software work properly?) and the users' side (do the people understand and believe what it's telling them, and do they know what to do?).

If MRP doesn't work properly during the pilot, it's not a major problem. All the parts are still being ordered via the old system, except for the few hundred in the pilot. These can be handled by putting them back on the old system or perhaps doing them manually. What's also necessary is to focus on *why* MRP isn't working properly and fix it. The people have the time to do that if they're not being inundated with output on 5,000 or 50,000 or 500,000 items.

What do I mean when I ask: "Is it working?" Simply, is it predicting the shortages? Is it generating correct recommendations to release orders, and to reschedule orders in and out? Does the master schedule for the pilot product(s) reflect what's actually being made? Can customer orders be promised with confidence? Answering yes to those kinds of questions means it's working.

Three Kinds of Pilots

Doing it right means using three different types of pilots—the computer pilot, the conference room pilot, and the live pilot.

1. *The computer pilot.*

This simply means checking out the hardware and software very thoroughly. If a company has written its software, this means testing and debugging. If they've bought software, it means running the programs on the computer, and debugging them. (Remember, there *will* be bugs in the software, no matter whether it's homegrown or purchased.) This process should begin as soon as the programs are available.

Often, the computer pilot[3] will deal initially with dummy items and dummy data. In purchased software, this should come as part of the package. The dummy products are things like bicycles, pen and pencil sets, etc., and the dummy data are transactions made up to test the

---

[3] In companies who've purchased software for MRP II.

programs. Then, if practical, run the new programs using real data from the company, using as much data as can readily be put into the system.

Next, do volume testing. Sooner or later, you'll need a program to copy your current data into the new formats required by the new software. Get that program sooner. Then copy your files over, and do volume testing. You're looking for problems with run times, storage, degradation of response times on the terminals, whatever. Who knows, your computer may need more speed, more storage, more of both. (Doing one's homework at the onset of the project means recognizing these possibilities, and putting contingency money into the project budget to cover them if needed.)

In addition to hardware, other major objectives of the computer pilot are to ensure the software works on the computer and to learn more about it. The key players are the systems and data processing staff, usually with some help from one or more project team members. (See figure 9-3 for the location of each of these pilots.)

2. The conference room pilot.

This follows the computer pilot. The main objectives of the conference room pilot are education and training: for the users to learn more about the software, to learn how to use it, and to manage their part of the business with it and make sure it fits the business. This process can also help to establish procedures and to identify areas that may require policy directions.

The key people involved are the users, primarily the folks in customer service, the master scheduler(s), and the material planners, probably some folks from purchasing. They meet three to five times per week in a conference room equipped with at least one CRT[4] for every two people. The items involved are real-world items, normally ones that will be involved in the live pilot. The data, however, will be dummy data, for two reasons:

a. Live data shouldn't be used because the company's still not ready to run this thing for real. Everyone's still in the learning and testing mode.

---

[4] Cathode ray tube. CRT is verbal shorthand for an entire terminal: screen, keyboard, processor, and related hardware.

b. It's important to exercise the total system (people, as well as software) as much as possible. Some of the dummy data for the conference room pilot should be manufactured so it will present as many challenges as possible to the people and the software.

One technique that works nicely is for a key person, perhaps the project leader, to play Murphy (as in Murphy's Law—"whatever can go wrong will go wrong"). As the conference room pilot is being operated, Murphy periodically appears and scraps out an entire lot of production or becomes a supplier who'll be three weeks late shipping or causes a machine to go down or generates a mandatory and immediate engineering change.[5]

Murphy needs to determine if the players know the right responses to both major pieces of the system:

a. The computer portion of the system—the hardware and the software. Do the people know how to enter and promise customer orders, how to update the master schedule, how to use pegging, firm planned orders, and the other technical functions within the software?

b. The people portion of the system—and this gets at feedback. Do the MRP planners know whom to give feedback to if they can't solve an availability problem on one of their items? Does the master scheduler know how and whom to notify in Customer Service if a customer order is going to be missed? Do the Customer Service people know to notify the customer as soon as they know a shipment will be missed?

This last point gets at the important MRP II principle of silence is approval. This refers to mandatory feedback when something goes wrong. In a Class A company, it's part of everyone's job: sales, planning, plant, and suppliers. As long as things are going well, no one needs to say anything. However, as soon as people become aware that one of their schedules won't be met, it's their job to provide immediate feedback to their customer, which could be the next work center, the real end customer, or someone in between.

Presenting the people and the software with difficult challenges in the

---

[5] I can remember one project leader who had a sweatshirt made up. It was navy blue with MURPHY printed in red gothic lettering.

conference room pilot will pay dividends in the live pilot and cutover stages. One company we worked with used a slogan during their business meetings and conference room pilot: Make It Fail. Super! This is another version of bulletproofing. During the conference room phase, they worked hard at exposing the weak spots, finding the problems, making it fail. The reason: so that in the live pilot phase *it would work.*[6]

The conference room pilot should be run until the users really know the system. Here are some good tests for readiness:

a. Ask the users, before they enter a transaction into the system, what the results of that transaction will be. When they can routinely predict what will result, they know the system well.

b. Select several MPS and MRP output reports (or screens) at random. Ask the users to explain what every number on the page means, why it's there, how it got there, etc. When they can do that routinely, they've got a good grasp of what's going on.

c. Are the people talking to each other? Are the feedback linkages in place? Do the people know to whom they owe feedback when things go wrong? The essence of successful MRP II is people communicating with each other. Remember, this is a *people* system, made possible by the computer.

If the prior steps have been done correctly and the supporting elements are in place, the conference room pilot shouldn't take more than a month or so.

3. The live pilot.

This is that moment of truth I mentioned earlier. It's when master scheduling and material requirements planning go into operation for the first time in the real world. (See figure 9-3.)

The objective of the live pilot is to *prove* MPS and MRP will work within the company. Until then, that can't be said. All that one could say

---

[6] When I used to fly airplanes for a living, I crashed many times. Fortunately, it was always in the simulator. The fact that it never happened to me in the real world is due in large part to the simulator. The conference room pilot is like a simulator; it allows us to crash but without serious consequences.

Figure 9-3
Company-Wide MRP II Implementation Phase I

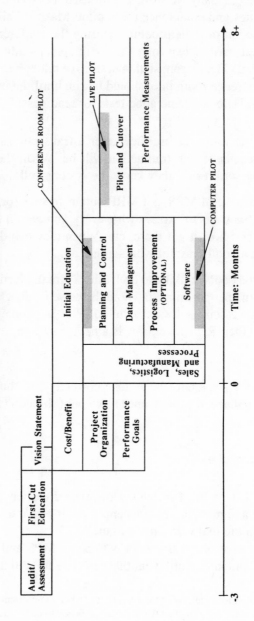

up to that point are things like: "It should work," "We think it'll work," "It really ought to work," etc. Only after the live pilot has been run successfully can the people say, "It works."

Before I get into the details of the live pilot, let me recap what I've covered so far by taking a look at figure 9-4.

Selecting the Live Pilot

What are the criteria for a good live pilot? Some of the considerations are:

1. *Size.*

It requires enough items to get a good test of how the overall man/machine system performs, but not so many items as to get overwhelmed. Try to keep the total number of items to less than 500.

Figure 9-4
Three Types of Pilots

Type	*Key People*	*Items/Data*	*Objectives*
Computer	Systems people Project leader	Dummy/dummy	1. Learn more about the software.
			2. Discover bugs.
			3. Check for problems with run time, response time, and storage.
Conference room	Customer svc. (Order entry) Master sched'r. MRP planners Systems analyst Project leader	Live/dummy	1. Do further user education and training.
			2. Build in feedback.
			3. Verify that the software fits the business.
Live	Customer svc. (Order entry) Master sched'r. MRP planners Project leader	Live/live	1. Use the system in the real world.
			2. Prove that it works.
			3. Obtain a sign-off from the users.

2. *Product orientation.*

The pilot should represent all the items for an entire product family (in the case of a simple product, such as clothing or cosmetics), a single product (moderately complex products, like bicycles or typewriters), or a part of a product (highly complex products, such as aircraft or machine tools). In the last example, the pilot might be one leg in the bill of materials or a modular planning bill for an option.

3. *Good cross-section.*

The pilot group should contain a good mix of finished products (or a portion thereof), subassemblies or intermediates, manufactured items, purchased items, and raw materials.

4. *Relatively self-contained.*

The fewer common parts contained in the pilot, the better. Items used in both the pilot product and others will not give a good test of MRP. MRP will not be aware of all the requirements for those items. The usual way of handling this is to post the MRP-generated requirements back to the old system. Some degree of commonality is almost always present (raw materials, in many cases) but try to pick a pilot where it's at a minimum.

5. *Best planner.*

If the company has material planners already and they're organized on a product basis, try to run the pilot on the product handled by the best planner. This is a people-intensive process, and it needs to have just as much going for it as possible.

Look Before You Leap

Let's consider what has to be in place prior to the live pilot. One element is a successful conference room pilot, where the users have proven they understand the system thoroughly. The other key elements are data integrity, education, and training. Please refer to the Implementers' Checklist at the end of this chapter.

The project team should address the first six entries on the checklist. All must be answered yes. The project leader then reports the results to the executive steering committee and asks for formal permission to launch the live pilot. Only after that's received should they proceed.

Operating the Live Pilot

When everything's in place and ready to go, start running the pilot items on MPS/MRP and stop running them on the old system. The objectives are to prove MPS/MRP is working and to obtain user sign-off. Is it predicting the shortages, giving correct recommendations, and so forth? Are the users, the master scheduler(s), and the material planners making the proper responses and taking the correct action? Are the users prepared to state formally that they can run their part of the business with these tools? If the users are unwilling and/or unable to sign off on the system, then one of several factors is probably present:

- It's not working properly.
- They don't understand it.
- Both of the above.

In any of these cases, the very worst thing would be to proceed into the cutover phase—to put all the remaining items onto the new system. First, aggressively go after the problem: either fix the system that's not working properly or correct the deficiency in education and training that's causing the user not to understand it, or both.

Run the live pilot as long as it takes.

Don't go beyond the pilot stage until it's working and the users have signed off. This is one area where the aggressive implementation mentality must take a back seat. Everyone—executive steering committee, project team, users—should understand the company won't go beyond the live pilot until it's been proven to work and until the users are comfortable with it.

Plan to run the live pilot for about a month or longer if manufacturing cycles are long and speeds are slow. It's essential to observe how the man/machine system performs over a number of weeks to prove it really works. A week is not enough time, a quarter is probably too long, for planning purposes, for most companies.

During the live pilot, don't neglect training. Get the other planning people as close to the pilot operation as possible, without getting in the way of the folks who are operating it. People not involved in the pilot need all the input they can get because they'll be on the firing line soon when the rest of the items are cut over to MRP II.

The pilot must be successful to go to cutover, and visible success supports behavior change. Therefore, make sure the other planning folks can see the success.

CUTOVER

Once the live pilot is working well, and the users are comfortable with it, it's time to cut over the rest of the items onto the MPS/MRP.

There are two different ways to cut over. It can be done in one group, or the remaining items can be divided into multiple groups and cut over one at a time.

The multiple-group approach is preferable because it has the following advantages:

1. *It's less risky.*

It represents a more controlled process.

2. *It's easier on the people.*

If the first group to cut over belongs to planner A, then planners B and C should be deeply involved in helping planner A. It reduces planner A's workload, and also provides additional training for B and C. When planner B cuts over, planners A and C can help him.

The multiple-group approach, on the other hand, may not always be practical and/or necessary. In some companies, there is so much commonality of components that it's difficult to isolate groups. This means that during the cutover process, many items will be partially but not totally on the new system. The difficulties in passing requirements from the new system to the old (or vice versa) can easily outweigh the benefits gained from using multiple groups. In this case, the one-group approach would probably be best. It's usually better at this point to move ahead quickly rather than to spend lots of time and effort transferring requirements for common parts.

Sometimes the multiple-group approach may not be necessary. A company with only a few thousand items or less may conclude their entire population of items is small enough, and there's no real need to break it down any finer.

A WORD ABOUT TIMING

Sometimes companies get hung up on a timing issue with cutover, specifically an accounting cutoff. Don't delay cutover for any appreciable amount of time—waiting for the beginning of the month, the beginning of the quarter or, shudder, the new fiscal year. Rather, the systems folks should have any necessary bridging programs ready to go to feed data from MPS/MRP into the fiscal systems. In this way, cutover can occur as soon as practical and not be delayed waiting for the passage of time.

THE NEED FOR FEEDBACK DURING CUTOVER

There's a potential dilemma here for you job shop people:

• This cutover is a phase I activity. The MPS and MRP planning tools are being made operational.

• MPS and MRP can't function effectively by themselves. They're merely components of an overall closed loop system.

• However, closing the loop in a job shop is a phase II activity, which comes later. (Even in a flow shop, where plant scheduling can be made operational in phase I,[7] supplier scheduling won't be fully implemented until phase II.) How can MPS and MRP be made operational prior to that?

The answer is that there must be a form of loop closing even during phase I. It's essential. Without feedback from the plant and purchasing, the planning people won't be notified when jobs won't be completed on schedule. They must have that feedback, or they will not be able to keep the order dates valid. Therefore, the principle of silence is approval applies here, even at this early stage.

This means that anticipated delay reporting from both the plant and

---

[7] We'll cover this shortly.

purchasing must be implemented as part of phase I. However, there's even a bit more to it than that for you job shop folks.

At this point, the company's beginning to operate with the formal priority planning system (MPS/MRP) but doesn't yet have the priority execution system (the dispatching portion of shop floor control) in place. Given good feedback, order due dates can be kept valid and up to date, but the tools to communicate those changing priorities to the shop floor still aren't available. Further, without capacity requirements planning, there's no specific, detailed visibility into future overloads and underloads at all the work centers on the shop floor.

A good approach here is to develop an interim, simple, possibly crude shop scheduling system. It's used to get the job done until the full-blown shop floor control system is on the air. This interim system is usually manual, not computerized, and operates with order due dates and possibly a simplified back scheduling approach. (Example 1: Job A has a four-week lead time. It's due two weeks from now. It should be 50 percent finished. Is it 50 percent finished? If not, it should be given priority. Example 2: Back schedule from the order due date assuming all operations take the same amount of time. Set operation due dates accordingly.)

In addition, it's highly desirable to assign one or more shop people full-time to the project during this transition phase. This person's responsibility is to help the folks on the plant floor work on the right jobs. This person maintains close contact with the interim shop scheduling system, with the material planners, and with the foremen. He finds out about the reschedules coming from the planners, makes sure the foremen are up to date, generates the anticipated delay report for the planners, helps break bottlenecks, etc.[8]

The last point, breaking bottlenecks, brings up another post-cutover issue: overloads. This can be a problem because capacity requirements planning isn't operational yet. Overloads are bad because the work won't get through on time. Underloads are almost as bad because people will run out of work and get a negative feeling about MRP II.

This can be a major problem, and one that the project team needs to be aware of and follow very closely. Advance planning can help a lot. Some companies have done a pre-cutover dry run or simulation to see

---

[8] This person can also make progress on shop floor cleanup activities during this period. Example: getting some of the large queues off the floor and back into the stockroom. The newly generated MRP priority information can help a lot in this job.

what's likely to occur. Contingency plans can help a lot: plan A might be what to do in case of an overload; plan B for an underload.

Once again, that key shop person mentioned earlier can be a big help—by eyeballing the queues, talking to the foremen about their problems, talking to the material planners about what MRP II shows is coming soon, breaking the bottlenecks, making certain the shop doesn't run out of work, etc. During this tricky transition period, do whatever possible to anticipate problems. Identifying them ahead of time can minimize their impact.

The buyers have a similar role to play with their suppliers. They need to follow up closely with their suppliers, learn which orders will not be shipped on time, and communicate these to the planners via the anticipated delay report.

There's also a potential capacity problem with suppliers. Since MRP is now involved in planning orders, the orders might not be coming out in the same pattern as before. The company could inadvertently be creating severe overloads or, just as bad perhaps, severe underloads at key suppliers. The buyers need to stay in close contact with these suppliers to solve these kinds of problems should they arise.

The three most important things the people can do during this period are:

1. Communicate

2. Communicate

3. Communicate

Talk to each other. Don't relax. Keep the groups—steering committee and project team—meeting at least as frequently as before, perhaps more frequently. Consider creating a spin-off task force to focus solely on these transitional problems, meeting perhaps every day.

Cutover is a very intense period. Plan to work long, long hours and to make additional resources available. The project leader should be present constantly—"carrying the water bucket" and helping the users in any way he can. That also applies to the assistant project leader, if there is one, the department head (P & IC manager or whatever), and the key system people. Don't overwhelm the planners. Rather, overwhelm the *problems*. Get through all of the output. Take all the necessary actions. Make it work.

The Potential Inventory Blip

What's the company's number one priority when implementing MRP II? Is it to reduce the inventories? Nope, that's not even priority number two. Number one priority, of course, is to run the business. Number two is to implement Manufacturing Resource Planning. Reducing inventories, during the implementation process, probably isn't even in the top 5 or top 10.

Should inventories start to drop during implementation? Toward the end, they should. But beware, *they may go up before they go down*. In a given company, there's about a 50-50 chance this will happen.

Here's why.

When the company starts to run material requirements planning, its logic will identify a certain number of reschedule-ins and reschedule-outs. These would be for the scheduled receipts, both open shop orders and open purchase orders. Some will be needed sooner, some later. The logic of MRP will also recognize items that are needed but for which there is no scheduled receipt. It will recommend releasing a new order.

What the logic of MRP will not do is make recommendations about inventory already in the stockrooms and warehouses. It's in the on-hand balance; it can't be rescheduled out because it's already in stock. It'll probably be needed but not until later. This phenomenon will cause some companies, in the short run, to expedite more than they're able to de-expedite. That introduces the possibility of a temporary inventory rise. (See figure 9-5.)

Be aware this may happen. It's not illegal, immoral, or fattening. It should be anticipated. Then, if it doesn't happen, so much the better.

Figure 9-5
What Might Happen to Your Inventories

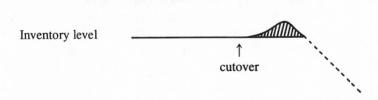

Inventory level

↑
cutover

DON'T STARVE THE SOURCES

Let's double back to a problem we touched on a short while earlier. Inventories that drop too quickly can also be a problem. A sharp drop in the inventory level may be an indication the implementation job is not being done properly.

The problem is the potential for "starving out" the shop and/or some key suppliers because less work is being released to them. This is most likely to happen in companies that had far too much inventory before implementation. After basic MRP is on the air, material requirements planning will indicate there is far less need for parts or raw material. Therefore, few new orders are released to the shop and suppliers. These people, who have become accustomed to a regular flow of work over the years, now see few orders.

Consider how a shop foreman or key supplier would feel in this situation. After hearing all the talk about how great MRP II is going to be, the first thing that happens is that orders dry up, and there's no work. MRP II will have a lot of negative impressions to live down in this case, and these first impressions may be lasting ones.

My message is: Don't lose sight of this issue during cutover and risk starving the shop and/or the key suppliers. If necessary, be prepared to release work early to keep the flow of work going to them. The necessary adjustments to work loads and, therefore, inventories can be made gradually over a longer period, without turning these vital sources of supply against MRP II.

THE INADVERTENT COLD-TURKEY CUTOVER

Here's a potential booby trap. Some companies have accidentally backed into a cold-turkey cutover, as follows:

1. They need to implement a new inventory transaction processing system in order to reach 95 percent inventory accuracy.

2. They need to do this prior to going on the air with MRP. This is proper since the records must be made accurate first.

3. The current inventory system contains *ordering logic;* it gives them signals of when to reorder. However, the new inventory transaction

processing software is a module of an overall software package for MRP II. As such, there is no ordering logic in the inventory processor, whose function is to maintain inventory balances. The ordering logic is contained within a module called material requirements planning.

4. The company implements the new inventory processor and simultaneously discontinues using the old one.

5. The result is the company has lost its ability to order material and parts.

The wrong solution: Discover this too late, scramble, and plug in the new software module that contains the ordering logic (MRP). The result is to implement MRP across the board, untested, with the likelihood of inaccurate inventory records, bad bills, a suspect master schedule, and inadequate user education, training, and buy in. The ultimate cold-turkey cutover.

The right solution to this problem is to recognize ahead of time that it might happen. Then, make plans to prevent this inadvertent cold turkey from happening.

The alternatives here include running both the old and new inventory processors until MRP comes up, writing some throw away programs to bridge from the new system to the old, or, worst case, developing an interim set of ordering logic to be used during this period.

CLOSING THE LOOP IN MANUFACTURING (FLOW SHOPS)

In most flow shops, it's a practical matter to implement plant scheduling in phase I. The reason: In flow environments, the manufacturing resources usually line up very closely with specific product families (unlike job shops, where any one work center may do work for a wide variety of product families).

Plant schedules for flow shops are often derived directly from the master schedule and material requirements planning. Thus, as one product group comes up on MPS/MRP, the new plant scheduling processes can be kicked in at the same time. (This is not the case in job shops, which normally require that all manufactured components be on material requirements planning before valid dispatch lists can be generated.)

PERFORMANCE MEASUREMENTS

Begin to measure performance at three levels:

1. *Performance goals.*

As soon as practical, start to relate actual performance to the measurements identified in the performance goal step (chapter 5). Make them simple and visible to all the people involved. Questions to ask:

• "Is our performance improving?"

• "Are we getting closer to our goals?"

• "If not, why not? What's not working?"

Remember, there's urgency to start getting results, to get the bang for the buck. In other words, "We paid for this thing—have we taken delivery?"

2. *Operational measurements—ABCD Checklist.*

This checklist is designed to help a company evaluate its performance and to serve as a driver for continuous improvement. (See Appendix E.)

3. *Technical measurements.*

These cover the technical specifics of how the man/machine system is performing. Examples:

a. Number of master schedule changes in the emergency zone. This should be a small number.

b. Master schedule orders rescheduled in, compared to those rescheduled out. These numbers should be close to equal.

c. Number of master schedule items overpromised.

d. MRP exception message volume, the number of action recommendations generated by the MRP program each week. For job shops, the exception rate should be 10 percent or less. For flow shops, the rate may be higher because of more activity per item. (The good news is that these kinds of companies usually have far fewer items.)

e. Late order releases, the number of orders released with less than the planning lead time remaining. A good target rule of thumb here is 5 percent or less of all orders released.

f. Production orders and purchase orders rescheduled in, versus rescheduled out. Here again, these numbers should be close to equal.

g. Stock outs, for both manufactured and purchased items.

h. Inventory turnover—finished goods and raw materials, at a minimum. For job shops, tracking work-in-process inventory turns may be deferred until phase II.

Except for inventory turns, most of these measurements are done weekly. Typically, they're broken out by the individual planner.

Here's one last point on this entire subject of measuring performance during this early stage. Walt Goddard says it very well:

My advice to the project team is to look below the surface. Frequently, at first glance, a new system looks like it's working well—the people are busy using it and hopefully saying good things about it. Yet, often this is on the surface and it has yet to get into *the bone and marrow of the company* [author's italics]. A smart manager needs to probe. One of the effective ways of doing it is to sample the actions that a master scheduler or planner has taken to see if, in fact, he would have done the same thing. If not, does that person have a good explanation for the difference? Don't assume that things are okay but, rather, expect they're not. Then, you can have a pleasant surprise if things are in good shape.

This concludes our discussion of implementing basic MRP. Remember, at this point, most companies really don't have a complete operating system. There's urgency to close the loop completely, and that'll be covered in the next chapter.

Implementers' Checklist

Function: Going on the Air—Phase I

	Complete	
Task	YES	NO
1. MPS/MRP pilot selected.	____	____
2. Computer pilot completed.	____	____
3. Conference room pilot completed.	____	____
4. Necessary levels of data accuracy 95 percent minimum on inventory records, 98 percent minimum on bills—still in place on *all* items, not merely the pilot items.	____	____
5. Initial education and training at least 80 percent complete throughout the company.	____	____
6. Executive steering committee authorization to start the live pilot.	____	____
7. Live pilot successfully operated, and user sign-off obtained.	____	____
8. Feedback links (anticipated delay reports) in place for both plant and purchasing.	____	____
9. Plant schedules (for flow shops) or interim shop floor control system (for job shops) in place and operating.	____	____
10. Executive steering committee authorization to cutover.	____	____
11. Cutover onto MPS/MRP complete.	____	____
12. Performance being measured at all three levels.	____	____

Chapter 10

Going on the Air—
Phases II & III

Phase II involves closing the loop in purchasing for all companies and, for job shops, closing the loop on the plant floor. (See figure 10-2.) Phase III covers the financial interface and the simulation capability.

CLOSING THE LOOP IN PURCHASING

Closing the loop in purchasing means implementing supplier scheduling. This is a phase II activity, because suppliers are somewhat like work centers in a job shop—any one of them can provide a range of items which go into many different product families. Therefore, it's usually necessary to have all products and components on MPS/MRP to generate complete schedules for a given supplier.

However, this may not always be the case. For example, let's say you have one or several suppliers providing items that go into the pilot product family only. In that case, it may be possible to pilot supplier scheduling with that supplier in phase I, as a logical part of the MPS/MRP pilot.[1] (In some cases, this could even be done manually if the supplier scheduling software won't be developed until later.) Even if you can do this, and it's definitely a good thing to do if practical, you'll most likely have to wait until MPS/MRP are fully implemented before you can do a great deal in this area.

---

[1] The MPS/MRP cutover might provide some additional opportunities here.

Figure 10-1
The Proven Path

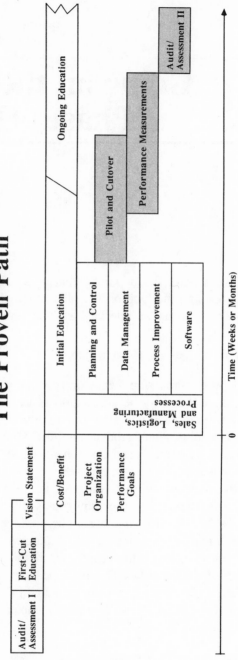

Time (Weeks or Months)

Figure 10-2
Company-Wide MRP II Implementation Phase II

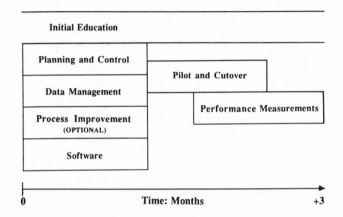

Here's a simplified look at supplier scheduling:

1. Establish long-term contractual relationships with suppliers.

2. Create a group of people (supplier schedulers) who are in direct contact with both suppliers and MRP, eliminating purchase requisitions for production items.

3. Give suppliers weekly schedules, eliminating hard-copy purchase orders.

4. Get buyers out of the expedite-and-paperwork mode, freeing up their time to do the important parts of their jobs: sourcing, negotiation, contracting, cost reduction, value analysis, etc.

In flow shops, supplier scheduling is the main thing that happens in phase II. For you job shop folks, supplier scheduling should be implemented either simultaneously with shop floor control, CRP, and I-O or immediately after it. Most companies can do it simultaneously. Different people are involved: the foremen and some others for plant scheduling; the buyers, supplier schedulers, and suppliers for supplier scheduling.

If there is a resource conflict, it's often in the systems group. Perhaps there's simply too much programming involved for both shop floor control and supplier scheduling to be done simultaneously. In this situation, close the loop in manufacturing first, then do purchasing. It's urgent to bring up the shop floor control system, so priority changes can be communicated effectively to the shop floor. Purchasing, even without supplier scheduling, should be in better shape than before. Basic MRP has been implemented, and probably for the first time ever, purchasing is able to give suppliers really good signals on what's needed and when.

Delaying supplier scheduling a bit is preferable to delaying shop floor control, if absolutely necessary. Try to avoid any delay, however, because it's best to be able to start in purchasing as soon as possible after the cutover onto basic MRP.

IMPLEMENTING SUPPLIER SCHEDULING

This process, as with every other part of implementing MRP II, should be well managed and controlled. These are the steps:

1. *Establish the approach.*

The company has to answer the following kinds of questions: What will be the format of the business agreement? Will it be an open-ended format or for a fixed period of time? To whom will the supplier schedulers report: purchasing, production control, elsewhere? Will the company need to retain purchase order numbers even though they'll be eliminating hard-copy purchase orders?

2. *Acquire the software.*

There's good news and bad news here. The bad news is it will probably be necessary to write your own software for supplier scheduling. Most software packages don't have it. (Be careful: Many software suppliers claim to have a purchasing module as a part of their overall MRP II software. What this usually means is their package can automate purchase requisitions and purchase order printing. Unfortunately, this is not the right objective. With supplier scheduling, the goal is to *eliminate* requisitions and hard-copy POs, not automate them.)

The good news is that writing the supplier scheduling programs is largely retrieval-and-display programming, drawn from existing files, which is typically less difficult. On the other hand, if the software package doesn't have the capability to maintain a vendor master file, the programming job will be correspondingly tougher.

3. Develop supplier education.

People who'll be involved need education for MRP II. Suppliers are people (a potentially controversial point in some companies that treat their suppliers like dogs). Suppliers will be involved. Therefore, suppliers need education about MRP II.

Most companies who've had success with supplier scheduling put together a one-day program for supplier education and training. The education part covers MRP II, how material requirements planning generates and maintains valid due dates,[2] and the concepts of customer-supplier partnerships and win-win.

Further, the principle of silence is approval must be explained thoroughly and be well understood by key supplier people. This refers to the mandatory feedback from suppliers, as soon as they become aware that they will be unable to meet the supplier schedule. As long as the suppliers are silent, this means they will meet their scheduled deliveries. When something goes wrong, and they won't hit the schedule, it's their job to provide *immediate* feedback to their supplier scheduler.

The training part gets at the supplier schedule, how to read it, when and how to respond, when to provide feedback, etc.

4. Pilot with one supplier.

Select a supplier and get their concurrence in advance to participate in the supplier scheduling pilot. This supplier should supply substantial volume, should be cooperative, and, ideally, will be located nearby. In the best of all possible worlds, this supplier would already be in supplier scheduling mode with one or more customers with Class A or B MRP II, but, of course, that's a nice-to, not a have-to.

Bring in their key people—plant manager, sales manager, key sched-

---

[2] Make certain that MRP is truly making that possible—that your due dates are now valid. Don't make the mistake of calling suppliers in and telling them how great MRP is if the dates now on your purchase orders are no better than before. Let's make certain our own house is in order before we start to ask for major changes from suppliers.

uling person, as well as the local sales person. Educate them, train them and, in the same session, cut them over onto supplier scheduling.

5. *Fine-tune the system.*

Based on what's learned in this pilot, modify the approach if necessary, refine the education process, and tweak the software. Begin to measure the performance of your pilot supplier(s) and you[3]— delivery performance, inventory levels, service to the plant floor, etc.

6. *Educate and cut over the major suppliers.*

Go after the approximately 20 percent of the suppliers who are supplying about 80 percent of the purchased volume. Get their tentative concurrence in advance. Bring them into your company in groups of three to six suppliers per day. Or, if necessary, go to their plant. As in the pilot, educate them, train them, and cut them over on the same day.

If it isn't possible to get tentative concurrence in advance from a given supplier, attempt to convince them of supplier scheduling's benefits to them, as well as to the customer. Demonstrate how it's a win-win situation. Consider taking the one-day education session to their plant. If the supplier is still reluctant, involve your company president in direct contact with the supplier's president. (Carrying the water bucket is what presidents are for, right?) If all these efforts fail, give them ninety days or so to shape up. Show them some positive results with other suppliers already on supplier scheduling. If they're not getting cooperative by that time, start to look for a new supplier.

7. *Measure performance.*

As each supplier is cut over onto supplier scheduling, start to measure how well they *and you* are doing. Possibly for the first time ever, a company can legitimately hold suppliers accountable for delivery performance—because probably for the first time ever, it can give suppliers valid due dates.

---

[3] The suppliers cannot perform well if you don't perform well. Just because a supplier isn't hitting the delivery dates doesn't mean that it's their fault; maybe your due dates aren't any good after all.

Also, begin tracking buyer performance and supplier scheduler performance. (For more details, see chapter 13.)

Communicate the measurements to everyone being measured. Raise the high bar—the level of expectation. When performance matches that, raise the bar again.

8. *Educate and cut over the remaining suppliers.*

As soon as the major suppliers are on supplier scheduling, go after the remainder. The target should be 100 percent of all suppliers of production items on supplier scheduling. That will probably take longer than the several months implied on the Proven Path bar chart, but it's important to stick with it.

CLOSING THE LOOP IN MANUFACTURING (JOB SHOPS)

You flow shop people can skip this section if you like. Or you can read it and feel good about not having to do all this work. For you job shop folks, stay tuned.

Let's talk first about two issues that deal with the overall approach: sequence and timing. I recommend you implement in the following sequence:

1. Shop floor control (dispatching).

2. Capacity requirements planning.[4]

3. Input-output control.

Shop floor control comes first because, as mentioned earlier, it's urgent to communicate those changing priorities out to the shop floor. Until it's possible to do that via the dispatching system, the company will have to live with the interim system. In all likelihood, that will be somewhat cumbersome, time consuming, and less than completely efficient.

---

[4] This refers to the specific technique known as detailed capacity requirements planning. The other capacity planning technique—rough-cut capacity planning—has already been implemented in phase I.

Capacity requirements planning comes next. It's less urgent. Also, when rough-cut capacity planning was implemented as a part of basic MRP, the company probably began to learn more about future capacity requirements than ever before.

Input-output control has to follow CRP. Input-output tracks actual performance to the capacity plan. The capacity plan (from CRP) must be in place before input-output control can operate.

A SPECIAL SITUATION

Closing the loop in manufacturing becomes easy where the company has it all, or most of it, already. Some companies implemented shop floor control years before they ever heard of MRP II. This was frequently done in the mistaken belief that the causes of the problems— missed shipments, inefficiencies, excessive work-in-process inventories, etc.—were on the shop floor. Almost invariably, the *symptoms* are visible on the shop floor, but the *causes* get back to the lack of a formal priority planning system that works.

If most or all of the shop floor control/CRP tools are already working, that's super! In this case, closing the loop in manufacturing can occur just about simultaneously with cutover onto basic MRP. Several companies I've worked with had this happy situation, and it sure made life a lot easier.

A few words of caution. If you already have a shop floor control system and plan to keep it, don't assume that the data's accurate. Verify the accuracy of the routings, and the validity of the standards and work center data. Also, make certain that the system contains the standard shop floor control tools that have been proven to work (i.e., valid back scheduling logic, good order close-out tools, etc.). The Standard System from Oliver Wight Limited Publications can often help greatly in this evaluation.

SHOP DATA COLLECTION

Shop data collection means collecting data from the shop. (How's that for a real revelation?) However, it does not necessarily mean *automated* data collection (i.e., terminals on the shop floor with bells and whistles and flashing lights). In other words, the shop data collection process doesn't have to be automated to operate closed loop MRP successfully. Some very effective shop floor control systems have used paper and pencil as their data collection device.

A company that already has automated data collection on the shop floor has a leg up. It should make the job easier. If you don't have it now, I recommend that you implement it provided it won't delay the project. (If it'll slow down the project, do it later—after MRP II is on the air.) Bar coding is particularly attractive here; it's simple, it's proven, and it's not threatening to most people because they've seen it in use when they buy groceries.

PILOT

I recommend a brief pilot of certain shop floor control activities. Quite a few procedures are going to be changing, and a lot of people are going to be involved. A two- to three-week pilot will help validate the procedures, the transactions, the software, and most importantly, the people's education and training.

It's usually preferable to pilot shop floor control with selected jobs rather than selected work centers. With these few selected jobs moving through a variety of work centers, one can usually get a good handle on how well the basics are operating.

Note the use of the word basics. The pilot will not be able to test the dispatch lists. Obviously, that won't be possible until after cutover, when all of the jobs are on the system and hence can appear on the dispatch lists.

CUTOVER

Once the pilot has proven the procedures, transactions, software, education and training, it's time for cutover. Here are the steps:

1. Load the shop status data into the computer.

2. Start to operate shop floor control and to use the dispatch list. Correct whatever problems pop up, fine-tune the procedures and software as required, and make it work.

3. Begin to run capacity requirements planning. Be careful— don't go out and buy a million dollars' worth of new equipment based on the output of the first CRP run. Review the output carefully and critically. Get friendly with it. Within a few weeks, people should start to gain confidence in it and be able to use it to help manage this part of the business.

4. Start to generate input-output reports. Establish the tolerances and define the ground rules for taking corrective action.

5. Start to measure shop performance in terms of both priority and capacity. (See chapter 11.)

6. Last, and perhaps most important of all, don't neglect the feedback links. Feedback is not a software module; it won't come as part of your software package. This is a verbal and handwritten person-to-person communication process. It will not involve the computer, except perhaps in large companies where a computer may possibly be used for message handling.

Feedback includes foreman-to-foreman communication, daily foremen's meetings, the generation of anticipated delay reports, etc. The feedback links established in phase I should be reviewed, tested, strengthened, made to work even better. The better the feedback, the better the closed loop system will operate. Without feedback, there is no closed loop.

IMPLEMENTING FINANCE AND SIMULATION

If things have gone well up to now, these last two elements should not present a major problem. If things haven't gone well, fix what's wrong before trying to implement these tools. (See figure 10-3.)

Figure 10-3
Company-Wide MRP II Implementation Phase III

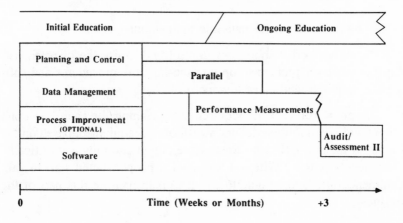

Initial Education		Ongoing Education	
Planning and Control			
	Parallel		
Data Management			
	Performance Measurements		
Process Improvement (OPTIONAL)			
		Audit/ Assessment II	
Software			

0   Time (Weeks or Months)   +3

THE FINANCIAL INTERFACE

Step one is to educate the people in finance and accounting early. Don't make the mistake of waiting until month 12 or 14 to start education in this part of the company. These folks need the education as soon as possible for two reasons:

1. So they can see where the company's headed regarding the entire MRP II effort.

2. So they can implement whatever financial applications may be required in phase I. As we said earlier, some degree of financial integration may have existed prior to MRP II.

With education, the finance and accounting people can participate effectively in the systems design, making sure the necessary financial hooks are built into the records early on. Finance and accounting people will need to do a bit of homework here.

Detailed analysis is required to determine that each record in the overall system will contain all the fields necessary for financial planning and control. These are typically dollar fields, which translate operational data (in pieces, pounds, gallons, liters, etc.) into financial terms. If this process isn't done early, it may be necessary to make major systems changes late in the game. Record layouts may need to be changed, perhaps causing a good deal of reprogramming, extra expense, confusion, and delay.

The pilot and cold-turkey approaches do *not* apply in this area. The parallel approach *does*, because the current financial systems already work. Naturally, they'll work a lot better with the improved data they'll get from MRP II. Begin to run the new financial programs while still running the current system. Compare the new output to what's coming out of the current system. Make certain that the correct numbers are coming out of the new system. Most companies find that after several months of a satisfactory parallel, they're comfortable with discontinuing the old system.

IMPLEMENTING SIMULATION

This is like implementing capacity requirements planning. Don't bet the ranch based on the output from the first simulation run. Rather, ease into it. Review the output critically; get familiar and friendly with it. As confidence builds, managers will find themselves more and more willing to make decisions based on the output from the simulation runs.

A word to the good folks in data processing: Computer run time can be a problem here. There probably won't be a problem if:

- There are relatively few items and work centers.

- And/or the software contains net change MRP and CRP.

Many companies don't fit the above pattern. They have lots of items and lots of work centers. They have regenerative MRP or CRP or both.

Companies in this latter group need to scope out just how much of a potential problem the run-time issue will be. If it's minor, then everything will probably be okay as is. If major, they'll need to program their way around it. Generally, this means making the regenerative CRP or MRP/CRP systems act like net change, probably via an approach called requirements alteration.

The basic trade-off is computer run time versus programming effort. Step one is to determine if there's a run-time problem. This may not be possible until after master scheduling, MRP, and CRP have been implemented. Step two, if run times prove be a problem, is to get to work on programming around it.

There's no one detailed solution that will apply to all, or even most, companies. Variations in software, hardware, file sizes, and the magnitude of the run-time problem preclude a clear-cut, widely applicable course of action. Therefore, an individualized solution will probably be required. In addition to a company's own systems and programming people, it may be necessary to get help from the software supplier's technical support people. Perhaps the MRP II consultant can be helpful either directly or by making available other expertise.

AUDIT/ASSESSMENT II

Of all of the steps on the Proven Path, this one may be the easiest to neglect. However, it may also be the most critical to the company's long-term growth and survival.

The reason: Audit/assessment II is the driver that moves the company into its next improvement initiative. And, there must be a next improvement initiative. It's no longer possible to stop improving and survive; they are mutually exclusive.

Under no circumstances should this step be skipped, even though the temptation to do so may be great. Why? Because the pain has gone away. We feel great! We're on top of the world! Let's kick our shoes off, put our feet up on the desk, and relax for a while.

Don't do it. Skipping audit/assessment II is high risk. Nothing more may be done; the next improvement initiative may not be forthcoming. As a result, the company's drive for operational excellence will stall out, and they will be left in a competitively vulnerable position.

Audit/assessment II is the mirror image of audit/assessment I, which asks: "What should we do first?" Audit/assessment II asks: "What should we do *next*?" Answers to this question could be:

Now that we've implemented MRP II successfully, we must begin a formal Just-in-Time/Total Quality Control initiative. We've already had success with some isolated JIT activities. Let's formalize the process and really focus on it.

When we started MRP II 14 months ago, we thought our distribution system was good enough. Now that we have MRP II working, and can really appreciate its power, we're convinced that we must move to true DRP to get even more bang for the buck.

Well, the first thing we did was Total Quality Control, several years ago. Now we have MRP II. The missing link is JIT, so let's get going.

We're doing really well. We've got DRP, JIT, TQC, MRP II. What we want to do now is to get even closer to the customer. We need to extend our DRP process even farther upward—up to our customers. The same basic tools that we use to replenish our field warehouses can be used to replenish inventories of our product at our major accounts. We've had great success with supplier scheduling where we're the customer; let's do reverse supplier scheduling where we're the supplier and we're exchanging information with our customers.

We need to get better at new product launch. We're going to tie the power of our MRP II/JIT/TQC tools together with a formal design for manufacturability (DFM) program. This will give us the capability to launch new products faster and better than our competitors.

Having implemented MRP II gives us a superb capability to plan and control at the operational, tactical level of the business. Where we must improve now is at the strategic level. We need to do a much better job at tying manufacturing into the strategic direction of the business. Next, we must implement a strategic manufacturing planning process into the company.

The participants in this step are the same as in audit/assessment I, who we identified in chapter 4 as "the executives, a wide range of operating managers, and, in virtually all cases, outside consultants with Class A credentials . . ."
The process here is also the same:

Fact finding, identifying areas of consensus and disagreement, matching the company's current status and strategies with the tools it has available for execution. The end result will be the development of an action plan to move the company onto a path of continuous improvement. Typically, the action plan is presented by the consultant(s) in a business meeting with the executives and managers who've been involved to date. The purpose for this session is to have the action plan explained, questioned, challenged, modified as required, and bought into.

The elapsed time frame for audit/assessment II will range from several days to one month. As with audit/assessment I, this is not a prolonged, multimonth affair involving a detailed documentation of current systems. Rather, its focus and thrust is on what's *not* working well and what needs to be done now to become more competitive.

This concludes our discussion of the Proven Path as it applies to a company-wide implementation of MRP II. Next, we'll look at an alternative and radically different method of implementation: Quick-Slice MRP.

IMPLEMENTERS' CHECKLIST

Function: Going on the Air—Phases II & III

Task	Complete	
	YES	NO
1. Supplier education program developed.	___	___
2. Supplier scheduling pilot complete.	___	___
3. Major suppliers cut over to supplier scheduling.	___	___
4. Supplier measurements in place.	___	___
5. All suppliers cut over to supplier scheduling.	___	___
6. Routing accuracy of 98 percent minimum for all items still in place.	___	___
7. Shop floor control pilot complete.	___	___
8. Shop floor control implemented across the board.	___	___
9. Dispatch list generating valid priorities.	___	___
10. Capacity requirements planning implemented.	___	___
11. Input-output control implemented.	___	___
12. Plant measurements in place.	___	___
13. Financial planning interfaces complete and implemented.	___	___
14. Simulation implemented.	___	___
15. Audit/assessment II completed; next improvement initiative underway.	___	___

PART III

Quick-Slice Implementation

Chapter 11

Quick-Slice
MRP—Overview

Way back in chapter 2 we talked about the principle of the three knobs: the amount of work to be done, the time available in which to do it, and the resources that can be applied. We said that any two of those knobs can be held constant by varying the third.

In a company-wide implementation of MRP II, the amount of work and time available are considered constants. The approach is to vary the resource knob. This will enable the project to be done correctly (the work knob) and completed quickly (the time knob). The approach, as my colleague Roger Brooks says, is to "never change the schedule; never change the load; simply add more horse."

Roger goes on to say that this may not always be possible. In fact, even when possible, it may not always be the best way. This is where Quick-Slice MRP enters the picture.

To understand Quick-Slice MRP, we need to take a detour into the world of Just-in-Time. How, one asks, should Just-in-Time be implemented? Is it done on a company-wide basis, as we've just seen with MRP II? No, not when it's done correctly. Rather, it's done in a series of smaller implementations, which Bill Sandras calls Breakthrough JIT Pilots.[1] This is an implementation process that focuses on only one portion of the business at a time, either a product line or major operational area.

---

[1] To reiterate: The Proven Path applies not only to a company-wide implementation of MRP II. It also covers breakthrough JIT and Quick-Slice MRP. Ditto for DRP, both company-wide and fast-track.

The main mission of the Breakthrough JIT pilot is to generate significant and visible results, and to do it quickly—in about four months. This is possible since the scope of the pilot is limited; it's not company wide.

Please note: The word pilot in this context has a specific meaning—to generate significant operational benefits. This is different from the pilot in a company-wide implementation of MRP II. There the word pilot refers to a live test of certain processes and systems to prove out the new approach but not necessarily to generate operational benefits. In Breakthrough JIT, the pilot is the cutover. It is the goal in itself.

Here's Bill Sandras again: "There is a marketing strategy behind the Breakthrough JIT Pilot implementation approach as well. The initial successes are designed to make it obvious that the only logical course of action is to continue. The implementation approach is designed to create a model of the future."

Thus, one Breakthrough JIT Pilot[2] is followed by another and another and another—until the long-range goal of JIT/TQC is achieved: to make continuous improvement a way of life throughout the company.

Now back to Quick-Slice. Here's the point:

QUICK-SLICE MRP
IS THE JIT IMPLEMENTATION APPROACH
APPLIED TO MRP II

It involves:

1. Selecting a pareto high-impact product line—a very important slice of the business.

2. Implementing as many of the MRP II functions as possible for that product.

3. Completing the pilot in a very short time, about 120 days.

Hence the label Quick-Slice MRP. Please note: It's not called Quick-Slice MRP II. That's because not every one of the MRP II functions can

---

[2] For more details, see William A. Sandras, Jr., *Just-in-Time: Making It Happen* (Essex Junction, VT: Oliver Wight Publications, Inc., 1989).

be implemented via Quick Slice. Most can, but not all, and we'll detail that in the next chapter.

WHERE QUICK SLICE APPLIES

There are quite a few cases where the Quick-Slice implementation approach makes a lot of sense. See if any of these fits your situation.

1. *Quick payback/self-funding.*

Top management understands and wants MRP II, but wants a quick payback for any one of a number of reasons:

• Funds are not available from corporate.

• The current year's budget has no provision for a major expenditure of this type.

• The senior managers are new and want to make their mark quickly and decisively.

• And/or the company's approach to major improvement projects is that they be self-funding.

This last point is a somewhat radical notion, not widely practiced. However, it is your author's belief that it represents perhaps the best way to mount major improvement initiatives within a manufacturing company.

The basic principle is: *Manufacturing excellence can be self-funding; it can cost zero dollars.* In fewer words, *excellence is free.* A portion of the savings and cash flow generated by one initiative is used to fund the next. Approaches like Breakthrough JIT and Quick-Slice MRP make this concept a practical matter from a budgeting standpoint because they can be started and completed within the same fiscal year.

2. *Middle management sells up.*

Operating-level people understand the need for MRP II and want it desperately. Top management doesn't see the need,[3] nor are they inter-

---

[3] This is an example of Wallace's law of organizational pain: Things often look rosier to the people at the top than those down in the trenches.

ested in shelling out big bucks for what they might feel is a computer deal to order parts. They won't take the time to learn about MRP II, nor will they authorize an audit/assessment. A Proven Path implementation on a company-wide basis is just not in the cards.

The solution here could be a Proven Path implementation on a Quick-Slice basis. Quick Slice is low dollars, low risk, high return, quick results. It just might get their attention.

It did at Engelhard Industries Chemical Group in Great Britain. The project leader there, Andy Coldrick,[4] made it happen on a Quick-Slice basis. In so doing, he and his team demonstrated to senior management the enormous power of Manufacturing Resource Planning. Once they saw it with their own eyes, they were convinced. They then proceeded to lead a company-wide implementation which resulted in Class A MRP II.

3. Re-implementers.

The company implemented MRP II some years ago but didn't do a good job of it. Now it wants to re-implement so it can get all the benefits of MRP II. However, strong negative sentiment exists within the company; people are saying things like, "It didn't work the first time. Why should it work now? Let's not waste our time."

This is typical. In a re-implementation, one of the hardest things is to break through people's resentment and frustration, and it almost always makes for a more difficult job than a first-time implementation.

Quick-Slice MRP can give a major boost here. A solid success, quickly, on a major part of the business can go a long way toward rekindling enthusiasm. Nothing succeeds like success.

Further, Quick-Slice MRP in a re-implementation should be low cost because re-implementers already have MRP software. It might not be good; they might not like it; they might be saying things like "Our software stinks." But the chances are quite high that it'll be good enough for the first one or several slices.

4. JIT without MRP.

Let's say the company is implementing JIT/TQC and does not have MRP II. As such, it can make substantial progress. However, before

---

[4] One of the pioneers of Quick-Slice MRP, and now managing director of Oliver Wight UK.

long the company will start to bump up against its inability to plan and schedule effectively. Not being able to communicate valid schedules to its plant, its suppliers, its customers, its engineers, its accountants, and others will seriously constrain its ability to eliminate waste and make continuous improvements.

One option for this company is to put JIT/TQC on hold for a year or so until MRP II is implemented on a company-wide basis. Not acceptable.

The other alternative, and the only proper one, is Quick-Slice MRP. Implement Quick Slice rapidly on those parts of the business that have already been through the Breakthrough JIT Pilot process; from then on, bring up JIT/TQC and Quick-Slice MRP on the same products.

This is an excellent fit. Not only does Quick Slice borrow from JIT for the implementation process; in most Quick-Slice implementations, some JIT processes are implemented also. This is the case even in companies who have not yet begun JIT/TQC.

5. *Jumbo-sized company.*

Companies[5] whose head count is well into the thousands typically have a more difficult time implementing MRP II (or just about any other major improvement initiative, for that matter.) The reason is, simply, more people—more layers in the organization, more communications interfaces, more competing initiatives underway, more opportunities for people not to get on board, more time required to make things happen, and so on.

The Quick-Slice approach dramatically reduces the size of the effort. One can "get one's arms around" an organization of a few dozen or even a few hundred people, and things can happen quickly. Obviously, the first slice would be followed by another and another and another.

6. *We're unique; we're different.*

The company is in a somewhat specialized industry; perhaps it makes widgets. The company thinks it wants to implement MRP II, but it's not sure. The reason: No one in the widget business has ever tried MRP II. Management is reluctant to invest big bucks until they can see it working.

Quick-Slice MRP provides the opportunity to do this quickly and with very little cost.

---

[5] Specific business units, not necessarily entire corporations.

7. Bleeding from the neck.

The company is in dire financial straits and needs help quickly: negative cash flow, red ink, and/or rapidly eroding market share come to mind. Survival may be at issue. Although MRP II may clearly be the answer, there might be too little time left for the company to take the 10 to 20 months necessary for a company-wide implementation. Quick-Slice, on the other hand, gives major results in a short time.

One of the earliest documented implementations[6] of this type occurred for exactly this reason. The Quick-Slice approach saved the company.

8. Others.

I'm sure there are some other good reasons that mitigate for a slice approach to implementation. One might be: "Why not?" Why not do it this way? It's fast; it's low dollars; it's low risk; it generates big results.

Here's what I recommend: When evaluating whether or not to do a Quick-Slice implementation, don't ask yourselves: "Why should we do it?" Ask yourselves: "Why not?" Start from there.

Are there any reasons not to do Quick Slice? Yes, they're not major, but they do exist.

1. No logical slice.

This could be a company whose products, components, raw materials and manufacturing processes are highly interwoven. There may be no valid way to "slice out" a product family.

2. Two systems.

The company will be operating with the new system on the slice product(s) and components and the current system on the rest. This will continue until all of MRP II has been implemented on all of the business. This can be awkward. Further, some companies/industries have strin-

---

[6] Mark Kupferberg, *MRP And JIT: A Survival Strategy*, APICS 1987 Conference Proceedings (Falls Church, VA: American Production and Inventory Control Society, p. 111.).

gent reporting requirements to their customers, their owners, regulatory agencies, and others; compliance may be difficult when using two systems for an extended time.

3. *Very small company.*

This is the flip side of the jumbo company mentioned above. In a very small organization, the difference in elapsed time between company wide and Quick Slice may be quite small. This could mitigate for doing it all at once.

4. *Lack of urgency.*

Implementing Quick Slice is intense because of the time pressures to get results quickly. If a strong sense of urgency isn't present, Quick Slice won't be the best way to go. More on urgency in a moment.

5. *Longer (maybe) to Class A.*

Using Quick Slice will, at least in theory, take longer to reach Class A MRP II. Consider the following Quick-Slice implementation:

Step	*Time*
Implement first slice	4 months
Implement second slice	4 months
Implement third slice	4 months

The company is now one year into implementation. They're getting enormous benefits from what they've done. However, they still don't have all of their products and components on the system, nor have they implemented all the functions of MRP II. What they'll need to do at some point is to shift to a company-wide implementation to capture the missing items and functions, which may take another six months or so.

To me, this is acceptable; I'll opt for Quick Slice and perhaps a slightly longer time to reach Class A.[7] Others may not.

---

[7] But perhaps not more time. As the first several slices are successful, momentum and enthusiasm can build. And this may result in the company-wide implementation on the rest of the products and functions going quite quickly.

HOW CAN IT BE DONE SO QUICKLY?

Some of you may be thinking: "Only four months? Only 120 days? How can anything this major be accomplished in such little time?"

Good question. There are two main parts to the answer: first urgency and focus, and then work load.

Urgency and focus.

Shorter projects often require a real feeling of urgency among the team members, and Quick-Slice MRP is no exception. The Quick-Slice mind-set says: "We're going to concentrate on this slice; we're going to do it right; we're going to get it done in four months; and we're not going to let obstacles stand in our way, because we're going to run over 'em, run around 'em, or knock 'em down." The team needs to do anything and everything to get the job done quickly and correctly. This small group knows that deadlines will be met, that ingenuity is the norm, and that it will accomplish an extraordinary deed.

Urgency and focus are essential. If you're going to do Quick Slice, don't leave home without 'em.

Workload.

It's essential to turn down the work load knob because the time knob has been cranked down to about four months. This is why Quick Slice focuses on only a small portion of the products and components. Virtually everything in a Quick-Slice implementation is scaled down, but there are three areas that really make the difference: education for the people (the A item, remember?), data integrity (the B item), and software (the C). Typically, the critical path in a company-wide implementation is through one of these three. Let's take a look at each one.

1. *Accelerated education for key people.*

One of the time-consuming steps in a company-wide implementation is initial education—reaching all or virtually all the people in the company. Quick Slice acknowledges that can't happen; there's just not enough time.

Therefore, the Quick-Slice approach is to provide, at the outset, education for only those people who'll be directly involved with the slice. This is a small percentage of the total employment in the company, and can be done quickly.

For the rest of the folks in the company, it's best not to delay their education. Whenever possible, educate them simultaneously with bringing up the first several slices. That will accelerate implementing both the subsequent slices and the company-wide cutover when it comes.

2. Data integrity on slice items only.

Another time-consuming task in a company-wide implementation is to get all the data up to the high levels of accuracy required for MRP II— inventory records, bills of material, formulas, routings, work orders, purchase orders, and more. It's a big job.

The Quick-Slice approach: Get data accuracy on only the slice products and components. You don't have time to do much more than that. Get the slice numbers right and worry about the rest later.

3. Software soon.

Urgency demands that the Quick-Slice implementation not get hung up on software. (Or hardware for that matter.) It cannot be allowed to delay the project.

"Well," you may be thinking, "those are nice words, but how in the world do we do that? After all, there's a lot at stake: MRP II software is expensive; it's a major purchase decision; it has to be installed, interfaced, enhanced, and all that takes a good deal of time. Our systems people will be hard pressed to get all that done to fit with the timing for a company-wide implementation, much less Quick Slice."

My answer, one more time: It's up to you. How important is a Quick-Slice implementation? We're back to urgency. If it's really important to you, you won't allow the software to delay the Quick-Slice implementation.

Make a quick decision on software—within a few days, not weeks or months. This decision for most re-implementers will be simple; since you already have MRP software, use that. If you don't already have software, focus on the low-cost, highly functional software that runs on personal computers (see chapter 8). If need be, plan to use it on an interim basis only, for a year or so, until the mainframe or minicomputer software becomes available as part of your company-wide implementation. We'll talk more about this in the next chapter.

In general terms, that's how it happens when companies do a Quick Slice on a Proven Path basis. Here's Roger Brooks again: "Time is the ultimate enemy. The longer the implementation takes, the more it will cost and the greater the 'window of risk.' "

In the next chapter, we'll look at the details of Quick-Slice implementation.

Chapter 12

Quick-Slice MRP— Implementation

In Quick-Slice MRP, the steps involved in implementation are identical with the ones in a company-wide implementation of MRP II.

The Proven Path methodology applies. (See figure 12-1.) The difference is that time is compressed. We're talking about days/weeks instead of weeks/months.

The front-end steps—audit/assessment I through performance goals—are done quite similarly to a company-wide implementation,[1] except that most of them will involve fewer people and may be done more quickly.

Audit/assessment I.

Of all these early steps in Quick Slice, it is most similar to company wide because at this point, it's unlikely that the company has decided to do Quick Slice. They may not know much about it, or may not have even heard of it. The job of this step is to set the direction. The participants in audit/assessment I include the executives, a number of operating

[1] If you need to refresh your memory, you may want to check back into chapter 4, where these steps are discussed in detail as they relate to a company-wide implementation. Here, we'll mainly be discussing the differences between Quick Slice and company wide.

Figure 12-1

Quick-Slice MRP

Audit/ Assessment I	First-Cut Education	Vision Statement

Cost/Benefit

Project Organization

Performance Goals

Initial Education

Ongoing Education

Planning and Control

Data Management

Process Improvement

Software

Sales, Logistics, and Manufacturing Processes

Pilot / Cutover

Performance Measurements

Audit/ Assessment II

Time: Weeks

-4   0   +12

managers, and one or several outsiders with Class A credentials. The process—fact finding, synthesis and report preparation, report presentation—are similar to company wide.

The one difference may be in timing. Back in chapter 4, I pointed out that the elapsed time for this step could range from several days to about one month. Well, during the fact-finding stage, Quick Slice may emerge as a strong possibility. This is where the Class A consultants come in. If they're doing their jobs correctly, they'll recognize this. They should crank up the urgency lever and make a preliminary recommendation for Quick Slice. This recommendation should identify one or several likely candidates for the slice product(s). This should happen at the conclusion of the fact-finding phase, so that the next step—first-cut education— can start early and overlap the remainder of audit/assessment I.

First-cut education.

For Quick Slice it should include all, or at least most, of top management. Unlike company wide, however, it does not involve all or most of the operating managers. Rather, it includes only those key people who will be directly involved with the slice: managers from the plant floor, planning, purchasing, systems, customer service, plus the likely full-time project leader if already identified.

This step should finish quickly, ideally being completed at about the same time as the audit/assessment I wrap-up. When that happens, it opens up a real opportunity for the next steps, as we'll see in a minute.

Vision statement, cost/benefit, project organization, performance goals.

These steps should be done together and, with few exceptions, can be completed in one or several days. Keep the vision statement brief (less is more, remember?), and establish the performance goals.

Included here is the selection of the slice products or family. Characteristics to look for in making this selection are shown in figure 12-2. Chances are you'll have to compromise on one criterion or another but get as close as you can.

Do the cost/benefit study on a joint venture basis (see chapter 4). It'll take less time than in company wide because there are fewer people and

Figure 12-2
Criteria for Selecting the Quick-Slice Product(s)

1. HIGH IMPACT, HIGH VISIBILITY
   (A pareto Class A product, not a B or a C)

2. LARGELY SELF-CONTAINED
   (The fewer components and work centers shared with other products the better)

3. GOOD PEOPLE
   (With resistance to change at least no greater than normal)

4. STABILITY
   (No major changes pending, no deep structural problems present that would inhibit the Quick-Slice implementation)

5. APPLICABILITY
   (Lessons learned here apply to the rest of the company)

---

functions involved. Make a yes or no decision on Quick Slice: If yes, create a one-page written project charter, spelling out urgency as a primary requirement in the implementation process.

Set up the steering committee, a complete one as with company wide and with a designated torchbearer.[2] And create the project team but much smaller than in company-wide, perhaps no more than the handful of managers mentioned above plus the full-time project leader.

Do you need a full-time project leader on a Quick-Slice implementation? Definitely.

Why? After all, you may be thinking, it says earlier in this book that if you're dealing with a small business unit, less than 100 people, you can get by without a full-timer—so why do we need one? Because if you don't have one, it's almost certain you won't get this thing done in four months . . . or five months . . . or six. The issue is urgency.

The opportunity I referred to earlier is this: If you can finish your first-cut education while the audit/assessment report is being completed, then the following activities can take place within one several-day period:

- Presentation of the audit/assessment I report.

- Creation of the vision statement.

---

[2] Unlike the torchbearer in a company-wide implementation (see chapter 5), the Quick-Slice torchbearer should plan on being directly involved with the implementation more frequently, perhaps several times per day.

• Development of the cost/benefit study.

• Creation of the steering committee, the project team, and the full-time project leader.

• Establishment of the performance goals.

You're killing a bunch of birds with one stone. You're accomplishing multiple tasks, you're getting maximum use out of your consultant, and you're saving him from having to make an extra trip to your company.

He should appreciate that. If your consultant's good, he'll probably be busy, and you'll need to see him frequently during your first slice implementation. In general terms, you can figure on the consultant being with you about two days per month, maybe three for the first month or so.

As we said earlier, an important part of the consultant's role is to help the company avoid the pitfalls and booby traps. This is even more critical in Quick Slice because there's less time to recover from a mistake here than in a company-wide implementation.

Initial education.

This consists mainly of accelerated internal education for key people. A few folks may need to attend outside classes beyond those in first-cut education but probably not many. The participants in the series of internal business meetings are:

1. The project team.

2. The steering committee.

3. The other folks who'll be directly involved with the slice.

These typically are the three groupings for the meetings. Relative to company wide, the people are fewer and the time frame is compressed; the objectives, the process, and the media (videotapes, printed material[3]) are much the same, except that for slice some Just-in-Time material will be necessary for issues like cells, kanban, material storage at point of use, and others.

---

[3] Regarding media, however, the internal education materials will need to be tailored to cover only those elements necessary for the slice.

The series of business meetings for the project team can happen in four weeks or less, since they're accelerated and there are fewer of them. To save time, the other two groups can start a bit before the project team is finished.

Defining sales, logistics and manufacturing processes.

This nails down the details of what's going to be done and generates the detailed project schedule. (See Appendix D for the Quick-Slice MRP Detailed Implementation Plan.) This can happen concurrently with the series of business meetings for the project team.

Planning and control processes.

In Quick Slice, these center around the implementation of sales & operations planning and the conference room pilot. The development of policy statements is optional and can be pursued if time allows.

Sales & operations planning should be implemented on all product families, not just the slice. There are important reasons for this:

1. *Ease.*

It will be almost as easy to implement S & OP on all products as it will on the slice product(s) only.

2. *Benefits.*

S & OP, of and by itself, will provide significant benefits prior to having any of the other MRP II elements in place.

3. *Early win.*

Quick Slice represents an early win. Implementing S & OP completely, within Quick Slice, is an early, early win. Early successes promote behavior change.

4. *Balance.*

With so much attention on the Quick Slice, it's important to watch the rest of the products to ensure that resources aren't being drained from them. S & OP will facilitate minding that part of the store.

5. *Motivator.*

Once all aspects of Quick Slice are implemented, an important difference will be apparent to the top management group members:

a. As they do sales & operations planning on the slice products, they will have the confidence that their decisions will be translated— logically, correctly, on a rack-and-pinion basis—to become the detailed schedules for the plant floor and the suppliers. That's what master scheduling and material requirements planning do.

b. When they make S & OP decisions on the nonslice products, they won't have that assurance. They'll see a "disconnect" between what they decide and what may or may not happen in the plant and at the suppliers.

This can serve as a strong motivator to the top management team to press on with additional slices and/or company-wide implementation. It helps to reduce complacency and, hence, the risk of stalling out after one or several successful slices.

The conference room pilot also is similar to that in a company-wide implementation. It involves fewer people, perhaps no more than three or four, and therefore, can take less time. Five sessions per day for several weeks should do the job; if more time is needed, perhaps the slice is too big and/or too complex.

Data management.

To quote from the prior chapter, the key here is to "get data integrity on the slice products, components and materials only. You don't have time to do much more than that. Get the slice numbers right and worry about the rest later."

Sure, if you can get some of the other inventory records or bills of material squared away while you're doing the slice items, fine— provided it doesn't slow you down. You simply can't allow yourselves to get into major activities here that are not necessary to bring up the slice.

Even though your data integrity focus needs to be largely or totally on the slice items, what you're doing will have indirect but important benefits for all other items as well:

• Learning how to get the records accurate. The learning curve applies; it'll be easier with the next bunch.

• Achieving an early win. Early successes promote behavior change.

What you need to get accurate are the on-hand inventory records, the open orders, the bills of material. The need to restructure bills is not likely, but it could be necessary in some cases. Make certain the item data, along with whatever work center data you may need, is reasonable and realistic.

The toughest data accuracy challenge for most companies in Quick Slice will be on-hand inventory balances. To get them accurate, we've seen companies do some creative things—all the time guided by the principle of urgency.

One example is what a company called their chicken wire stockroom. This was, in effect, a smaller stockroom within their unsecured primary stockroom. They cleared an area, fenced it in with chicken wire to obtain limited access, and proceeded to get the records accurate. In some environments, a painted line on the floor could have the same effect.

Another company had an accuracy problem with common items, ones used both in the slice product and elsewhere. Their solution: Stock 'em in two different locations and, to preserve integrity, add a letter (S for slice) to the slice item numbers.[4] In that way, the slice items were segregated in both the real world and the computer.

Process improvement.

Here's potentially a big difference between Quick-Slice and a company-wide implementation. In company-wide, this step is optional. In many slice implementations, particularly in job shops, a major process improvement step is mandatory. It involves cellular manufacturing; the creation of manufacturing cells.[5]

In a job shop, assembly operations are almost always focused on a product basis. Fabrication, however, is done at functionally organized work centers, any one of which may be performing production operations on many different components that go into many different products. Most of the products will not be in the slice. Although not impossible, it will be difficult to implement Quick Slice successfully in

---

[4] This, of course, meant a minor modification to the slice bills of material, to call out the *S* items, not the regular. At that company, no problem.

[5] For a detailed explanation of this issue, see William A. Sandras, Jr., *Just-in-Time: Making It Happen* (Essex Junction, VT: Oliver Wight Publications, Inc., 1989).

that environment. It will be totally dependent on these functionally organized work centers that have little or no identification with the slice products and activities.

The solution is to create flow from the job shop, and the way this is done is with cells. This means to dedicate specific pieces of equipment to the manufacture of specific items and, typically, to arrange those pieces of equipment adjacent to each other in a flow arrangement. We call this a physical cell.

However, it's not always necessary to move equipment. In Appendix B, we talk about conceptual cells, where the equipment does not get relocated. Instead, the equipment is linked together conceptually via kanban, which is also explained in Appendix B.

The message: Don't even think of having to delay the slice implementation if it'll take a lot of time to move equipment. Rather, use conceptual cells to get started, go on the air with the slice, and move the machines later.

One last point here concerns visibility. Make the slice equipment highly visible. Identify the physical cells and the machines belonging to the conceptual cells by putting up signs, banners, or flags. Or by painting the equipment a different color. Use the same color (green for go?) here, in the stockroom, and for the slice shop paperwork.

Software.

In a company-wide implementation, some activities that take quite a bit of time are:

- Software selection.
- Software interfacing.
- Software enhancements.

We have to find a way to shortcut the time required for these, or our Quick Slice will wind up being a Slow Slice. Push your urgency button a couple of times, and let's take a look at how to do that.

First, software selection. You either already have MRP II software, or you don't. (Be careful here. Sometimes homegrown software is called MRP, but it really isn't; it's HARP software.) Companies in the first category—those who already have it—include re-implementers and those who bought MRP II software but never used it. If you're one of these, use what you have—even if you don't like it. Use it even if most people are going around saying, "Our software stinks."[6] Almost invariably, it will be good enough to support the slice.

If you don't have software for MRP II, simply buy one of the rapidly growing number of personal-computer-based packages. You can probably get everything you need for less than $30,000, in some cases, much less. And most of it is quite good—fairly complete functionally and very user friendly. Since the price is so low, you can buy it and use it for a year or so—and then if need be, replace it with software to run on your mainframe or minicomputer as you migrate to MRP II company wide.

Second, do minimal (or even zero) interfacing of the new software with the current system. Don't allow interfacing to get on the critical path. If necessary, do manual interfacing via duplicate data entry, use temporaries, do whatever to feed the slice data into the current systems.

Third, make minimal (or even zero) enhancements to the software. Remember, this is not a company-wide implementation where there's time to do these kinds of things. We're dealing here with a limited number of people and items. Given a good set of software, plus enthusiasm and dedication on the part of the people directly involved, this typically is not a problem; they're willing to operate with a less than ideal set of software in return for being part of a team that's making such major and rapid progress.

Pilot/cutover.

In Quick-Slice MRP, as with Breakthrough JIT, the pilot is the cutover; they're one and the same. The Quick-Slice pilot is the actual implementation itself.

Let's see which of the MRP II functions actually get implemented at this point. Keep in mind that sales & operations planning has already been started. Figure 12-3 shows what will be implemented in this pilot/cutover step.

Figure 12-3 indicates that supplier scheduling should be done where practical. It probably won't be practical to implement supplier scheduling on all slice purchased items, most of which come from suppliers who

---

[6] Maybe it does, but probably it doesn't. The reasons why most Class C and D users didn't get to Class A or B do not lie in the software. Typically, it's because the people part of the implementation was not handled correctly.

Figure 12-3
MRP II Functions Implemented During Quick-Slice

Sales & Operations Planning
(On all product families)

Demand Management
(On the slice products)

Master Production Scheduling
(On the slice products)

Rough-cut Capacity Planning
(On the key resources)

Material Requirements Planning
(On the slice components and materials)

Plant Scheduling/Kanban
(On the slice products and components)

Supplier Scheduling
(On the slice components and materials, where practical)

are also providing items for nonslice products. The dilemma is that the nonslice items can't be effectively supplier scheduled because:

1. They're not on MRP; hence, there are no planned orders; hence, a key element of supplier scheduling (visibility out beyond quoted lead time) is missing.

2. They're on the current MRP system that's not working well; hence, the dates on the scheduled receipts and planned orders are not valid; hence, a key element of supplier scheduling (valid dates on orders) is missing.

However, where you can align a given supplier's items solely into the slice family, those items and that supplier should be supplier scheduled. Further, in some cases, it may be possible to work with a supplier on a split approach. That supplier could be supplier scheduled for the slice items they're supplying but would continue to receive traditional hard-copy purchase orders for the nonslice material.

The message here for you guys and gals in purchasing: Do as much supplier scheduling as you can in the slice, but realize that you probably won't be able to do 100 percent.

Still on the topic of scheduling, we need to talk about another kind of supplier: internal rather than external. Let's take the case of a company, largely a job shop, which is implementing Quick-Slice MRP. They've created flow, via cells, for their higher volume fabricated components. However, it's simply not practical to produce all of the slice components via cells; there may be many of them with too little volume to justify a cellular approach.

What to do? Treat the job shop as a supplier for those fabricated items that will continue to be made there. In effect, buy them from the job shop.

But this brings up another problem. How can we be sure that the job shop is going to deliver the slice items on time? After all, many of the jobs in the job shop are typically late. Well, there are several parts to the answer.

First, the dates on the slice components will be valid. This isn't the case for virtually all the other jobs.[7] Second, the people in the job shop need to understand those dates are valid and that they must complete slice jobs on time. Third, the shop paperwork accompanying the slice jobs should be easy to spot, perhaps bordered with the same color used to identify the slice cells (green for go?). And last, some clear direction and follow-up from the plant manager that the slice jobs will be done on time should be all it takes to make this happen.

Performance measures.

Begin to measure results against the goals defined at the outset. In Quick Slice, this could include on time deliveries, lead time reduction, measures of productivity, cost reduction, inventory turns and others. For the slice products, things should be significantly and visibly better on the plant floor and with customer service. If not, stop right here and fix whatever's not working. Do not, repeat, do not go beyond the first slice if the results aren't forthcoming. Things should also get visibly better, it is hoped, before too long, in the profit and loss statement and on the balance sheet.

Audit/assessment II.

The performance measurement step addresses the question: "Is it working?" The next question is: "What next—what do we do for an encore?"

---

[7] If all the dates are valid, why are you implementing MRP? You already have it, perhaps under a different name.

The answer should come out of audit/assessment II and, most probably, will be to do another slice. If so, loop back to the front end of the Proven Path and get started. Obviously, the first audit/assessment step shown on the chart no longer applies, having been replaced by audit/ assessment II. First-cut education will probably involve no one, assuming that all the key players went through this process for the first slice.

However, and this is a big however, if one or more key people didn't get educated in the first slice (some top management people, maybe?), this is the ideal time to make that happen. The first slice is working, things are visibly better, and enthusiasm is high. Go for it!

A Quick-Slice implementation can result in a series of loops. The first slice is done and it's successful. Audit/assessment II leads the company to loop back and do the second slice. That's successful, and that leads to a third slice and possibly more. That's great; that's the way it should be.

At some point, after a number of slices, the need to shift to a company-wide implementation will become compelling. Several reasons:

1. The company continues to operate with two systems. Maybe as much as one-third or one-half of the products are now on Quick-Slice MRP, and this may represent well over 80 percent of the sales volume. However, many products/components are still on the old system.

2. The common parts problem is becoming difficult. Many of the materials and component items may go into both slice products and ones not on MRP. This can be cumbersome.

3. Not having all purchased items on MRP is inhibiting progress on supplier scheduling.

4. Even though much of the job shop may have been converted to cells during the slice implementations, some or much of it may need to remain for the long term. Shop floor dispatching and capacity requirements planning normally won't work effectively without all the manufactured components on MRP.

5. The full financial interface can't happen until all products, manufactured components, purchased items, work centers, and routings are contained within MRP II.

Sooner or later, following one of the slice implementations, the audit/ assessment II step will lead you to shift to a company-wide approach to get all products and all MRP II functions implemented. And, in some cases, it can be done simultaneously. Audit/assessment II could lead you to start a company-wide implementation at the same time that you're starting another slice.

Quick Slice without top management.

In chapter 11, I indicated that one reason to do a Quick Slice versus company wide is middle management sells up (i.e., top management doesn't want to be bothered and won't take the time to learn about MRP II). In that situation, a company-wide implementation simply doesn't have much chance of getting beyond Class C. Quick Slice may be the only way to go, serving as a demonstration project to convince senior managers that MRP II works and is very important.

However, any implementation—company-wide or Quick Slice— without active, visible, and informed top management leadership is *not a Proven Path implementation.* The odds for success drop, and that's the bad news. The good news is they drop less with Quick Slice.

What, then, are the differences in a Quick-Slice implementation without a top management team that's MRP II knowledgeable? The answer to that question raises another: Can you persuade and lead and teach them to do sales & operations planning? If yes, you're a leg up and your slice implementation can probably proceed in a fairly standard fashion, with perhaps a few other exceptions. For example, top management may not want to participate in the steps that involve vision statement, cost/benefit, and performance goals. Do it without them. That's not ideal, but it sure beats doing nothing.

What if top management won't get involved with sales & operations planning? You're still not dead in the water. What you will have to do, however, is to get their agreement that they'll keep hands off of the slice family during and after the implementation. By this, I refer primarily to issues of demand management. If customer orders will be promised without regard to their impact on the plant and the suppliers, Quick Slice won't have much chance for success. Ditto if sales forecasts will be changed dramatically inside of cumulative lead time.

In cases like this, reconsider your options. Perhaps you could select a different product line for the first slice, maybe one of less significance to them. It might be an easier sell to convince them to allow the slice team to manage the demand stream on a category B product line rather than an A.

Regardless of how you do it—top management educated and involved or top management not educated but involved or top management completely uninvolved—it will be necessary to get schedule stability on the slice items. Build a fence around the slice products and components to keep out volatile, wildly erratic demand.

What about a torchbearer? If at all possible, get one. Isn't there at least one potential MRP II enthusiast within the ranks of top management or, at a minimum, one who's open-minded and willing to get some education? If yes, then sign him up. Involve that person. An informed, knowledgeable torchbearer is as important in this situation as in a Proven Path implementation, maybe more so.

Similarly, how about professional guidance? Frequently, an uninterested top management team will be willing to spend the relatively few dollars required for an outside consultant; they just don't want to spend their time on MRP II. In this case, go for it. Enlist the services of an experienced consultant with Class A credentials.

Now, in this scenario, you've got two heavyweights involved: the torchbearer and the consultant. The first slice still won't be Proven Path, but you've got a reasonable shot at success. If it goes well, top management should get on board. If they do, the second slice and subsequent company-wide implementation will be Proven Path. And they will work.

CONCLUSION

Quick-Slice MRP represents a breakthrough in implementation methodology. As with company wide, it's proven; it's been shown to work in actual practice. It's not a free lunch, in that it has some minor drawbacks: two systems, possibly longer to reach Class A. However, Quick Slice offers the enormous advantage of significant early payback with all its advantages.

Another advantage is flexibility. Quick-Slice MRP, coupled with other Fast-Track Implementation routes like Breakthrough JIT/TQC and Fail-safe Mini-DRP, makes it much more practical to do simultaneous implementations of more than one tool. We've already discussed implementing Breakthrough JIT/TQC together with Quick-Slice MRP on the same products and processes. Another example: Quick-Slice MRP and Fail-safe Mini-DRP on the same product family at the same time.

As I write this, a majority of MRP II implementations continue to be company wide. That may change. The benefits from Quick Slice are so compelling that, at some point, it's likely that Quick Slice will become the primary implementation method.

IMPLEMENTERS' CHECKLIST

Function: Quick-Slice MRP

This checklist serves the same purpose as the Implementers' Checklists for company-wide implementation in chapters 4 through 10: to detail the major tasks necessary to ensure total compliance with the Proven Path. A company that can check yes for each task on this list can be virtually guaranteed of a successful implementation of Quick-Slice MRP.

Because this checklist spans a total Quick-Slice Implementation, it's divided into monthly increments to serve as approximate guidelines on timing. These guidelines reflect the principle of urgency.

TASKS TO BE COMPLETED IN MONTH 1

Task	Complete	
	YES	NO
1-1. Audit/assessment I conducted with participation by top management, operating management, and an outside consultant with Class A experience.	____	____
1-2. The general manager, key staff members, and key operating managers have attended first-cut education.	____	____
1-3. Vision statement and cost justification prepared on a joint-venture basis, with both top management and operating management from all involved functions participating and approved by general manager.	____	____
1-4. Written project charter created and formally signed off by all executives and managers participating in the justification process, citing urgency as a key element in the Quick-Slice implementation process.	____	____

Task	Complete	
	YES	NO
1-5. Slice product(s) selected.	⎯⎯	⎯⎯
1-6. Full-time project leader selected from a key management role in an operating department.	⎯⎯	⎯⎯
1-7. Torchbearer identified and formally appointed.	⎯⎯	⎯⎯
1-8. Project team formed, consisting of key people who will be directly involved in the slice.	⎯⎯	⎯⎯
1-9. Executive steering committee formed, consisting of the general manager, all staff members, and the project leader.	⎯⎯	⎯⎯
1-10. Project team meeting at least twice per week, and executive steering committee meeting at least twice per month.	⎯⎯	⎯⎯
1-11. Outside consultant, with Class A MRP II experience, retained and on-site approximately two or three days every month.	⎯⎯	⎯⎯
1-12. Detailed performance goals established, linking directly back to each of the benefits specified in the cost/benefit analysis.		

TASKS TO BE COMPLETED IN MONTH 2

Task	Complete	
	YES	NO
2-1. Key members of project team to outside MRP II class (those who have not yet attended, if any).	⎯⎯	⎯⎯
2-2. Accelerated series of business meetings conducted for project team.	⎯⎯	⎯⎯
2-3. Process definition statements completed for all processes to be impacted by Quick Slice.	⎯⎯	⎯⎯

	Complete	
Task	YES	NO
2-4. Software decision made; software and necessary new hardware installed.	____	____
2-5. Detailed project schedule established by the project team, naming names, in days, and showing completion of Quick-Slice project in less than five months.	____	____
2-6. Detailed project schedule being updated at least twice weekly at project team meetings, with status being reported at each meeting of the steering committee.	____	____
2-7. Sales & operations planning meetings initiated.	____	____

TASKS TO BE COMPLETED IN MONTH 3

	Complete	
Task	YES	NO
3-1. Series of business meetings conducted for steering committee.	____	____
3-2. Series of business meetings conducted by project team people for all other persons involved with the slice.	____	____
3-3. Enthusiasm, teamwork, and a sense of ownership becoming visible throughout all groups involved in the slice.	____	____
3-4. Inventory record accuracy, including scheduled receipts and allocations, at 95 percent or better for all slice items.	____	____
3-5. Bill of material accuracy at 98 percent or better for all slice items, and all slice bills of material properly structured and sufficiently complete for MRP.	____	____

Task	Complete	
	YES	NO
3-6. All slice item data, plus any necessary work center data, complete and verified for reasonableness.	——	——

TASKS TO BE COMPLETED IN MONTH 4

Task	Complete	
	YES	NO
4-1. Executive steering committee authorization to implement MPS and MRP on the slice products and components.	——	——
4-2. MPS and MRP operating properly.	——	——
4-3. Plant schedules, and kanban where appropriate, for the slice items in place and operating properly.	——	——
4-4. Feedback links (anticipated delay reporting) in place for both plant and purchasing.	——	——

TASKS TO BE COMPLETED IN MONTH 5

Task	Complete	
	YES	NO
5-1. Suppliers cut over to supplier scheduling as practical.	——	——
5-2. Financial planning interfaces complete and implemented as practical.	——	——
5-3. Performance measurements in place and being reviewed carefully by the steering committee and project team.	——	——
5-4. Audit/assessment II completed; next improvement initiative underway.	——	——

PART IV

Ongoing Operation

Chapter 13

Operating MRP II

Imagine the feelings of the winning Super Bowl team. What a kick that must be! They've reached their goal. They're number one.

Now, imagine it's six months later. The team, the coaches, and the team's owner have just held a meeting and decided to cancel this year's training camp. Their attitude is who needs it? We're the best in the business. We don't have to spend time on fundamentals—things like blocking, tackling, and catching footballs. We know how to do that. They've also decided not to hold daily practices during the season. We'll just go out every Sunday afternoon and do the same things we did last year.

Does this make any sense? Of course not. But this is exactly the attitude some companies adopt after they become successful MRP II users. Their approach is: "This MRP II thing's a piece of cake. We don't need to worry about it anymore."

Wrong, of course. George Bevis said it very well. "MRP II is not a destination; it's a journey." No Class A or B MRP II system will maintain itself. It requires continual attention, constant care and feeding.

There are two major objectives involved in operating MRP II:

1. Don't let it slip.

2. Make it better and better.

It's easy to let it slip. Some Class A companies have learned this lesson the hard way. They've "taken their eye off the ball," and assumed their MRP II system will maintain itself. In the process, they've lost a letter grade. They've slipped to Class B. (Companies who achieve Class B and make the same mistake can become Class C very quickly.) Then comes the laborious process of reversing the trend and re-acquiring the excellence that once was there. The flip side of these experiences is represented by the excellent MRP II user companies. Their attitude is: "We're Class A, but we're going to do better next year than we did this year. We're not satisfied with the status quo. Our goal is to be even more excellent in the future than we are now."

How should a company address these issues? How can they not let it slip? What's involved in making it better and better?

Five important elements are involved:

- Understanding.

- Organization.

- Measurements.

- Education.

- Just-in-Time/Total Quality Control.

Let's look at each one.

UNDERSTANDING

In this context, understanding means lack of arrogance. In the example of the championship football team, things were reversed. They *had* arrogance; they *lacked* understanding. They also lacked any real chance of becoming next year's Super Bowl champions.

Operating at a Class A level is much the same. A company needs to understand:

- Today's success is no guarantee of tomorrow's.

- MRP II will not maintain itself; if left unattended, it will deteriorate.

- People are the key.

• The name of the game is to win, to be better than the competition, and operating a Class A MRP II system is one of the best ways to do that.

ORGANIZATION

Don't disband the MRP II project team and the executive steering committee. Keep these groups going. They're almost as important after a successful implementation as before. However, some changes in the way they operate should be made.

The MRP II Operating Committee

After implementation is complete, the MRP II project team should remain in place, with the following changes:

1. The group now has no full-time members; therefore, it's probably a bit smaller than it was. Its membership is now 100 percent department heads.

2. Since MRP II is no longer a project but rather is operational, the name of the group might be changed to MRP II operating committee or something along those lines.

3. Group meetings are held about once a quarter rather than once a week.

4. The chairmanship of the group rotates among its members, perhaps once or twice a year. First, a marketing manager might be the chairperson, next a manager from accounting, then perhaps someone from engineering or purchasing. This approach enhances the collective sense of ownership of MRP II. It states strongly that MRP II is a company-wide system.

The group's job is to focus formally on the performance of the MRP II system, report results to top management, and develop and implement improvements.

Spin-off Task Forces

Just as during implementation, these temporary groups can be used to solve specific problems, capitalize on opportunities, etc.

The Executive Steering Committee

Following implementation, the executive steering committee should meet about once every six months.[1] It receives updates on MRP II performance from the MRP II operating committee. Its tasks are much the same as during implementation: reviewing status, re-allocating resources when necessary, and providing leadership.

MEASUREMENTS

Manufacturing Resource Planning has two sides: operational and financial. MRP II enables a company to express the operating plan in financial terms. It can translate pieces and gallons and standard hours into dollars.

It follows, then, that measuring the effectiveness of MRP II performance requires both operational and financial measurements. Let's look at operational measurements first.

Operational Measurements—The ABCD Checklist for Operational Excellence[2]

Section 5 of the ABCD Checklist is the essential operational measurement of "how we're doing" operating MRP II.

This part of the ABCD Checklist should be reviewed by the MRP II operating committee formally, as a group, at least twice a year. Agreement should be reached on each of the 22 overview questions. For any answer that's lower than excellent this group should focus on:

1. What's causing the no answer? What's going wrong? Use the checklist's detailed audit questions for diagnosis.

2. What's the best way to fix the problem? Does the problem exist only within one department? If so, that department manager should be charged with correcting the problem. On the other hand, if the problem crosses departmental boundaries, should the company activate a spin-off task force?

[1] This can happen in a separate meeting or as part of a regularly scheduled executive team meeting, which, in many companies, is held weekly.

[2] The entire list of questions with instructions to their use, is titled *The Oliver Wight ABCD Checklist for Operational Excellence* (Essex Junction, VT: Oliver Wight Publications, Inc., 1992).

3. How quickly can it be fixed? (Set a date—don't let it drift.)

Each time the ABCD Checklist is reviewed, the results are formally communicated to the executive steering committee: the score achieved, the class rating (A,B,C, etc.), what the no answers are, what's being done about them, and what help, if any, is needed from top management.

Who does this communication? Who presents these results? The part-time successor to the full-time project leader. In other words, the chairperson of the MRP II operating committee.

Operational Measurements—Other

Listed below is a series of detailed technical measurements, not explicitly covered in the ABCD Checklist, relating to the specific operation of certain MRP II functions. This list will probably not be 100 percent complete for any one company, and, further, it contains some elements that may not apply in some organizations. I include them here to serve as a foundation for companies to use, along with the ABCD Checklist, in developing their own measurements program.

In master production scheduling, some companies measure:

1. Number of MPS changes in the emergency zone. This should be a small number.

2. MPS orders rescheduled in compared to those rescheduled out. These numbers should be close to equal.

3. Finished goods inventory turnover for make-to-stock.

Typically, these measurements are done weekly, except for inventory turnover, which is normally a monthly calculation. In material requirements planning, check on:

1. Number of stock outs for both manufactured and purchased items.

2. Inventory turnover, again for both make and buy items.

3. Exception message volume. This refers to the number of action recommendations generated by the MRP program each week. For conventional (fabrication and assembly) manufacturers, the exception rate should be 10 percent or less. For process and repetitive plants, the rate

may be higher because of more activity per item. (The good news is that these kinds of companies usually have far fewer items.)

4. Late order releases—The number of orders released within less than the planned lead time. A good target rule of thumb here is 5 percent or less of all orders released.

5. Production orders and supplier orders[2] rescheduled in versus rescheduled out. Here again, these numbers should be close to equal.

Except for inventory turns, most of these measurements are done weekly. Typically, they're broken out by the planner, including, of course, the supplier schedulers.

In capacity requirements planning, some companies track the past-due load. Target: less than one week's work. Frequency: weekly.

In shop floor control, the following are frequently measured:

1. On-time shop order completions, to the operation due date. A good measurement here is to track late jobs in (arriving) to a work center compared to late jobs out (completed). This recognizes that manufacturing departments shouldn't be penalized for jobs that arrive behind schedule. Some companies expand this to track total days of lateness in and out rather than merely members of jobs. This helps to identify people who may be making up some of the lost time even when jobs are completed late.

2. Capacity performance to plan. Standard hours of actual output compared to planned output. A good target: plus or minus 5 percent.

The frequency of the above: weekly; the breakout: by manufacturing department. Please keep in mind these are MRP II-related measurements only, and are not intended to replace measures of efficiency, productivity, and others.

For purchasing, I recommend measuring stock outs and inventory turns on purchased material by supplier and by buyer, as well as for the supplier schedulers, as mentioned above. Here, also, don't neglect the other important measurements on quality, price, etc.

For data, I recommend weekly reports on inventory, bill of material, and routing accuracy. The targets for all should be close to 100 percent.

---

[2] Supplier orders refers to the firm orders (scheduled receipts) in the supplier schedule and, for those items not yet being supplier scheduled, conventional purchase orders.

Financial Measurements

At least once a year, the MRP II operating committee should take a check on "how we're doing" financially with the system. Actual results in dollars should be compared to the benefits projected in the cost justification.

Just as with the operational measurements, a hard-nosed and straightforward approach should be used here: Is the company getting at least the benefits expected? If not, why not? Start fixing what's wrong, so the company can start to get the bang for the buck. Results are reported to the executive steering committee.

EDUCATION

Failure to establish an airtight ongoing education program is a major threat to the long-term successful operation of MRP II. Ongoing education is essential because:

New people enter the company.

Plus, current employees move into different jobs within the company, with different and perhaps expanded responsibilities. Failure to educate these new job incumbents spells trouble. It means that sooner or later the company will lose that critical mass of MRP II knowledgeable people. The company then will be unable to operate MRP II as effectively as before.

People tend to forget.

They need refresher education and training. To borrow a concept from the physical sciences, there's a half-life to what one learns. If that half-life is one year, people will remember about half of what they learned about MRP II last year, 25 percent from two years ago.

Business conditions change.

For any given company, its operating environment three years from now will probably differ substantially from what it is today. Companies develop new product lines, enter new markets, change production processes, become subject to new governmental regulations, acquire new subsidiaries, find that they're operating in a buyers' market (not a sellers' market), or vice versa, and on and on and on.

Operating MRP II means running the business with that set of tools, which tends not to change.

However, business conditions do change. It's necessary periodically to match up the tools (MRP II) to today's business environment and objectives. These may be very different from what they were a few years ago when MRP II was implemented.

What's needed is an ongoing process.

That is, one where people can review the tools they're using to do their jobs, match that up against today's requirements, and ask themselves, "Are we still doing the right things? How might we use the tools better? How could we do our jobs differently to meet today's challenges?" We're back to behavior change. (See chapter 6.) It's necessary after implementation, as well as before. And the way to facilitate behavior change is via education.

Ongoing MRP II education should be woven tightly into the operational fabric of the company. Minimum MRP II educational standards should be established for each position in the company, and written into the job specification. New incumbents should be required to meet these standards within the first few weeks on the job. These minimum standards will require some new people to go to outside classes. However, as with initial education, most of the ongoing education can be accomplished via inside education sessions, including virtually all the refresher education.

How can ongoing MRP II education be woven into the operational fabric of the company? Perhaps it can best be done by involving the folks in human resources. In the personnel office, there are files for each employee. Checklists are maintained there to help ensure that employees have signed up for programs like health insurance, the blood drive, and the United Fund. Given these files and these checklists, the human resources department may be the best group to administer the ongoing MRP II educational program, schedule people into classes, track attendance, report and reschedule no-shows, etc. Of course, the inside education sessions would be conducted by operating managers and other key people.

Let me add a word about ongoing education for top management. A change in senior management, either at the CEO level or on his staff, is a point of peril for MRP II. If the new executive does not receive the proper education, then he will, in all likelihood, not understand MRP II and may inadvertently cause it to deteriorate. New executives on board need MRP II education more than anyone else. This requirement is absolute and cannot be violated if the company wants to operate MRP II successfully over the long run. Here, also, this critically important educational requirement should be built directly into the executive's job specifications as a hard-and-fast rule with no latitude permitted.

JUST-IN-TIME/TOTAL QUALITY CONTROL

JIT/TQC is arguably the best thing that ever happened to MRP II. The reason? Because JIT/TQC, done properly, will not allow you to neglect your MRP II processes.

Let's take the case of a company that first implements MRP II successfully, and then attacks JIT/TQC.[4] Let's say the company allows MRP II to slip, to deteriorate—perhaps by not keeping the inventory data accurate or by not managing demand properly or by allowing the bills of material to get messed up or by violating time fences in the master schedule, or all of the above. What will happen?

Well, before long, the problems created by not having excellent plans and schedules will begin to affect (infect?) JIT/TQC. Poor plans and schedules will inhibit JIT/TQC from working nearly as well as they can and should. The reason: No longer will there be inventories, queues, and safety stocks to cover up the bad schedules.

JIT/TQC, in effect, will "send up a rocket" that there are major problems here, that waste is being created, not eliminated. JIT/TQC will scream to get MRP II back to Class A. And that's great.

But that's not all. JIT/TQC does more than keep MRP II from slipping. It also helps it to get better and better. How so? By simplifying and streamlining the real world.

---

[4] This sequence isn't mandatory. Frequently, companies will go after Just-in-Time and/or Total Quality Control first. Some companies implement them simultaneously, typically via Breakthrough JIT/TQC and Quick-Slice MRP.

- As setup times drop, so do order quantities and, hence, inventories.

- As quality improves, safety stock can be decreased and scrap factors minimized.

- As flow replaces job shop, queues go down and so do lead times.

As these real world improvements are expressed into the MRP II system, it will run better and better. As the real world gets simpler, data integrity becomes easier and planning becomes simpler.

SUMMARY

To those of you whose companies haven't yet started on JIT/TQC, I urge you to begin as soon as possible. You must do these things, and many others, in order to survive in the ultracompetitive worldwide marketplace of the 1990s and beyond.

Ollie Wight once again hit the nail right on the head: "MRP II is essential but not sufficient." You bet! No one of these tools—Just-in-Time, Total Quality Control, Manufacturing Resource Planning, design for manufacturability, CAD/CAM, activity based costing, and all the others—is sufficient. They're all essential.

"How are we doing?" is one necessary question to ask routinely. Another is: "How can we do it better?"

Don't neglect this second question. The truly excellent companies seem to share a creative discontent with the status quo. Their attitude is: "We're doing great, but we're going to be even better next year. We're going to raise the high bar another six inches, and go for it."

There are few companies today who are as good as they could be. There are few companies today who even have any idea how good they could be. In general, the excellent companies are populated with individuals no smarter or harder working than elsewhere. They merely got there first, then stayed there (at Class A), and then got better and better.

With a Class A MRP II system, a company can operate at an excellent level of performance—far better than before, probably better than it ever dreamed possible. High quality of life, being in control of the business and not at the mercy of the informal system, levels of customer service and productivity previously thought unattainable—to many companies today this sounds like nirvana. However, it's not good enough.

Are all Class A companies perfect? Nope. Are there things these companies could do better? Certainly.

The message is clear. Companies should not rest on their laurels after reaching Class A with MRP II. Don't be content with the status quo. It's more important than ever to go after those additional productivity tools, those "better mousetraps," those better and more humane ways of working with people. Many of these projects can be funded with the cash freed up by the inventory reductions made possible by MRP II. Look upon your excellent MRP II system as an engine, a vehicle, a launch pad for total excellence. Without that attitude, you'll never know how good you can be. You'll never know where the outer limits lie.

Good luck and Godspeed.

IMPLEMENTERS' CHECKLIST
Function: Operating MRP II

Task	Complete YES	NO
1. MRP II project team reorganized for ongoing operation, with no full-time members and rotating chairmanship.	___	___
2. Executive steering committee still in place.	___	___
3. ABCD Checklist and financial measurements generated by project team at least twice per year and formally reported to executive steering committee.	___	___
4. Ongoing MRP II education program underway and woven into the operational fabric of the company.	___	___
5. Just-in-Time/Total Quality Control processes initiated and successfully completed within the company and with suppliers.	___	___
6. Discontent with the status quo and dedication to continuing improvement adopted as a way of life within the company.	___	___

Appendix A

The Fundamentals of Manufacturing Resource Planning and Just-in-Time/ Total Quality Control

To be truly competitive, manufacturing companies must deliver products on time, quickly, and economically. Manufacturing Resource Planning (MRP II) and Just-in-Time/Total Quality Control (JIT/TQC) have proven to be essential tools in achieving these objectives.

Their capabilities offer a means for effectively managing the required resources: materials, labor, equipment, tooling, engineering specifications, space, and money. For each of these resources, Manufacturing Resource Planning can calculate what's required, when it's needed, and how much is needed. Having matched sets of resources at the right time and the right place is essential for an economical, rapid response to customer demands. Just-in-Time/Total Quality Control forces the elimination of waste and removal of obstacles that get in the way. MRP II's strength is in planning and control; JIT/TQC's strength is in execution and continuous improvement. Both are essential to be a winner in manufacturing.

Part One—Manufacturing Resource Planning (MRP II)

The logic of MRP II is quite simple; it's in every cookbook. The sales & operations plan says that we're having Thanksgiving dinner on the third Thursday in November. The master schedule is the menu, including turkey, stuffing, potatoes, squash, vegetables, and all the trimmings. The bill of material says, "Turkey stuffing takes one egg, seasoning, bread crumbs, etc." The routing says, "Put the egg and the seasoning in a mixer." The mixer is the work center where the processing is done.

In manufacturing, however, there's a lot more volume and a lot more change. There isn't just one product, there are many. The lead times aren't as short as a quick trip to the corner store, and the work centers are busy. Thanksgiving won't get rescheduled, but customers sometimes change their minds. The world of manufacturing is a world of constant change, and that's where MRP II comes in.

The elements that make up an MRP II operating and financial planning system are shown in figure A-1. We'll briefly walk through each to get an understanding of how MRP II operates.

Business Planning

Business planning represents the overall plan for the company, taking into account the needs of the marketplace (customer orders and forecasts), the capabilities within the company (people skills, available resources, technology), financial targets (profit, cash flow, and growth), and strategic goals (levels of customer service, quality improvements, cost reductions, productivity improvements, etc.). The business plan is expressed in dollars and lays out the long-term direction for the company. The general manager and his staff are responsible for maintaining the business plan.

Sales & Operations Planning

Sales & operations planning addresses that part of the business plan which deals with sales, production, inventories, and backlog. It's the operational plan designed to execute the business plan. As such, it is

Figure A-1
Manufacturing Resource Planning (MRP II)

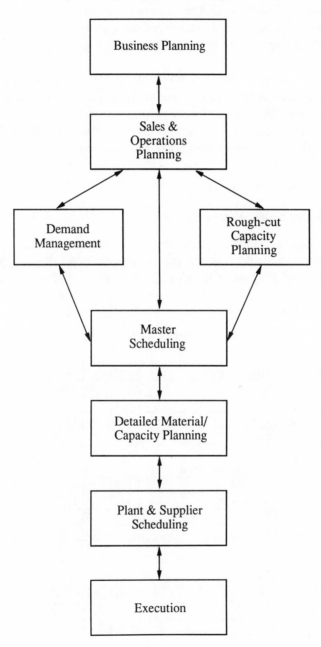

stated in units of measure such as pieces, standard hours, etc., rather than dollars. It's done by the same group of people responsible for business planning in much the same way. Planning is done in broad categories of products and establishes an aggregate plan of attack for sales and marketing, engineering, manufacturing and purchasing, and finance.

A simple example of a sales & operations plan is contained in figure A-2. In the sales & operations plan, the sales plan and production plan are aggregated by product family (group of products, items, options, features, etc.), showing the ending inventory/backlog (depending on whether it's a make-to-stock or make-to-order product).

DEMAND MANAGEMENT

Forecasting/Sales Planning

Forecasting/sales planning is the process of predicting what items the sales department expects to sell and the specific tasks they are going to take to hit the forecast. The sales planning process should result in a

Figure A-2

Sales Plan

Sales Plan	-3	-2	-1
Planned	120	120	120
Actual	124	123	138
Diff.	+4	+3	+18
Cum. Diff.		+7	+25

Production Plan

Production Plan			
Planned	125	125	125
Actual	121	119	118
Diff.	-4	-6	-7
Cum. Diff.		-10	-17

Inventory/Backlog

Inventory/Backlog				
Planned		103	108	113
Actual	98			
Diff.				

monthly rate of sales for a product family (usually expressed in units identical to the production plan), stated in units and dollars. It represents sales and marketing's commitment to take all reasonable steps to make sure the forecast accurately represents the actual customer orders to be received.

Customer order entry and promising

Customer order entry and promising is the process of taking incoming orders and determining specific product availability and configuration. It results in the entry of a customer order to be built/produced/shipped, and should also tie to the forecasting system to net against the projections. This is an important part of an MRP II system; to look at the orders already in the system, review the inventory/backlog, available capacity, and lead times, and then determine when the customer order can be promised. This promise date is then entered as a customer commitment.

ROUGH-CUT CAPACITY PLANNING

Rough-cut capacity planning is top management's rough estimate of determining what it will take to achieve the plans discussed in the sales & operations planning meetings and if it is realistic. The process relies on aggregate information in hours and units to highlight potential problems in the plant, engineering, finance, etc. prior to the proposed schedule being approved. It takes the machine and labor hours available and balances that with what the company is trying to achieve in production.

MASTER SCHEDULING

Master scheduling is a detailed statement of what products the company will build, stated by individual item rather than families. It is broken out into two parts—how many and when. It takes into account existing customer orders, forecasts of anticipated orders, current inventories, and available capacities. This plan must extend far enough into the future to cover the sum of the lead times to acquire the necessary resources. The master schedule must be laid out in time periods of weeks or smaller in order to generate detailed priority plans for the execution departments to follow. The sum of what's specified in the master schedule must reconcile with the sales & operations plan for the same time periods. Figure A-3 is an example of a master schedule including the available-to-promise calculation used in customer order promising.

Figure A-3

Master Schedule

Week		1	2	3	4
Forecast		20	20	20	20
Customer Orders		15			
Master Schedule		40		40	
Inventory	0	20	0	20	0
Available to Promise		25		40	

DETAILED MATERIAL/CAPACITY PLANNING

Material Requirements Planning (MRP)

Material requirements planning starts by determining what components are required to execute the master schedule, plus any needs for service parts/spare parts. To accomplish this, MRP requires a bill of material to describe the components that make up the items in the master schedule and inventory data to know what's on hand and/or on order. By reviewing this information, it calculates what existing orders need to be moved either earlier or later, and what new material must be ordered. Figure A-4 is an example of an MRP display for an item.

Figure A-4

Week		1	2	3	4
Requirements		80		80	
On Order					200
Inventory	100	20	20	-60	140
Planned Orders					

Capacity Requirements Planning (CRP)

Capacity requirements planning takes the recommended needs for manufactured items from MRP and converts them to a prediction of how much capacity will be needed and when. A routing which defines the operations involved is required, plus the estimate of time required for each. A summary by key work center by time period is then presented to compare capacity needed to capacity available. Figure A-5 is an example of a capacity plan for a work center.

Figure A-5

Week	1	2	3	4
Capacity (Required)	90	90	90	110
Capacity (Available)	90	90	90	90
Overload/Underload	0	0	0	-20

PLANT AND SUPPLIER SCHEDULING

Plant scheduling is two-way communication with the factory. Utilizing MRP, the plant is advised of which jobs have been scheduled, where they are located, and the priority of each. Furthermore, a company must also monitor the flow of capacity by comparing how much work was to be completed versus how much has actually been completed. This technique is called input-output control, and its objective is to ensure that what is actually occurring matches with what should be occurring in terms of capacity.

There are two basic ways for companies to arrange their production facilities: job shop and flow shop. A brief description of each follows.

Job Shop

A job shop is where the resources are grouped by like type. The classic example of this approach is a machine shop, where the lathes are in one area, the drills in another, etc. Work moves from work center to work center based on routings unique to the individual items being produced. Job shop scheduling is called dispatching, and there is a daily dispatch list for each work center. The dispatch list is simply a schedule of the work to be done in the work center, sorted in due date sequence. An example of a dispatch list is shown in figure A-6.

Figure A-6

Shop Order	Part Number	Operation Sequence Number	Qty.	Operation Start	Operation Due	Order Due	Std. Hrs. Set Up	Std. Hrs. Run	Status
17621	91762	020	50	8/13	8/16	8/25	—	3.5	R
18430	98340	030	500	8/13	8/18	8/31	4.3	14.3	H
18707	78212	010	1100	8/16	8/18	9/6	1.1	18.2	T
18447	80021	020	300	8/17	8/19	8/28	1.5	9.0	T
19712	44318	020	120	8/24	8/26	9/10	3.3	15.1	

Flow Shop

A flow shop is where the resources are grouped by their sequence in the process. An example of this type of environment is an automobile assembly line, oil refineries, a filling line in a consumer package goods plant, or a manufacturing cell. Work moves through the process automatically, so there is no need to use formal routings and move from operation to operation. Basically the raw material(s) are at one end, and the finished product comes out the other. To schedule the shop in this type of environment, a line/cell schedule is used. The line/cell list shows the jobs to be started in the priority sequence as they should begin, taking into account various run times and expected outcomes. An example of a line/cell list is shown in figure A-7.

Figure A-7

	WEEK 1 M	T	W	TH	F	WEEK 2 M	T	W	TH	F	WEEK 3	WEEK 4
BLEND X:												
REQMTS.						1100	1100	1100	1100	1100	4400	
SCHED.					1100	1100	1100	1100	1100	1100	3300	
BLEND Z:												
REQMTS.	1050	1050	1050	1050	1050							5250
SCHED.	1050	1050	1050	1050							1050	4200

Supplier Scheduling

Suppliers also need valid schedules. Supplier scheduling replaces the typical and cumbersome cycle of purchase requisitions and hard copy purchase orders. Within MRP II, the output of MRP for purchased items is summarized and communicated directly to suppliers. Long term contracts define prices, terms, conditions, and total quantities, and supplier schedules authorizing delivery are generated and communicated at least once per week, perhaps even more frequently in certain Just-in-Time/Total Quality Control environments. Supplier scheduling includes those changes required for existing commitments with suppliers—materials needed earlier than originally planned as well as later—plus any new commitments that are authorized. To help suppliers do a better job of long-range planning so they can better meet the needs of the company, the supplier scheduling horizon should extend well beyond the established lead time. An example of a supplier schedule is shown in figure A-8.

Figure A-8

	WEEK 1					WEEK 2					WEEK 3	WEEK 4
	M	T	W	TH	F	M	T	W	TH	F		
RAW MATL R:												
REQMTS.	1050	1050	1050	1050	1100	1100	1100	1100	1100	1100	4350	4200
INV. 3600 LBS.	2550	1500	450	9400	8300	7200	6100	5000	3900	2800	8450	4250
SCHED.			10,000								10,000	

EXECUTION AND FEEDBACK

The execution phase is the culmination of all the planning steps, where the items or processes are actually created. Any problems with materials or capacity are resolved through interaction between the plant and the planning department. This is done on an exception basis, and feedback will only be necessary when some part of the plan cannot be executed. This feedback consists of stating the cause of the problem and the best possible new completion date. This information must then be analyzed by the planning department to determine the consequences. If an alternative cannot be found, the planning department should feed the problem back to the master scheduler. Only if all other practical choices have been exhausted should the master schedule be altered. If the master schedule is changed, the master scheduler owes feedback to sales if a promise date will be missed, and sales owes a call to the customer if an acknowledged delivery date will be missed.

By integrating all of these planning and execution elements, MRP II becomes a process for effectively linking long-range aggregate plans to short-term detailed plans. From top to bottom, from the general manager and his staff to the front-line operators, it ensures that all activities are in lockstep to gain the full potential of a company's capabilities. The reverse process is equally important. Feedback goes from bottom to top on an exception basis—conveying unavoidable problems in order to maintain valid plans. It's a rack-and-pinion relationship between the top-level plans and the actual work done in the plant.

In addition to MRP II's impact on the operations side of the business, it has an equally important impact on financial planning. By including the selling price and cost data, MRP II can convert each of the plans into dollars. The results are time-phased projections of dollar shipments, dollar inventory levels, cash flow, and profits.

Incorporating financial planning directly with operating planning produces one set of books. The same data is driving both systems—the only difference being the unit of measure. Too often financial people have had to develop a separate set of books as they couldn't trust the operating data. Not only does this represent extra effort, but much judgment and guesswork have to be applied to determine the financial projections.

In addition to operating and financial planning information, simulations represent the third major capability of MRP II. The ability to produce information to help answer "what if" questions and to contribute to contingency planning is a valuable asset for any manager to have. What if business goes up faster than expected; what if it goes up as planned, but the mix of products shifts; what if our costs increase, but our prices do not; do we have enough capacity to support our new products and maintain sales for current ones? These are common and critical issues that constantly arise in all manufacturing companies. The key part of the management job is to constantly think through alternative plans. With MRP II, people can access the data needed to help analyze the situation, play "what if," and, if required, initiate a better plan.

PART TWO—JUST-IN-TIME/TOTAL QUALITY CONTROL

The Just-in-Time/Total Quality Control process seeks to eliminate waste in all areas. Waste is defined as any non value-added activity, and further classified into two categories, necessary and unnecessary. An example of necessary waste is double-entry bookkeeping, which doesn't add value to the product but is required. Unnecessary waste would be excess steps or paperwork that may be in the accounting process. Essentially, any resource that is not actively involved in a process that adds value is in a waste state. Therefore, waste includes all inventory not actually being worked on, all inventory not needed at a particular moment in time, all inspection to detect defective products, and all movement from one operation to another. Waste exists in all aspects of the business, and should be eliminated wherever possible because it not only adds cost without value, but also because it constrains the ability to respond economically to change.

The ability to respond to change can be measured by the speed at which we can economically convert materials into shipments. As a result, Just-in-Time/Total Quality Control drives us toward high velocity manufacturing. It often begins in manufacturing, but quickly encompasses all organizations in the company, as well as suppliers and customers.

Just-in-Time/Total Quality Control also means repeated reductions in order quantities, safety stocks, queues, rejects, set-ups, transactions, complexity of the product, number of suppliers, time in order entry, days of customer lead time, warranty claims, and customer returns, all of which occur over and over, day after day.

We cannot, however, suddenly eliminate waste, or economically have zero inventories or lot sizes of one overnight. We cannot immediately eliminate inspection without adverse consequences. In fact, blindly following the process can lead to higher costs, worse quality, and unsatisfactory product deliveries.

With that discussion of what Just-in-Time/Total Quality Control is, let's talk about how to correctly implement it.

THE JUST-IN-TIME/TOTAL QUALITY CONTROL PROCESS

The process of Just-in-Time/Total Quality Control is to eliminate waste, but we must first understand it before we can use it to economically improve quality, delivery, and cost. As shown in figure A-9, the Just-in-Time journey begins and progresses by learning how to economically manufacture "one less at a time." The one-less-at-a-time process is designed to:

- Continuously expose and prioritize wasteful constraints.

- Stimulate everyone to think effectively about solutions to the prioritized constraints.

- Provide visual feedback on our progress.

The one-less process is as critical to Just-in-Time/Total Quality Control as the computer is to Manufacturing Resource Planning. We can eliminate waste without the one-less process, but we are missing the continuous improvement driver and we are not likely to get as far nor travel as fast. Most companies try to eliminate waste. "One less at a time" is what makes it different from just operating the same old way.

Just-in-Time/Total Quality Control contains a technique called *kanban* which sets an upper limit on inventory. Kanban is a Japanese word that means "card," "signal," or "visual record." Each kanban in the system authorizes pieces of inventory, or orders in order entry, or specifications in design engineering, etc. The total number of kanbans in the system limits the total amount of inventory in the manufacturing pipeline. Simply, the essence of the kanban system is like the old-fashioned milk delivery system. Whenever the milkman would see an empty bottle of milk, he would replace it with a full one. Unfortunately, to some people, kanban cards may imply a new scheduling system. While kanban controls will replace or simplify conventional shop floor work order systems, the main benefit by far of the Just-in-Time/Total Quality Control process occurs when we continue to make shipments, while slowly removing kanbans (wasteful inventory), to expose constraints to higher manufacturing velocities. Just-in-Time/Total Quality Control is designed to expose constraints, but wishful thinking will not make the constraints disappear; we must use adequate problem-solving tools.

Just-in-Time/Total Quality Control involves all areas of the company. However, different companies with varying needs will choose different parts of the process, depending on where they are feeling the most pain.

Figure A-9   The Just-in-Time Process: "One Less at a Time"*

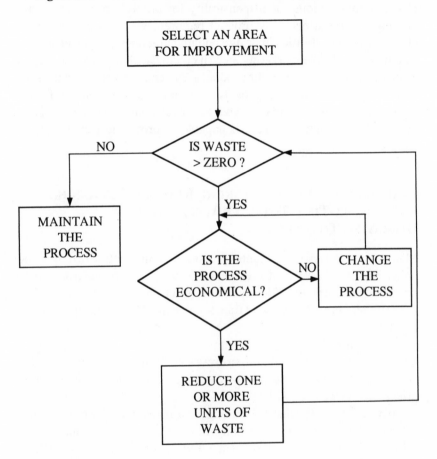

*BILL SANDRAS

For one company, it may be the materials area, focusing on inventory, sourcing, stockkeeping, and paperwork. For another, it's production, where the focus is on setup reduction, equipment layout and configuration, and mixed-model loading. It may be in accounting, focusing on standards, payment frequency, work-in-process accounting, labor accounting, and performance measures. Almost every company is affected in one way or another in the personnel area, whether it's in employee stability issues, flexibility between workers and job catego- ries, communications, or responsibility for problem resolution. Engi- neering can be affected by product requirements, flow requirements, changing responsibilities in design and manufacturing engineering, and design teams. In the marketing area, it can mean changes to the way we forecast, sell, and market our products. Systems, processes, and facili- ties may need to change, especially in the areas of work orders, factory layout, and traffic. No matter what the area though, the Just-in-Time/ Total Quality Control process is capable of providing tremendous re- sults.

Part Three—Manufacturing Resource Planning and Just-in-Time/Total Quality Control Operating Together

Manufacturing Resource Planning is the planning and scheduling tool which enables a company to get the maximum performance from *today's* operating environment. However, it doesn't challenge the way things are—if there is a 52-week lead time for an item, MRP II just plans based on that.

Just-in-Time/Total Quality Control forces constant improvements to today's environment, so that tomorrow's environment is better. It's like the conscience of the system, always asking "can we do this better, more effectively, more economically, etc."

Manufacturing Resource Planning then plans and controls that new environment to enable a company to maximize performance out of *tomorrow's* improved environment. And so on, and so on. MRP II provides the tool, and JIT provides the process to make the environment better so the tool is more effective.

Conclusion

Faster, more reliable, and more economical responses to changes are the major advantage of having MRP II and JIT in place. Changes in the marketplace are always occurring, and some represent important oppor- tunities and require quick analysis to determine the best way to take advantage of them. In addition, unavoidable problems are also occur- ring. Being unaware that the plans cannot be carried out only leads to bigger problems—not only do you lose valuable time before you recognize the situation, but during this period of time you are likely to compound the problem. "Bad news early is better than bad news late" is a better approach. It permits you to react to the problem before it's a crisis, rather than after.

Companies that operate MRP II and Just-in-Time/Total Quality Control in an outstanding manner are equipped to manage change—they have controls enabling them to lay out alternative plans, predict the consequences of each, select the best one, make it happen, and then continuously challenge each of the essential steps to make them even more effective. In short, they have greater control in running the business and continuously improving the business.

Thanks go to Walt Goddard, Bill Sandras, and Tom Wallace for the information contained in this appendix.

Job Shop Versus Flow Shop

There are two basic ways for companies to arrange their production facilities: job shop and flow shop. Other terms you may have come across, such as batch, intermittent, etc., are essentially subsets of job or flow. We don't need to concern ourselves with them here.

JOB SHOP

First, let's define job shop. Many people say a job shop is a place where you make specials. Well, it's true that specials can be made in a job shop but so can standard products. The issue is not so much the product but rather how the resources are organized. Let's try this one on for size: Job shop—a form of manufacturing organization where the resources are grouped by like type. Other terms for it include functional form of organization or single-function departments. The classic example of this approach is a machine shop. Here all the lathes are in one area, the drills in another, the mills in another, and the automatic screw machines are in the building next door.

In a job shop, the work moves from work center to work center based on routings unique to the individual items being produced. In some job shops, there can be dozens or even hundreds of different operations within a single routing. Each one of these operations must be formally scheduled via a complex process known as back scheduling. These back-scheduled operations must then be grouped by work center, sorted by their scheduled operation completion dates, and communicated to the shop floor via what's called a dispatch list. This process is repeated once per day, in some cases, once per shift.

269

Do job shops exist in other than metalworking? You bet. I can remember one from my years in the pharmaceutical industry, specifically that part of the plant where we made tablets and capsules. We had single-function departments, called the granulating department, compressing, coating, capsule filling, etc. The nature of the product would determine its routing. Tablets went to the compressing department; capsules didn't. Some tablets got coated; some didn't. Capsules got filled but didn't get compressed.

This is a job shop, by the above definition. And please note: We didn't make specials. We made the same products, to the same specifications, time and time again. The Food & Drug Administration prefers it that way.

Advantages typically attributed to the job shop form of organization include a higher rate of equipment utilization and enhanced flexibility.

FLOW SHOP

A flow shop is a form of manufacturing organization where the resources are grouped by their sequence in the process. Some refer to it as a process layout. Examples include oil refineries, certain chemical manufacturing operations, an automobile assembly line, a filling line in a consumer package goods plant, or a manufacturing cell.

Back to my former company, making tablets and capsules. The filling and packaging operation was flow, not job, shop. Each work center (line) consisted of some very dissimilar pieces of equipment in a precise sequence: a bottle cleaner, a filler, a cotton stuffer, a capper, a labeler, a case packer, etc. Note: We didn't have all of the cotton stuffers in one corner of the department, as the job shop layout would call for. This would have been very slow, inefficient, a waste of space, etc.

Many flow shops don't use formal routing information inside the computer because the routing is defined by the way the equipment is located within the line or the cell. Where formal routings are maintained in this environment, they often consist of only one operation, which might read make the product or make the part.

In most situations in most companies, flow is superior to job shop:

• Products can be made much faster via a flow process than job shop. Hence, shorter lead times and better response to customers' needs.

• Inventories, both work-in-process and other, are much smaller. Hence, less space is required; fewer dollars are tied up; obsolescence is less likely.

• Less material handling is required. Hence, less risk of damage and, more important, non-value-adding activities are reduced with an attendant rise in productivity.

• Workers are more able to identify with the product. Hence, more involvement, higher morale, better ideas for improvement.

There are other benefits from flow, one of which is simplicity. (See figures B-1 and B-2.)

Which is simpler? Which is easier to understand? Which is less difficult to plan and schedule? Which allows for more visual control and more immediate feedback?

The obvious answer, and the correct one, to all of these is flow shop. Well, so what? Unless you're fully a flow shop today, what should you be doing? The answer is, wherever possible, you should be converting to flow, because if you don't, and your competition does, you might be in trouble. And your competitors may be doing just that because, as a general principle, *the manufacturing world is moving to flow*. It's too good not to do it.

And how do you convert from job shop to flow? Answer: Go to cellular manufacturing. More and more, we see companies migrating from job shop to flow via the creation of manufacturing cells (also called

Figure B-1
Job Shop

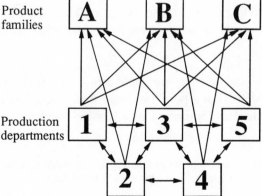

Figure B-2
Flow Shop

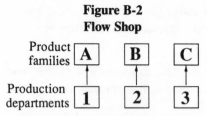

flow lines, demand pull lines, kanban lines, and probably some other terms that are just now being dreamed up).[1]

IMPLICATIONS FOR MRP II IMPLEMENTATION

Flow is far simpler than job shop, all other things being equal. It's more straightforward, more visual and visible. It can use much simpler scheduling and control tools.

Flow requires fewer schedules, all other things being equal. To make a given item via flow normally requires only one operation to be scheduled. For example, the same item, made in a job shop and having a ten-operation routing, would require ten schedules to be developed and maintained via the back-scheduling process.

To sum up:

• Flow means FIFO—first in, first out. Jobs go into a process in a given sequence and, barring a problem, are finished in that same sequence.

• Flow means fast. As we said earlier, jobs typically finish far quicker in a flow process than in a job shop.

• FIFO and fast means simple schedules. These are frequently simple sequence lists derived directly from the master schedule or the material plan (MRP).

It's easier—and quicker—to implement simple tools. Therefore, implementing MRP II in a pure flow shop should take less time, perhaps several months less, compared to a similar[2] implementation in a job shop.

---

[1] For an excellent treatment of this topic, please see William A. Sandras, Jr., *Just-in-Time: Making It Happen* (Essex Junction, VT: Oliver Wight Publications, Inc., (1989).

[2] Same size, same product complexity, same software, etc.

MRP II Detailed Implementation Plan— Company-Wide

MRP II
Proven Path Detailed Implementation Plan

TASK	RESPONSIBLE	COMMENTS
1. AUDIT/ASSESSMENT I	Top Mgmt. Middle Mgmt.	Assess the company's current situation. In most cases, this is done with the help of an outside consultant with Class A credentials.
2. FIRST-CUT EDUCATION	Top Mgmt. Middle Mgmt.	What is MRP II, how does it work, why should a company commit to it? Top management should attend the Top Management Course, key middle managers should attend the Five-Day Course, Executive Torchbearer and Team Leader should attend Successful Implementation Class.
3. VISION STATEMENT	Top Mgmt. Middle Mgmt.	A short, concise document defining what we want to accomplish, and when it should be in place.
4. COST/BENEFIT	Top Mgmt. Middle Mgmt.	A clear listing of the costs and benefits, agreed to by the key players.
A. Prepare cost/benefit.	Top Mgmt. Middle Mgmt.	Cost/benefit analysis.
B. Commit to implementation.	Top Mgmt.	Approve the implementation. Communicate the commitment. Deliver clear, consistent messages.
5. PROJECT ORGANIZATION	Top Mgmt.	Create the appropriate management and operational teams.
A. Executive Steering Committee.	Top Mgmt.	Include designation of Executive Torchbearer. Schedule review meetings once a month.
B. Project Team.	Top Mgmt.	Team Leader should be full-time.
C. Outside counsel.	Top Mgmt.	Outside consultant with Class A experience.
D. Spin-off task groups.	Ex. Steering Committee	Identify initial groups, more may be needed later.
6. PERFORMANCE GOALS	Top Mgmt. Middle Mgmt.	Using the ABCD Checklist, agree on expected performance levels and measurements.

274

MRP II
Proven Path Detailed Implementation Plan

TASK	RESPONSIBLE	COMMENTS
7. INITIAL EDUCATION	Team Leader	Provide the necessary understanding to all people who will be designing and using the new tools.
A. Outside education for people who will be leaders at the in-house series of business meetings and key managers.	Team Leader	To be effective discussion leaders, these managers need exposure at either the Top Management Course or the Five-Day Course. The key managers mentioned here are people critical to the design or operation, but who have not been covered under first-cut education and who are not leaders for the business meetings.
B. Outside education for people designated as in-house experts.	Team Leader	Generally, in-house experts are designated in the following areas: Manufacturing Strategy, Sales & Operations Planning, Master Production Scheduling, Material Requirements Planning, Capacity Management and Shop Scheduling, Purchasing, Inventory Record Accuracy, Bill of Material Accuracy, and Financial Integration. These in-house experts may or may not be part of the project team.
C. Project Team/Discussion Leaders video course.	Team Leader	A series of business meetings where the general principles are translated into the specifics of operation for your company. Acquire the MRP II Video Library.
D. Top Management video course.	Executive Torchbearer/ Project Leader	A series of business meetings where the top managers apply the concepts to their company.
E. Mixed Management Overview video course.	Discussion Leaders	A series of business meetings covering the overview materials, with a mixed group of managers from each of the different functional areas. The objectives are to understand the concepts, to better understand one another, and to help in team building.

275

MRP II
Proven Path Detailed Implementation Plan

TASK	RESPONSIBLE	COMMENTS
F. Department specific video courses.	Discussion Leaders	Series of business meetings organized by department. The objectives are to determine specifically what changes need to be made to run the business differently in these departments. Typical groups for these meetings include, but are not limited to: Production and Inventory Control, Purchasing, Manufacturing Supervision, Quality, Sales and Marketing, Engineering, Finance, Management Information Systems, Personnel, Stockroom, Group Leaders, and Direct Labor Employees.
8. SALES, LOGISTICS, AND MANUFACTURING PROCESSES	Top Mgmt. Middle Mgmt.	Develop a detailed statement of how these processes will operate following implementation. The Project Team/Discussion Leaders series of business meetings (Task #7C above) generally provides most of the information needed for this task. Key issues or changes should be approved by top management.

TASK	RESPONSIBLE	COMMENTS
9. PLANNING AND CONTROL PROCESSES		Identification of the systems necessary for effective planning and control. Some of these systems will be implemented using the pilot approach.
A. Sales & Operations Planning.	Top Mgmt.	Can be started right away. Format, policies, unit of measure, and family designations can be developed in the first few meetings and revised as needed thereafter.
B. Demand Management.	Sales Mgr.	Focus on improving the demand side of the business through: sales planning, item forecasting, eliminating or reducing detailed forecasting wherever possible by using DRP or interfacing with customer scheduling systems.
C. Master Production Scheduling.	P&IC Mgr.	Decisions on what level in the product structure to master schedule, and what items will be master scheduled. Typically started with material planning as part of the pilot.
1. Develop a master scheduling policy.	Top Mgmt. Sales & Mktg. P&IC Mfg. Suprvsn.	Should address the following: 1. Procedure for changing the master production schedule. Who can request a change, how the proposed change is investigated, and who should approve it. 2. Periodic reviews of actual production vs. the master production schedule with an emphasis on problem resolution.
D. Material Planning.	P&IC Mgr.	Begun as a pilot.
E. Capacity Planning.	P&IC Mgr. Mfg. Suprvsn.	Sometimes implementation is delayed until after master scheduling and material planning are fully implemented.

MRP II
Proven Path Detailed Implementation Plan

TASK	RESPONSIBLE	COMMENTS
F. Shop Scheduling.	P&IC Mgr. Mfg. Suprvsn.	Includes shop floor control and input-output control. Some companies today are using kanban on the factory floor in place of traditional shop floor control. Other companies are using both kanban in some areas, and traditional shop floor control in other areas.
G. Supplier Scheduling & Development	Purchasing Mgr.	Typically started as a pilot with one or several suppliers.

Proven Path Detailed Implementation Plan

TASK	RESPONSIBLE	COMMENTS
10. DATA MANAGEMENT		These are the steps required to attain the necessary levels of data accuracy.
A. Inventory Record Accuracy.	Stockroom Mgr.	Objective is a minimum 95 percent inventory record accuracy.
1. Measure a sample as a starting point.	Stockroom Mgr.	Develop an objective assessment of the starting point. Most companies use a sample of 100 items.
2. Provide the tools for limited access and transaction recording.	Stockroom Mgr.	Includes enough stockroom people, adequate space, counting scales, and typically a fence. In the case of a simultaneous MRP II/JIT implementation, see the JIT implementation plan for the handling of point-of-use and point-of-manufacture storage. Transaction system must be simple and easy to use.
3. Implement control group cycle counting.	Stockroom Mgr.	Used to find and fix the root causes of errors.
4. Begin cycle counting all items.	Stockroom Mgr.	Done after the causes of errors have been corrected. Several approaches are commonly used: process-control cycle counting, cycle counting by ABC code, random cycle counting.
B. Bill of Material Accuracy.	Engr. Mgr. Mfg. Suprvsn.	Objective is a minimum 98 percent bill of material accuracy, and an accurate bill of material structure.
1. Measure a sample of single-level bills as a starting point.	Engr. Mgr. Mfg. Suprvsn.	Develop an objective assessment of the starting point. Most companies use a sample of 100 single-level bills.
2. Assign responsibility for bill of material accuracy.	Top Mgmt.	Working with all the different departments who are users of the bills of material.

279

MRP II
Proven Path Detailed Implementation Plan

TASK	RESPONSIBLE	COMMENTS
3. Verify bills of material for correct item numbers and quantity per.	Engr. Mgr. Mfg. Suprvsn.	Typically done by exception: issue to manufacturing per the bill of material and track exceptions. A cycle audit, line-by-line audit, and/or disassembly of the product can also be used where appropriate. Objective is to highlight errors and correct them as well as correcting the root causes of the errors.
4. Verify correct structure in the bills of material.	Engr. Mgr. Mfg. Suprvsn.	Typical areas of work include: 1. Representing how material moves in the factory. 2. Showing raw material on the bills of material. 3. Including modules and self-consumed assemblies where appropriate. 4. Removing unnecessary levels from the bills of material.
5. Develop and implement bill of material policies.	Engr. Mgr.	Typical policies include: 1. Engineering (or formula) change procedure. 2. Documenting new or special products. 3. Temporary material substitutions.
C. Routing Accuracy.	Mfg. Engineering Mgr.	Objective is a minimum 95 percent routing accuracy.
1. Measure 100 routings as a starting point.	Mfg. Engineering Mgr.	Develop an objective assessment of the starting point.
2. Assign responsibility for routing accuracy.	Top Mgmt.	May involve assigning areas of responsibility if these do not already exist.
3. Verify routings.	Mfg. Engr. Mgr.	Typically done by auditing work on the factory floor for: correct work center, correct operation sequence, reasonable time standard (plus or minus 10 percent).

MRP II

Proven Path Detailed Implementation Plan

TASK	RESPONSIBLE	COMMENTS
D. Item Data.	P&IC Mgr. Purchasing Mgr.	Have knowledgeable people verify this information.
1. Verify order policies.	P&IC Mgr. Purchasing Mgr.	Decide between fixed-order quantity and lot-for-lot. Dynamic-order quantity calculations are not recommended. Fix the obvious errors in order quantities, use remainder as is, work to reduce the order quantities.
2. Verify lead times.	P&IC Mgr. Purchasing Mgr.	Manufactured items: use simple, consistent scheduling rules, fix the obvious problems, work to reduce the lead times. Purchased items: use current lead times, work with suppliers to implement supplier scheduling to get out beyond the lead times.
3. Verify safety stock levels.	P&IC Mgr. Purchasing Mgr.	Applies to independent demand items consistent with master schedule policy. For dependent demand items, restrict to special circumstances only.

MRP II
Proven Path Detailed Implementation Plan

TASK	RESPONSIBLE	COMMENTS
11. PROCESS IMPROVEMENT		MRP II is a planning and control system. JIT/TQC is process improvement; changing the business to make it more efficient, more productive, and less costly through the elimination of waste.
		Companies need to do both: Plan and control their business, and change their processes to continuously improve them. For the detailed implementation plan in the area of process improvement, see the JIT/TQC Detailed Implementation Plan.

282

MRP II
Proven Path Detailed Implementation Plan

TASK	RESPONSIBLE	COMMENTS
12. SOFTWARE	MIS Mgr.	Select and implement the software to support the planning and control systems identified above.
A. Select software.	MIS Mgr. P&IC Mfg. Suprvsn.	Select software that meets most of the needs from a user and MIS point of view.
1. Acquire *The Standard System* book.	MIS Mgr. P&IC Mfg. Suprvsn.	Available from Oliver Wight Limited Publications, this book provides an explanation of what a typical software package should provide.
2. If needed, schedule software consulting audit.	MIS Mgr. P&IC Mfg. Suprvsn.	Helpful in situations where new software is being used or extensive modification and/or interfacing is required.
B. Evaluate systems work and acquire necessary resources.	MIS Mgr.	Includes work needed for modifications, interfacing, and temporary bridges.
C. Implement necessary modules with modifications and interfacing.	MIS Mgr.	Typical modules include: Inventory Transactions, Bills of Material, Routings, Master Production Scheduling, Material Requirements Planning, Capacity Requirements Planning, Shop Floor Control, Input-Output Control, Purchasing, Financial Integration.
D. Agree on MIS performance standards.	MIS Mgr. P&IC Mfg. Suprvsn.	Response times, on-time completion of planning run, reports, etc.

MRP II
Proven Path Detailed Implementation Plan

TASK	RESPONSIBLE	COMMENTS
13. PILOT AND CUTOVER	Team Leader Project Team Involved Users	Conversion of the current processes to the new processes using a pilot approach.
A. Complete three pilots.	Team Leader Project Team Involved Users	Pilots are: 1. Computer pilot to test the software. 2. Conference room pilot to test procedures and people's understanding. 3. Live pilot to test the new processes and verify they are working. Systems that are typically implemented using the pilot approach are: 1. Master Production Scheduling. 2. Material Requirements Planning. 3. Shop Floor Control. 4. Supplier Scheduling and Development.
B. Monitor critical measurements.	Team Leader	Before moving into cutover, verify that the new processes and systems are working.
C. Group remaining products into several groups.	P&IC Involved Users	Three or four groups are typical.
D. Bring each group onto the new systems.	P&IC	Each group will require intense planner coverage to get them settled down.

MRP II
Proven Path Detailed Implementation Plan

TASK	RESPONSIBLE	COMMENTS
14. PERFORMANCE MEASURE-MENTS	Dept. Heads	Compare actual results to the previously agreed-upon key measurements. Typical performance measurements include: 1. Production Plan performance. 2. Master Production Schedule performance. 3. Manufacturing Schedule performance. 4. Engineering Schedule performance. 5. Supplier Delivery performance. Other measurements include: 1. Customer Service. 2. Quality. 3. Cost. 4. Velocity.
15. AUDIT/ASSESSMENT II	Top Mgmt. Middle Mgmt.	Re-assess the company's situation. Where are the current opportunities, what needs to be done next. This could be a phase 2 of the implementation, a concentrated effort to improve current levels of performance, etc. In most cases, this is done with the help of an outside consultant with Class A credentials.
16. ONGOING EDUCATION	Dept. Heads	Run a continuing program of outside education and business meetings to improve skill levels and company operating results.
A. Educate key managers new to the business.	Top Mgmt.	New managers in key positions need exposure at either the Top Management Course or Five-Day Course to continue achieving full operating benefits.

MRP II
Proven Path Detailed Implementation Plan

TASK	RESPONSIBLE	COMMENTS
B. Maintain in-house experts.	Dept. Heads	Also important to continue achieving full operating benefits.
C. Continue the series of business meetings.	Dept. Heads	These meetings focus on how to improve the operating results of the business through the use of these tools. It's good to stand back and look at the situation from time to time. Sometimes new people are run through a special series of meetings, more typically, they are included in the ongoing series of business meetings.

Quick-Slice MRP Detailed Implementation Plan

Quick-Slice MRP
Proven Path Detailed Implementation Plan

TASK	RESPONSIBLE	COMMENTS
1. AUDIT/ASSESSMENT I	Top Mgmt. Middle Mgmt.	Assess the company's current situation. In most cases, this is done with the help of an outside consultant with Class A credentials.
2. FIRST-CUT EDUCATION	Top Mgmt. Middle Mgmt.	What is MRP II, how does it work, why should a company commit to it? Top management should attend the Top Management Course, key middle managers should attend the Five-Day Course, Executive Torchbearer and Team Leader should attend Successful Implementation Class.
3. VISION STATEMENT	Top Mgmt. Middle Mgmt.	A short, concise document defining what we want to accomplish, and when it should be in place.
4. COST/BENEFIT	Top Mgmt. Middle Mgmt.	A quick listing of the costs and benefits as applied to the slice only.
5. PROJECT ORGANIZATION	Top Mgmt.	Create the appropriate management and operational teams to implement the slice.
A. Executive Steering Committee.	Top Mgmt.	Include designation of Executive Torchbearer. Schedule review meetings once a month.
B. Project Team.	Top Mgmt.	Team Leader should be full-time.
C. Outside counsel.	Top Mgmt.	Outside consultant with Class A experience.
6. PERFORMANCE GOALS	Top Mgmt. Middle Mgmt.	Using the ABCD Checklist, agree on expected performance levels and measurements.
7. INITIAL EDUCATION	Team Leader	Provide the necessary understanding to the team members who will be designing and implementing the slice.
A. Outside education for team members.	Team Leader	To be effective team members, these people need exposure at the Five-Day Course.

Quick-Slice MRP
Proven Path Detailed Implementation Plan

TASK	RESPONSIBLE	COMMENTS
B. Project Team video course.	Team Leader	A series of business meetings where the general principles are translated into the specifics of operation (for the slice only). Acquire the MRP II Video Library.
8. SALES, LOGISTICS, AND MANUFACTURING PROCESSES	Top Mgmt. Middle Mgmt.	Develop a detailed statement of how these processes will operate following implementation (for the slice only). The Project Team/ Discussion Leaders series of business meetings (Task #7B above) generally provides most of the information needed for this task.
9. PLANNING AND CONTROL PROCESSES		Identification of the systems necessary for effective planning (slice only). Some of these systems will be implemented using the pilot approach.
A. Sales & Operations Planning.	Top Mgmt.	Start for all items, not just slice product(s). Format, policies, unit of measure, and family designations can be developed in the first few meetings and revised as needed thereafter.
B. Demand Management.	Sales Mgr.	Slice items only.
C. Master Production Scheduling.	P&IC Mg.	Slice items only.
1. Develop a master scheduling policy.	Top Mgmt. Sales & Mktg. P&IC Mgr. Mfg. Supervsn.	Should address the following: 1. Procedure for changing the master production schedule. Who can request a change, how the proposed change is investigated, and who should approve it. 2. Periodic reviews of actual production vs. the master production schedule with an emphasis on problem resolution.
D. Material Planning.	P&IC Mgr.	Slice items only. Begun as a pilot.
E. Shop Scheduling.	P&IC Mgr. Mfg. Supervsn.	Slice items only, simple shop schedules.
F. Supplier Scheduling & Development.	Purchasing Mgr.	Slice items only, simple supplier schedules.

289

TASK	RESPONSIBLE	COMMENTS
10. DATA MANAGEMENT		These are the steps required to attain the necessary levels of data accuracy (slice items only).
A. Inventory Record Accuracy.	Stockroom Mgr.	Objective is a minimum 95 percent inventory record accuracy (slice items only).
1. Provide the tools for limited access and transaction recording.	Stockroom Mgr.	It may be necessary to physically isolate the items in the slice. Transaction system must be simple and easy to use.
2. Implement control-group cycle counting.	Stockroom Mgr.	Used to find and fix the causes of errors.
3. Inventory all slice items.	Stockroom Mgr.	Done to bring the accuracy of all slice items to a minimum of 95 percent. May have to be done several times to keep the accuracy at least 95 percent if the causes of errors have not been corrected.
B. Bill of Material Accuracy.	Engineering Mgr.	Objective is a minimum 98 percent bill of material accuracy, and an accurate bill of material structure (slice items only).
1. Verify bills of material for correct item numbers and quantity per.	Engineering Mgr.	Typically done by exception: issue to manufacturing per the bill of material and track exceptions. A line-by-line audit and disassembly of the product can also be used where appropriate. Objective is to highlight errors and correct them.
2. Verify correct structure in the bills of material.	Engineering Mgr.	Typical areas of work include: 1. Representing how material moves in the factory. 2. Showing raw material on the bills of material. 3. Including modules and self-consumed assemblies where appropriate. 4. Removing unnecessary levels from the bills of material.

Quick-Slice MRP
Proven Path Detailed Implementation Plan

TASK	RESPONSIBLE	COMMENTS
C. Item Data.	P&IC Mgr. Purchasing Mgr.	Have knowledgeable people verify this information (slice items only).
1. Verify order policies.	P&IC Mgr. Purchasing Mgr.	Fix the obvious errors in order quantities, use remainder as is.
2. Verify lead times.	P&IC Mgr. Purchasing Mgr.	Manufactured items: use simple consistent scheduling rules, fix the obvious problems. Purchased items: use current lead times, fix the obvious problems.
3. Verify safety stock levels.	P&IC Mgr. Purchasing Mgr.	Applies to independent demand items consistent with master schedule policy. For dependent demand items, restrict to special circumstances only.
11. PROCESS IMPROVEMENT		If a flow shop can be created quickly to replace a job shop, this will make it easier to plan and schedule.
A. Identify JIT activities.	Top Mgmt. Middle Mgmt. Mfg. Supervsn.	Activities like: cells, kanban, and reducing levels in the bills of material for the slice items.
B. Implementation of JIT activities identified above.	Execution Teams	Each team is measured against their charter and individual implementation plan. For more details, see the JIT/TQC Detailed Implementation Plan.
12. SOFTWARE	MIS Mgr.	Select and implement the software to support the slice items. This may be temporary software (like a PC-based software package) or the current software if it is already up and running.
A. Select software.	MIS Mgr. P&IC Mfg. Supervsn.	A quick selection is essential here. In the case of "temporary" software, this can with a minimum of evaluation.

TASK	RESPONSIBLE	COMMENTS
1. Acquire *The Standard System* book.	MIS Mgr. P&IC Mfg. Supervsn.	Available from Oliver Wight Limited Publications, this book provides an explanation of what a typical software package should provide.
B. Implement necessary modules:	MIS Mgr.	This should be done with little, if any, interfacing of systems. Typical modules include: Inventory Transactions, Bills of Material, Master Production Scheduling, Material Requirements Planning.
13. PILOT AND CUTOVER	Team Members	Typically, there is no pilot in a Quick-Slice implementation. All the slice items are brought up on the system at once. However, the following implementation steps for a pilot are still appropriate for the implementation of the slice items.
A. Complete three pilots.	Team Members	Pilots are: 1. Computer pilot to test the software. 2. Conference room pilot to test procedures and people's understanding. 3. Live pilot (or, in this case, slice implementation) to test the new processes and verify they are working.
14. PERFORMANCE MEASUREMENTS	Team Members	Compare actual results to the previously agreed-upon key measurements. Typical performance measurements include: 1. Production Plan performance. 2. Master Production Schedule performance. 3. Manufacturing Schedule performance. 4. Supplier Delivery performance.
15. AUDIT/ASSESSMENT II	Top Mgmt. Middle Mgmt.	Re-assess the company's situation. Is it now time to implement MRP II across all items? What's next?
16. ONGOING EDUCATION		In the case of Quick Slice, ongoing education typically means initial education for the next phase of implementation.

Sources for Additional Information

Preparing yourself to implement a Class A MRP II system requires careful study of a huge amount of information, far more than could be included in this or any other book. The Oliver Wight Companies can provide further assistance in getting ready, including books on the subject, live education, and video-based education.

OLIVER WIGHT EDUCATION ASSOCIATES

OWEA is made up of a group of independent MRP II educators and consultants around the world who share a common philosophy and common goals. Classes directed toward both upper- and middle-level management are being taught in various locations around the U.S. and Canada, as well as abroad. For a detailed class brochure, listing course descriptions, instructors, costs, dates, and locations, or for the name of a recommended consultant in your area, please contact:

Oliver Wight Education Associates
P.O. Box 435
Newbury, NH 03255
800-258-3862 or 603-763-5926

OLIVER VIDEO PRODUCTIONS, INC.

The Oliver Wight Video Library offers companies the video-based materials they need to teach the "critical mass" of their employees about the principles of MRP II and Just-in-Time. For more information on obtaining the Oliver Wight Video Library, contact:

Oliver Wight Video Productions, Inc.
5 Oliver Wight Drive
Essex Junction, VT 05452
800-343-0625 or 802-878-8161

PROFESSIONAL SOCIETIES

American Production and Inventory Control Society (APICS)
500 West Allendale Road
Falls Church, VA 22046-4274
(703) 237-8344

American Society for Quality Control
P.O. Box 555, Milwaukee, WI 53201
(414) 272-8575

Association for Manufacturing Excellence
P.O. Box 584 Elm Grove, WI 53122

Society of Manufacturing Engineers (SME)
One SME Drive, P.O. Box 930, Dearborn, MI 48121
(313) 271-1500

All of these societies have international branches.

Glossary

ABC CLASSIFICATION Classification of the items in an inventory in decreasing order of annual dollar volume or other criteria. This array is then split into three classes, called A, B, and C. Class A contains the items with the highest annual dollar volume and receives the most attention. The medium Class B receives less attention, and Class C, which contains the low-dollar volume items, is controlled routinely. The ABC principle is that effort saved through relaxed controls on low-value items will be applied to reduce inventories of high-value items.

ACTION MESSAGE An output of an MRP II system that identifies the need for and the type of action to be taken to correct a current or a potential problem. Examples of action messages are Release Order, Reschedule Out, Cancel, etc.

ALLOCATION In an MRP II system, an allocated item is one for which a picking order has been released to the stockroom but not yet sent out of the stockroom. It is an uncashed stockroom requisition.

ANTICIPATED DELAY REPORT A report, normally issued by both manufacturing and purchasing to the material planning function, regarding jobs or purchase orders which will not be completed on time, why not, and when they will be completed. This is an essential ingredient of a closed-loop system. Except perhaps in very large companies, the anticipated delay report is manually prepared.

[1] Many of the terms in this glossary have been drawn or adapted from the *APICS Dictionary*, Thomas F. Wallace and John R. Dougherty, Editors. It is reprinted with permission from American Production and Inventory Control Society, Inc., copyright 1987, 6th Edition.

AUTOMATIC RESCHEDULING   Allowing the computer to automatically change due dates on scheduled receipts when it detects that due dates and required dates are out of phase. Automatic rescheduling is not recommended.

AVAILABLE-TO-PROMISE   The uncommitted portion of a company's inventory or planned production. This figure is frequently calculated from the master production schedule and is maintained as a tool for order promising.

BACKFLUSH   The deduction from inventory of the component parts used in an assembly or subassembly by exploding the bill of materials by the production count of assemblies produced. *See* Postdeduct Inventory Transaction Processing.

BACKLOG   All of the customer orders booked but not yet shipped. Sometimes referred to as open orders or the order board.

BACK SCHEDULING   A technique for calculating operation start and due dates. The schedule is computed starting with the due date for the order and working backward to determine the required completion dates for each operation.

BILL OF MATERIAL   A listing of all the subassemblies, intermediates, parts, and raw materials, etc. that go into a parent item, showing the quantity of each component required. May also be called formula, recipe, or ingredients list in certain industries.

BREAKTHROUGH JIT PILOT   A method of JIT/TQC implementation where as many JIT/TQC practices as possible are implemented into one product and/or manufacturing process. Breakthrough JIT is one of three fast-track implementation processes.

BUCKETED SYSTEM   An MRP, DRP or other time-phased system in which all time-phased data are accumulated into time periods or buckets. If the period of accumulation were to be one week, then the system would be said to have weekly buckets.

BUCKETLESS SYSTEM   An MRP II, DRP, or other time-phased system in which all time-phased data are processed, stored, and displayed using dated records rather than defined time periods or buckets.

BUSINESS PLAN   A statement of income projections, costs, and profits usually accompanied by budgets and a projected balance sheet as well as a cash flow (source and application of funds) statement. It is usually stated in terms of dollars only. The business plan and the sales & operations plan, although frequently stated in different terms, should be in agreement with each other.

CAD/CAM   The integration of Computer Aided Design and Computer Aided Manufacturing to achieve automation from design through manufacturing.

CAPACITY REQUIREMENTS PLANNING (CRP)   The process of determining how much labor and/or machine resources are required to accomplish the tasks of production, and making plans to provide these resources. Open shop orders, as well as planned orders in the MRP system, are input to CRP which translates these orders into hours of work by work center by time period. In earlier years, the computer portion of CRP was called infinite loading, a misnomer.

CELLULAR MANUFACTURING   A method of organizing production equipment which locates dissimilar equipment together. The goal is to produce items from start to finish in one sequential flow, as opposed to a traditional job shop (functional) arrangement which requires moves and queues between each operation. *See* Group Technology.

CLOSED-LOOP MRP   A system built around material requirements planning and also including the additional planning functions of production planning, master production scheduling, and capacity requirements planning. Further, once the planning phase is complete and the plans have been accepted as realistic and attainable, the execution functions come into play. These include the shop floor control functions of input-output measurement, dispatching, plus anticipated delay reports from both the shop and suppliers, supplier scheduling, etc. The term closed loop implies that not only is each of these elements included in the overall system but also that there is feedback from the execution functions so that the planning can be kept valid at all times.

COMMON PARTS BILL (OF MATERIAL)   A type of planning bill which groups all common components for a product or family of products into one bill of material.

CUMULATIVE LEAD TIME   The longest length of time involved to accomplish the activity in question. For any item planned through MRP it is found by reviewing each bill of material path below the item, and whichever path adds up the greatest number defines cumulative material lead time. Also called aggregate lead time, stacked lead time, composite lead time, or critical path lead time.

CUSTOMER CONNECTIVITY   The process of linking customers and suppliers. This is often made possible by tools such as Distribution Resource Planning and supplier scheduling. Frequently, electronic data interchange (EDI) is used as the communications medium.

CYCLE COUNTING   A physical inventory-taking technique where inventory is counted on a periodic schedule rather than once a year. For example, a cycle inventory count may be taken when an item reaches its reorder point, when new stock is received, or on a regular basis, usually more frequently for high-value fast-moving items, and less frequently for low-value or slow-moving items. Most effective cycle counting systems require the counting of a certain number of items every work day.

DAMPENERS   A technique within material requirements planning used to suppress the reporting of certain action messages created during the computer processing of MRP. Extensive use of dampeners is not recommended.

DEMAND   A need for a particular product or component. The demand could come from any number of sources (i.e., customer order, forecast, interplant, branch warehouse, service part), or to manufacture the next higher level. *See* Dependent Demand, Independent Demand.

DEMAND MANAGEMENT   The function of recognizing and managing all of the demands for products to ensure that the master scheduler is aware of them. It encompasses the activities of forecasting, order entry, order promising, branch warehouse requirements, interplant requirements, interplant orders, and service parts requirements.

DEMONSTRATED CAPACITY   Capacity calculated from actual performance data, usually number of items produced times standard hours per item plus the standard set-up time for each job.

DEPENDENT DEMAND   Demand is considered dependent when it comes from production schedules for other items. These demands should be calculated, not forecasted. A given item may have both dependent and independent demand at any given time. *See* Independent Demand.

DIRECT-DEDUCT INVENTORY TRANSACTION PROCESSING   A method of doing bookkeeping which decreases the book (computer) inventory of an item as material is issued from stock, and increases the book inventory as material is received into stock. The key concept here is that the book record is updated coincident with the movement of material out of or into stock. As a result, the book record is a representation of what is physically in stock.

DISPATCH LIST   A listing of manufacturing orders in priority sequence according to the dispatching rules. The dispatch list is usually communicated to the manufacturing floor via hard copy or CRT display, and contains detailed information on priority, location, quantity, and the capacity requirements of the manufacturing order by operation. Dispatch lists are normally generated daily and oriented by work center. Also called the daily foremen's report.

DISTRIBUTION CENTER   A warehouse with finished goods and/or service items. A typical company, for example, might have a manufacturing facility in Philadelphia and distribution centers in Atlanta, Dallas, Los Angeles, San Francisco, and Chicago. The term distribution center is synonymous with the term branch warehouse, although the former has become more commonly used recently. When there is a warehouse that serves a group of satellite warehouses, this is usually called a regional distribution center.

DISTRIBUTION REQUIREMENTS PLANNING   The function of determining the needs to replenish inventory at branch warehouses. A time-phased order-point approach is used, where the planned orders at the branch warehouse level are exploded via MRP logic to become gross requirements on the supplying source. In the case of multilevel distribution networks, this explosion process can continue down through the various levels of master warehouse, factory warehouse, etc., and become input to the master production schedule. Demand on the supplying source(s) is recognized as dependent, and standard MRP logic applies.

DISTRIBUTION RESOURCE PLANNING (DRP) The extension of distribution requirements planning into the planning of the key resources contained in a distribution system: warehouse space, manpower, money, trucks and freight cars, etc.

ELECTRONIC DATA INTERCHANGE (EDI) The computer-to-computer exchange of information between separate organizations. Companies are now communicating their supplier schedules to suppliers via EDI, instead of mailing printed schedules or hard copy purchase orders.

ENGINEER-TO-ORDER PRODUCT A product that requires engineering design, and bill of material and routing work before manufacturing can be completed. Such products typically require master scheduling of average or typical items or expected activities and capacities, with many individual components being identified only after preliminary design work is complete.

FAST-TRACK IMPLEMENTATION An implementation approach which focuses on a small number of products and/or processes, with the goal of achieving significant benefits in a very short time, typically about one hundred days. The three fast-track implementation routes are Breakthrough JIT Pilot, Quick-Slice MRP, and Fail-safe Mini-DRP.

FINAL ASSEMBLY SCHEDULE (FAS) Also referred to as the finishing schedule as it may include other operations than simply the final operation. It is a schedule of end items either to replenish finished goods inventory or to finish the product for a make-to-order product. For make-to-order products, it is prepared after receipt of a customer order, is constrained by the availability of material and capacity, and it schedules the operations required to complete the product from the level where it is stocked (or master scheduled) to the end item level.

FINITE LOADING Conceptually, the term means putting no more work into a work center than it can be expected to execute. The specific term usually refers to a computer technique that involves automatic shop priority revision in order to level load operation-by-operation. Successful applications of finite loading are very difficult to find.

FIRM PLANNED ORDER A planned order that can be frozen in quantity and time. The computer is not allowed to change it; this is the responsibility of the planner in charge of the item. This technique can aid planners to respond to material and capacity problems by firming up selected planned orders. Firm planned orders are also the normal method of stating the master production schedule.

FIXED ORDER QUANTITY An order quantity technique where the same quantity is planned to be ordered each time.

FLOW SHOP A plant in which machines and operators handle a standard, often uninterrupted, material flow. The plant layout (arrangement of machines, cells, lines, etc.) are extreme examples of flow shops, where each product follows essentially the same path through the plant. Many repetitive manufacturing operations are also examples of flow shops. (Syn: process plant.) *See* Job Shop.

FOCUS FORECASTING   A system that allows the user to simulate the effectiveness of numerous forecasting techniques, thereby being able to select the most effective one.

FULL PEGGING   Refers to the ability of a system to automatically trace requirements for a given component all the way up to its ultimate end item (or contract number).

GROUP TECHNOLOGY   An engineering and manufacturing philosophy which identifies the sameness of parts, equipment or processes. It provides for rapid retrieval of existing designs and anticipates a cellular-type production equipment layout.

HEDGE   1) In master production scheduling, a quantity of stock used to protect against uncertainty in demand. The hedge is similar to safety stock, except that a hedge has the dimension of timing as well as amount. 2) In purchasing, any purchase or sale transaction having as its purpose the elimination of the negative aspects of price fluctuations.

INDEPENDENT DEMAND   Demand for an item is considered independent when such demand is unrelated to the demand for other items. Demand for finished goods and service parts are examples of independent demand.

INFINITE LOADING   *See* Capacity Requirements Planning.

INPUT-OUTPUT CONTROL   A technique for capacity control where actual output from a work center is compared with the planned output (as developed by CRP and approved by Manufacturing). The input is also monitored to see if it corresponds with plans so that work centers will not be expected to generate output when jobs are not available to work on.

INTERPLANT DEMAND   Material to be shipped to another plant or division within the corporation. Although it is not a customer order, it is usually handled by the master production scheduling system in a similar manner.

INVENTORY TURNOVER   The number of times that an inventory turns over or cycles during the year. One way to compute inventory turnover is to divide the average inventory level into the annual cost of sales. For example, if average inventory were three million dollars and cost of sales were thirty million, the inventory would be considered to turn ten times per year.

ITEM RECORD   The master record for an item. Typically it contains identifying and descriptive data, control values (lead times, lot order quantities, etc.) and may contain data on inventory status, requirements, and planned orders. Item records are linked together by bill of material records (or product structure records), thus defining the bill of material.

JOB SHOP A functional organization whose departments or work centers are organized around particular types of equipment or operation, such as drilling, forging, spinning, or assembly. Products move through departments by individual shop orders.

JUST-IN-TIME In the broad sense, Just-in-Time is an approach to achieving excellence in a manufacturing company based on continuing elimination of waste and consistent improvement in productivity. Waste is then defined as those things which do not add value to the product. Waste can be divided into two categories: necessary and unnecessary. Unnecessary waste should be eliminated, and necessary waste should be made unnecessary so that it, too, can be eliminated.

In the narrow (and less correct) sense, Just-in-Time is considered by some as a production and logistics method designed to result in minimum inventory by having material arrive at each operation just in time to be used.

KANBAN A method for Just-in-Time production in which consuming (downstream) operations pull from feeding (upstream) operations. Feeding operations are authorized to produce only after receiving a kanban card (or other trigger) from the consuming operation. Kanban in Japanese loosely translated means card. Syn: demand pull.

LEAD TIME A span of time required to perform an activity. In a logistics context, the activity in question is normally the procurement of materials and/or products either from an outside supplier or from one's own manufacturing facility. The individual components of any given lead time can include some or all of the following: order preparation time, queue time, move or transportation time, receiving and inspection time.

LEVEL Every part of assembly in a product structure is assigned a level code signifying the relative level in which that part or assembly is used within that product structure. Normally, the end items are assigned level 0 and the components/subassemblies going into it are level 1 and so on. The MRP explosion process starts from level 0 and proceeds downwards one level at a time.

LOAD The amount of scheduled work ahead of a manufacturing facility, usually expressed in terms of hours of work or units of production.

LOGISTICS In an industrial context, this term refers to the functions of obtaining and distributing material and product. In a military sense (where it has greater usage), its meaning can also include the transportation of personnel.

LOT-FOR-LOT An order quantity technique in MRP which generates planned orders in quantities equal to the net requirements in each period. Also called discrete, one-for-one.

MACHINE LOADING The accumulation by work centers of the hours generated from the scheduling of operations for released orders by time period. Machine loading differs from capacity requirements planning in that it does not use the planned orders from MRP but operates solely for scheduled receipts. As such, it has very limited usefulness.

MAKE-TO-ORDER PRODUCT   The end item is finished after receipt of a customer order. Frequently, long lead-time components are planned prior to the order arriving in order to reduce the delivery time to the customer. Where options or other subassemblies are stocked prior to customer orders arriving, the term assemble-to-order is frequently used.

MAKE-TO-STOCK PRODUCT   The end item is shipped from finished goods off the shelf, and therefore, is finished prior to a customer order arriving.

MANUFACTURING RESOURCE PLANNING (MRP II)   A method for the effective planning of all resource of a manufacturing company. Ideally, it addresses operational planning in units, financial planning in dollars, and has a simulation capability to answer what if questions. It is made up of a variety of functions, each linked together: business planning, production planning, master production scheduling, material requirements planning, capacity requirements planning, and the execution support systems for capacity and material. Output from these systems would be integrated with financial reports such as the business plan, purchase commitment reports, shipping budget, inventory projections in dollars, etc. Manufacturing resource planning is a direct outgrowth and extension of closed-loop MRP. MRP II has also been defined, validly, as a management system based on network scheduling. Also, and perhaps best, as organized common sense.

MASTER PRODUCTION SCHEDULE (MPS)   The anticipated build schedule. The master scheduler maintains this schedule and, in turn, it becomes a set of planning numbers which drives MRP. It represents what the company plans to produce expressed in specific configurations, quantities, and dates. The master production schedule must take into account customer orders and forecasts, backlog, availability of material, availability of capacity, management policy and goals, etc.

MATERIAL REQUIREMENTS PLANNING (MRP)   A set of techniques which uses bills of material, inventory data and the master production schedule to calculate requirements for materials. It makes recommendations to release replenishment orders for material. Further, since it is time phased, it makes recommendations to reschedule open orders when due dates and need dates are not in phase. Originally seen as merely a better way to order inventory, today it is thought of primarily as a scheduling technique (i.e., a method for establishing and maintaining valid due dates on orders). It is the foundation for closed-loop MRP.

MATERIALS MANAGEMENT   An organizational structure which groups the functions related to the complete cycle of material flow, from the purchase and internal control of production materials to the planning and control of work-in-process to the warehousing, shipping, and distribution of the finished product.

MODULAR BILL (OF MATERIAL)   A type of planning bill which is arranged in product modules or options. Often used in companies where the product has many optional features (e.g., automobiles). *See* Planning Bill.

MURPHY'S LAW   A tongue-in-cheek observation which states: If anything can go wrong, it will.

NET CHANGE MRP   A method of processing material requirements planning on the computer whereby the material plan is continually retained in the computer. Whenever there is a change in requirements, open order, or inventory status, bills of material, etc., a partial explosion is made only for those parts affected by the change.

NET REQUIREMENTS   In MRP, the net requirements for a part or an assembly are derived as a result of netting gross requirements against inventory on hand and the scheduled receipts. Net requirements, lot sized and offset for lead time, become planned orders.

ON-HAND BALANCE   The quantity shown in the inventory records as being physically in stock.

OPEN ORDER   An active manufacturing order or purchase order. *See* Scheduled Receipts.

OPTION   A choice or feature offered to customers for customizing the end product. In many companies, the term option means a mandatory choice (i.e., the customer must select from one of the available choices). For example, in ordering a new car, the customer must specify an engine (option) but need not necessarily select an air conditioner.

ORDER ENTRY   The process of accepting and translating what a customer wants into terms used by the manufacturer. This can be as simple as creating shipping documents for a finished goods product to a far more complicated series of activities including engineering effort for make-to-order products.

ORDER PROMISING   The process of making a delivery commitment (i.e., answering the question "When can you ship?") For make-to-order products, this usually involves a check of material and capacity availability.

ORDER QUANTITY   The amount of an item to be ordered. Also called lot size.

PEGGING   In MRP, pegging displays, for a given item, the details of the sources of its gross requirements and/or allocations. Pegging can be thought of as live where-used information.

PERIOD ORDER QUANTITY   An order quantity technique under which the order quantity will be equal to the net requirements for a given number of periods (e.g., weeks) into the future. Also called days' supply, weeks' supply, fixed period.

PICKING   The process of issuing components to the production floor on a job-by-job basis. Also called kitting.

PICKING LIST   A document which is used to pick manufacturing orders, listing the components and quantities required.

PLANNED ORDER   A suggested order quantity and due date created by MRP processing, when it encounters net requirements. Planned orders are created by the computer, exist only within the computer, and may be changed or deleted by the computer during subsequent MRP processing if conditions change. Planned orders at one level will be exploded into gross requirements for components at the next lower level. Planned orders also serve as input to capacity requirements planning, along with scheduled receipts, to show the total capacity requirements in future time periods.

PLANNER/BUYER   *See* Supplier Scheduler.

PLANNING BILL (OF MATERIAL)   An artificial grouping of items and/or events, in bill of material format, used to facilitate master scheduling and/or material planning. A modular bill of material is one type of planning bill.

POST-DEDUCT INVENTORY TRANSACTION PROCESSING   A method of doing inventory bookkeeping where the book (computer) inventory of components is reduced only after completion of activity on their upper level parent or assembly. This approach has the disadvantage of a built-in differential between the book record and what is physically in stock. Also called backflush.

PRODUCT STRUCTURE   *See* Bill of Material.

PROJECTED AVAILABLE BALANCE   The inventory balance projected out into the future. It is the running sum of on-hand inventory, minus requirements, plus scheduled receipts and (usually) planned orders.

PULL SYSTEM   Usually refers to how material is moved on the plant floor. Pull indicates that material moves to the next operation automatically upon completion of the prior operation. *See* Kanban.

PUSH SYSTEM   Usually refers to how material is moved on the plant floor. Push indicates that material moves to the next operation automatically upon completion of the prior operation.

QUEUE   A waiting line. In manufacturing the jobs at a given work center waiting to be processed. As queues increase, so do average lead times and work-in-process inventories.

QUEUE TIME   The amount of time a job waits at a work center before set-up or work is performed on the job. Queue time is one element of total manufacturing lead time. Increases in queue time result in direct increases to manufacturing lead time.

QUICK-SLICE MRP   A method of implementing most of the MRP II functions into a small slice of the business, typically one product or product line, in a very short time. Quick-Slice MRP is one of the fast-track implementation approaches.

REGENERATION MRP   A method of processing material requirements planning on the computer whereby the master production schedule is totally re-exploded down through all bills of material, at least once per week to maintain valid priorities. New requirements and planned orders are completely regenerated at that time.

REPETITIVE MANUFACTURING   Production of discrete units, planned and executed via schedule, usually at relatively high speeds and volumes. Material tends to move in a sequential flow. *See* Flow Shop.

RESCHEDULING ASSUMPTION   A fundamental piece of MRP logic which assumes that existing open orders can be rescheduled in nearer time periods far more easily than new orders can be released and received. As a result, planned order receipts are not created until all scheduled receipts have been applied to cover gross requirements.

RESOURCE REQUIREMENTS PLANNING   *See* Rough-cut Capacity Planning.

ROUGH-CUT CAPACITY PLANNING   The process of converting the production plan and/or the master production schedule into capacity needs for key resources: manpower, machinery, warehouse space, suppliers' capabilities and, in some cases, money. Product load profiles are often used to accomplish this. The purpose of rough-cut capacity planning is to evaluate the plan prior to attempting to implement it. Sometimes called resource requirements planning.

ROUTING   A document detailing the manufacture of a particular item. It includes the operations to be performed, their sequence, the various work centers to be involved, and the standards for set-up and run. In some companies, the routing also includes information on tooling, operator skill levels, inspection operations, testing requirements, etc.

SAFETY STOCK   In general, a quantity of stock planned to be available to protect against fluctuations in demand and/or supply.

SAFETY TIME   A technique in MRP whereby material is planned to arrive ahead of the requirement date. This difference between the requirement date and the planned in-stock date is safety time.

SALES & OPERATIONS PLANNING   The function of setting the overall level of manufacturing output (production plan) and other activities to best satisfy the current planned levels of sales (sales plan and/or forecasts), while meeting general business objectives of profitability, productivity, competitive customer lead times, etc. as expressed in the overall business plan.

SALES PLAN   The overall level of sales expected to be achieved. Usually stated as a monthly rate of sales for a product family (group of products, items, options, features, etc.). It needs to be expressed in units identical to the production plan (as well as dollars) for planning purposes. It represents Sales and Marketing managements' commitment to take all reasonable steps necessary to make the sales forecast (a prediction) accurately represent actual customer orders received.

SCHEDULED RECEIPTS   Within MRP, open production orders and open purchase orders are considered as scheduled receipts on their due date and will be treated as part of available inventory during the netting process for the time period in question. Scheduled receipt dates and/or quantities are not normally altered automatically by the computer. Further, scheduled receipts are not exploded into requirements for components, as MRP logic assumes that all components required for the manufacture of the item in question have either been allocated or issued to the shop floor.

SCRAP FACTOR   A percentage factor used by MRP to increase gross requirements of a given component to account for anticipated loss of that component during the manufacture of its parent.

SERVICE PARTS   Parts used for the repair and/or maintenance of a product. Also called repair parts, spares.

SHOP FLOOR CONTROL   A system for utilizing data from the shop floor as well as data processing files to maintain and communicate status information on shop orders (manufacturing orders) and work centers. The major subfunctions of shop floor control are: 1) assigning priority of each shop order, 2) maintaining work-in-process quantity information, 3) conveying shop order status information, 4) providing actual input and output data for capacity control purposes, 5) providing quantity by location by shop order for work-in-process inventory and accounting purposes, 6) providing measurement of efficiency, utilization, and productivity of manpower and machines.

SHOP ORDER CLOSE-OUT STATION   A stocking point on the shop floor. Completed production of components is transacted (received) into the shop order close-out station and subsequently transacted (issued) to assembly or other downstream operations. This technique is used to reduce material handling by not having to move items into and out of stockrooms, while simultaneously enabling a high degree of inventory record accuracy.

SHRINKAGE FACTOR   A factor used in material requirements planning which compensates for expected loss during the manufacturing cycle either by increasing the gross requirements or by reducing the expected completion quantity of planned and open orders. The shrinkage factor differs from the scrap factor in that the former affects all uses of the part and its components. The scrap relates to only one usage.

SIMULATION   Within MRP II, utilizing the operational date to perform what if evaluations of alternative plans, to answer the question: "Can we do it?" If yes, the simulation can then be run in financial mode to help answer the question: "Do we really want to?"

SUPPLIER SCHEDULER   A person whose main job is working with suppliers regarding what's needed and when. Supplier schedulers are in direct contact with both MRP and the suppliers. They do the material planning for the items under their control, communicate the resultant schedules to their assigned suppliers, do follow-up, resolve problems, etc. The supplier schedulers are normally organized by commodity, as are the buyers. By using the supplier scheduler approach, the buyers are freed from day-to-day order placement and expediting, and therefore have the time to do cost reduction, negotiation, supplier selection, alternate sourcing, etc. Syn: vendor scheduler, planner/buyer.

SUPPLIER SCHEDULING   A purchasing approach which provides suppliers with schedules rather than individual hard-copy purchase orders. Normally a supplier scheduling system will include a business agreement (contract) for each supplier, a daily or weekly schedule for each supplier extending for some time into the future, and individuals called supplier schedulers. Also required is a formal priority planning system that works very well, because it is essential in this arrangement to routinely provide the supplier with valid due dates. Some form of supplier scheduling is essential for Just-in-Time purchasing. Syn: vendor scheduling.

TIME BUCKET   A number of days of data summarized into one columnar display. A weekly time bucket in MRP would contain all the relevant planning data for an entire week. Weekly time buckets are considered to be the largest possible (at least in the near- and medium-term) to permit effective MRP.

TIME FENCE   Point in time where various restrictions or changes in operating procedures take place. For example, changes to the master production schedule can be accomplished easily beyond the cumulative lead time; whereas, changes inside the cumulative lead time become increasingly more difficult, to a point where changes should be resisted. Time fences can be used to define these points.

TWO-LEVEL MPS   A master scheduling approach for make-to-order products where an end product type is master scheduled along with selected key options, features, attachments, and common parts.

TURNOVER   The number of times inventory is replaced during a time period; in other words, a measurement of investment inventory to support a given level of sales. It is found by dividing the cost of goods sold for the period by the average inventory for the period.

VENDOR SCHEDULER   *See* Supplier Scheduler.

VENDOR SCHEDULING   *See* Supplier Scheduling.

WORK-IN-PROCESS   Product in various stages of completion throughout the plant, including raw material that has been released for initial processing and completely processed material awaiting final inspection and acceptance as finished product or shipment to a customer. Many accounting systems also include semi-finished stock and components in this category.

INDEX